FAILING BOYS?

FAILING BOYS?
Issues in gender and achievement

EDITED BY

DEBBIE EPSTEIN, JANNETTE ELWOOD,

VALERIE HEY AND JANET MAW

on behalf of the
Centre for Research and
Education on Gender,
University of London
Institute of Education

Open University Press
Buckingham · Philadelphia

Open University Press
Celtic Court
22 Ballmoor
Buckingham
MK18 1XW

email: enquiries@openup.co.uk
world wide web: http://www.openup.co.uk

and
325 Chestnut Street
Philadelphia, PA 19106, USA

First Published 1998
Reprinted 1999

A catalogue record of this book is available from the British Library

ISBN 0 335 20239 X (pb)   0 335 20238 1 (pb)

Library of Congress Cataloging-in-Publication Data
Failing boys?:issues in gender and achievement / Debbie Epstein . . .
    [et al.] (eds.) on behalf of Centre for Research and Education on
Gender, Institute of Education.
        p. cm.
    Includes bibliographical references and index.
    ISBN 0–335–20239–X (hardcover). – ISBN 0–335–20238–1 (pbk.)
    1. Boys. – Education – Great Britain.   2. Underachievers – Great
Britain.   3. School failure – Great Britain. 4. Academic
achievement – Great Britain. 5. Sex differences in education – Great
Britain. I. Epstein, Debbie, 1945– .   II. University of London.
Centre for Research and Education on Gender.
LC1390.F35   1998
371.823´41–dc21
                                                              98–18351
                                                                   CIP

Typeset by Graphicraft Limited, Hong Kong
Printed in Great Britain by Biddles Ltd, Guildford and King's Lynn

Contents

Contributors

MICHÈLE COHEN is Principal Lecturer in the Humanities Department at Richmond, the American International University in London. She has been working on masculinity for a number of years and is the author of *Fashioning Masculinity: National Identity and Language in the Eighteenth Century* (1996). She is presently writing a chapter for a book she is co-editing with Tim Hitchcock on *English Masculinities 1660–1800*.

HARRY DANIELS has taught in mainstream and special schools and units. His current research interests are: gender and learning; provision for pupils with emotional and behavioural difficulties in mainstream schools; the mental health of pupils with special needs in mainstream schools; and the development of peer support for teacher problem solving in schools. He has a general interest in the development of post-Vygotskian social theory.

JANNETTE ELWOOD is Lecturer in Education at the Institute of Education, University of London, with special interest in assessment. Her research interests are assessment, especially gender equity issues related to public examinations. Between 1994 and 1996 she directed the 'Gender Differences in Examinations at 18+' project (funded by the Nuffield Foundation). She teaches courses in assessment and research methodology for masters and doctoral students.

DEBBIE EPSTEIN is Reader in Education at the Institute of Education, University of London. She researches the intersecting constructions of gender, sexuality and race in education and in popular culture. Recent publications include: with Richard Johnson *Schooling Sexualities* (Open University Press 1998); edited with Deborah Lynn Steinberg and Richard Johnson *Border Patrols: Policing the Boundaries of Heterosexuality* (1997); and, edited with Joyce E. Canaan,

A Question of Discipline: Pedagogy, Power and the Teaching of Cultural Studies (1997).

VALERIE HEY is a senior researcher in the academic group Culture, Communication and Societies at the University of London, Institute of Education. She is currently co-directing an Economic and Social Research Council funded study into the relationships between schooling, pedagogies and cultures of masculinity in primary schools. She has recently published a well-received original study *The Company She Keeps: An Ethnography of Girls' Friendship* (Open University Press 1997).

DAVID JACKSON taught in secondary English departments for nearly twenty years. He is now retired through ill health. He has been involved in male and masculinity issues for 15 years. He has published *Unmasking Masculinity: A Critical Autobiography* and *Challenging Macho Values: Practical Ways of Working with Adolescent Boys* with Jonathan Salisbury.

DIANA LEONARD is a Reader in Women's Studies and Education and head of the Institute of Education's Centre for Research and Education on Gender. She has published extensively on the sociology of gender and the family and has recently completed two ESRC-funded research projects: on 'Gender and SEN in Mainstream Junior Schooling' and the 'Family Work of Young People, their Educational Achievement and Post-16 Careers'. Since October 1997 she and colleagues at the Institute and the University of Birmingham have been working on a new project on 'Gender and Learning'. Her other interests include differences between the experiences of women and men, and home and overseas' doctoral students.

PAT MAHONY is Professor of Education at Roehampton Institute London. She has worked for many years in the areas of equal opportunities and teacher education and is currently engaged in a number of research projects exploring the impact and significance of government policy in these areas. Her books include *Schools for the Boys?*; *Learning our Lines* (edited with Carol Jones); *Promoting Quality and Equality in Schools* (edited with Ruth Frith); *Changing Schools: Some International Perspectives on Working with Girls and Boys*; *Class Matters* (edited with Christine Zmroczek); and *International Perspectives on Women and Social Class* (edited with Christine Zmroczek).

JANET MAW has recently retired from the Institute of Education, where she was Senior Lecturer in Curriculum Studies. For the last decade her research and writing has focused on the production, discourse and consumption of texts in the policy and practices of education, employing a socio-cultural approach to language. In particular she has concentrated on the discourse of the National Curriculum, especially in history where issues of culture, ethnocentrism and national identity are central. From 1989–91 she co-directed a research project on 'Handling Ethnocentrism in History Classrooms'. She is also interested in the inspection of schools and the discourses used by Ofsted.

PATRICIA MURPHY is Director of the Centre for Curriculum and Teaching Studies at the School of Education, Open University. Prior to this she was Deputy Director of the Assessment for Performance Unit, Science Project, King's College, University of London. Her research into gender and science, assessment and problem solving in science and technical education is well known.

LYNN RAPHAEL REED is a senior lecturer and research fellow in the Faculty of Education at the University of the West of England, where she manages the MA programme including a pathway in 'Raising Achievement in City Schools'. Her research includes life histories of teachers committed to social justice, and an ethnographic study of boys and the orientations to learning in specific classroom contexts.

TONY SEWELL is a lecturer in the school of Education, University of Leeds. He has published widely on African-Caribbean boys and schooling as well as sociological approaches to special needs. He is currently specializing in the area of emotional and behavioural difficulties. Dr Sewell is a lead columnist for the *Sunday Mirror* and *Voice* newspapers.

MARJORIE SMITH has taught for several years in primary, secondary and higher education. She is now an educational psychologist in the London Borough of Newham.

JOAN SWANN is a senior lecturer in the Centre for Language and Communications at the Open University. Her main interests are language and gender, and other areas of sociolinguistics. Publications include: *Gender Voices* (1989, with David Graddol); *Girls, Boys and Language* (1992); and several papers on language and gender issues in education.

Acknowledgements

We would like to thank:

- the ESRC for funding the research seminar series 'Gender and Education: Are Boys Now Underachieving?' held at the Centre for Research and Education on Gender (CREG) at the University of London Institute of Education during 1995–6 and 1996–7;
- the participants in that seminar series for their stimulating, engaged and supportive participation in the seminars;
- Amanda Claremont and Ulrike Baechle for their administrative support during the seminar series;
- Ulrike Baechle for the mammoth task of preparing the manuscript (including dealing with significant computer gremlins with equanimity);
- all the contributors for sticking to a tight schedule;
- Taylor and Francis for permission to reuse material from Patricia Murphy and Jannette Elwood's article 'Gendered experiences, choices, and achievement – exploring the links' originally published in *International Journal of Inclusive Education* 2(2), 1998.

Abbreviations

AEN	additional educational needs
APU	Assessment and Performance Unit
DES	Department of Education and Science
DfE	Department for Education
DfEE	Department for Education and Employment
EO	equal opportunities
EOC	Equal Opportunities Commission
ESRC	Economic and Social Research Council
GCE	General Certificate of Education
GCSE	General Certificate of Secondary Education
GNVQ	General National Vocational Qualification
HMI	Her Majesty's Inspectorate of Schools
ILEA	Inner London Education Authority
INSET	in-service education and training
LEA	local education authority
OECD	Organization for Economic Cooperation and Development
Ofsted	Office for Standards in Education
SAT	Standard Assessment Task
SEN	special educational needs
TTA	Teacher Training Agency
WO	Welsh Office

PART I

Boys' underachievement in context

1

Schoolboy frictions: feminism and 'failing' boys

DEBBIE EPSTEIN, JANNETTE ELWOOD, VALERIE HEY
AND JANET MAW

During the academic years 1995–6 and 1996–7 we were responsible for organizing a series of seminars held by the Centre for Research and Education on Gender at the University of London Institute of Education, and funded by the Economic and Social Research Council. The series, entitled 'Gender and Education: Are Boys Now Underachieving?', was intended to help us and other researchers map the field within the UK context in this area of current interest. As word got out that we were responsible for the seminar series, our telephones began to ring: other academics, local education authority (LEA) administrators, journalists from the broadsheet and tabloid press and from the BBC, Her Majesty's Inspectorate of Schools (HMI), teachers, teacher unions, researchers for the Labour Party's education team (then in opposition), all wanted to find out what we had to say about the vexed question of boys' 'underachievement' in schools. One particular phone conversation took place between Debbie Epstein and a senior HMI, phoning from Ofsted (Office for Standards in Education) in the summer of 1995. A young feminist, overhearing Debbie's side of the conversation, remarked on the HMI's concern about boys' 'underachievement', 'Oh, you mean they're not doing better than girls any more, like they should!'

Indeed, much of the public debate about boys and schooling has been conducted in precisely the terms she indicated. In this chapter, we explore the nature of the public debate, its status as a kind of globalized moral panic, and the importance of moving away from simplistic, often alarmist, descriptions and proposed 'solutions' towards hearing more thoughtful, and especially feminist, voices and analyses of the issues involved. It is these voices to which this book gives space. Neither we, in this introductory chapter, nor the other contributors to the book, argue that there are no problems

associated with the education of boys. Rather, we suggest that the discourses
in which debates about the schooling of boys have been framed are both
narrow through the ways in which the terms 'achievement' and 'education'
have been understood, and masculinist in style; that they lack a historical
perspective; that it is unhelpful to set up a binary opposition between the
schooling of girls and that of boys, according to which, if one group wins,
the other loses; and that questions around equity and differences among
boys and among girls as well as between boys and girls are key to understanding what is happening in schools. In this regard, we shall point to the
importance of investigating the different versions of masculinity which are
open to and taken up by boys in schools; how they may work to produce
problems for educators and for boys themselves; and how boys come to
inhabit them.

New lads, new panics?

To understand the current debates about boys' 'underachievement' it is
important to place them within their historical context. Like much that is
'new' in 'new Britain', problems relating to the education of boys, particularly working-class boys, have been around for a long time. For example,
more than 20 years ago, Paul Willis (1977) wrote about the ways in which
working-class boys often responded to the alienation and middle-class values
of schooling through strategies of resistance and, in the process, became
embedded within their class status. In his influential ethnographic study,
Willis distinguished between those boys who saw themselves as 'lads', and
those with middle-class aspirations who worked hard at school, who were
labelled by the 'lads' as 'ear'oles'. Just as 'New Labour' looks a great deal like
'Old Tory', so too do the 'new lads' represented in, for example, the BBC
situation comedy *Men Behaving Badly*, in articles in the popular press, and
in television documentaries about boys and education, resemble nothing so
much as Paul Willis's lads of the 1970s – although the generic requirements of
situation comedy have, perhaps inevitably, given working-class masculinities
a somewhat softer edge than those depicted by Willis.

Several authors in this volume point to this feature of the debate. Indeed,
Michèle Cohen's title, 'A habit of healthy idleness', is drawn from a government report of 1923 (Board of Education 1923) and she traces the evidence
of boys' inferior 'achievement' in, at least, the learning of language, back to
John Locke's 1693 treatise, *Some Thoughts Concerning Education* (1989). What
is particularly interesting about Cohen's chapter is her analysis of the ways
in which debates about the educational differences between boys and girls
have been framed historically. Boys' educational failures, she suggests, generally have been located as extrinsic to themselves, for example, by attributing
them to the failures of pedagogies, methods, texts and/or teachers, while their
successes have been located as intrinsic, attributed to their innate brilliance,

intellect or natural potential. For girls, on the other hand, the opposite has been the case. Educational success for them historically has been attributed to the methods by which they have been taught or has been devalued as being due to lower-order abilities such as neatness (rather than the higher-order 'intelligence'), while their failures have been seen as inherent to their sex.

It is well known, but often overlooked (or wilfully forgotten) that, in the British context, the 11-plus examinations, by which children used to be selected for secondary schooling, were deliberately skewed so that girls had to achieve better results than boys in order to gain entry to selective grammar schools. To do otherwise would have meant that grammar schools would have been overwhelmingly populated by girls. In the 1950s and 1960s, the justification for this was that boys matured later than girls so it would not be fair to exclude them from grammar schools on the basis of test results at the age of 11. Girls' greater success in school-based 'achievement' has been most marked in the area of language – including the learning both of a first language and of other languages, and this, as both Michèle Cohen and Joan Swann point out in their chapters, is not a new phenomenon. In contrast, girls' relative success in gaining passes at grade C and above in mathematics at GCSE is more recent, and Jo Boaler (1997, 1998) has suggested that this is because structural obstacles to girls' success have been removed in this subject area, rather than because they have become better at mathematics.

So what is new, in the context of late 1990s Britain, is not that there are problems associated with the schooling of (many) boys, or that (some) girls do better than (some) boys in achievement measured by examination results, particularly in languages, arts and humanities – though it should be noted that the measured achievement of all pupils at GCSE and A level has improved, but girls' results have generally improved rather faster than boys. Rather, we can see changes in three important respects. First, some of the barriers to girls' achievement have been removed, partly through the introduction of comprehensive schooling and the consequent ending of the 11 plus (as a result of arguments about class rather than gendered or racialized equality); and partly through certain gains that have been made through feminist struggle both within and beyond the school and, related to that, through changing definitions of what it means to be a woman. Second, the popular, common-sense explanations of boys' problems with schooling have become a subject for major public concern. Third, we have seen a narrowing of definitions of school-based achievement, combined with an increasing concern about it. As Pat Mahony asks in her contribution to this book, 'Why is there such a concern, even an obsession, with academic achievement in the first place?'

Failing boys? The local and the global

So far, we have focused on the history of discourses about boys' educational achievement, or lack of it, in the context of the United Kingdom. However,

Pat Mahony's question is well placed, and she suggests that, in order to answer it, we have to consider 'the underachievement of boys' in the context of the global economy. She and David Jackson (this volume) both point out that the phenomenon of panic about boys' 'underachievement' is one which transcends national boundaries. Similar debates have been in process in much of the anglophone world (e.g. Australia, Canada, New Zealand, the United Kingdom, the United States) as well as in some other countries (e.g. Denmark, Germany and Japan),[1] as evidenced by the number of recent conference papers and publications about these issues. In many countries, the debate has followed lines similar to those familiar to British readers. There have been significant different threads to discourses about boys and schooling which have derived from a variety of theoretical positions about masculinity and about schooling and several of the dominant discourses played out in the public debates about boys and achievement have achieved an international currency: the 'poor boys' discourse; the 'failing schools' discourse; and the 'boys will be boys' discourse.

Pity the 'Poor Boys'

'Poor boys' is a discourse drawn from what can, broadly, be called the 'Men's Movement'; indeed, Jane Kenway (1995b) has labelled this positioning of boys as the victims in education as the 'Lads' Movement'. As Pam Gilbert (1998: 18–19) points out:

> [The] popular 'new-speak' about equity is now not about girls' education or about gender and education: it is about boys' education ... [Equity] matters are subsumed by stories about boys. Poor boys, lost boys, damaged boys, under-fathered boys. Boys at the mercy of feminist teachers; boys being outperformed by girls; boys who have not been allowed to tap into what Don and Jeanne Elium (1992: 17) call 'the moist, dark, mysterious call of the masculine soul'.

As can be seen, this version of boys' education rests heavily on the kind of reactionary argument developed by authors like Robert Bly in the United States (e.g. Bly 1990), Steve Biddulph in Australia (e.g. Biddulph 1994) and Neil Lydon in the UK (e.g. Lydon 1996). While these authors differ somewhat in their proposed 'solutions' to the problems of men and boys, their identifications of the source of these problems are strikingly similar. In each case, they argue that men have lost control of their lives because of attacks by assertive women, particularly feminists (see also, Sammons *et al.* 1994). They all call for a 'return' to a 'more natural' regime in which men and women knew their places, and men were able to use their inherent male power. In the context of education and debates about boys' 'underachievement', the supporters of the 'Lads' Movement' develop a range of arguments which blame women for the failures of boys. If it is not women teachers (see

Raphael Reed this volume), then it is mothers; if it is not mothers, it is feminists; most often it is a combination. Again, this is not a new phenomenon. As Jane Miller (1996) points out, (some) men have expressed concerns about the effects women teachers have on boys for as long as there has been schooling provided by the state. In general, these concerns have been about women teachers making boys 'soft', smothering them with matriarchal values. Miller's work points to these claims made in the United States early in the twentieth century, while Bob Connell (1996: 207) remarks on similar concerns in the 1960s. Pat Mahony, in this volume, quotes Anne-Mette Kruse's description (1996: 439) of one prominent representative of the 'Lads' Movement' to show how such claims continue to be made in the context of contemporary Europe:

> school is a terrible place for boys. In school they are trapped by 'The Matriarchy' and are dominated by women who cannot accept boys as they are. The women teachers mainly wish to control and to suppress boys.

When these theoretical frameworks are applied to the question of 'boys' underachievement', they come up with 'solutions' which, rather than questioning hegemonic versions of (white, heterosexual, able-bodied) masculinity work to recuperate and reinstate them. Some of these 'solutions', as Lynn Raphael Reed (this volume) suggests, take the form of a masculinization of teaching styles, both by using curriculum content thought to be more interesting to boys and by adopting teaching styles likely to favour boys, particularly in secondary schools (see also Boaler 1998). Another proposed 'solution' is that of introducing male 'mentors' into schools who, it is thought, can offer boys a better male role model. However, as Raphael Reed points out '[Unproblematized] notions of masculinity are embedded in certain "positive" role models.' She describes one mentoring scheme for boys which involved being picked up from home at 6.45 a.m. to attend a meeting scheduled for breakfast time. Such schemes, along with proposals involving such measures as the introduction of compulsory attendance at cadet corps, can be seen as:

> a way of muzzling the bite of pro-feminist initiatives, and more particularly, the active challenge of feminism in education. It is also a covert way of reconfirming unequal gender relations between boys/girls and men/women.
>
> (Jackson this volume: 78)

Failing schools failing boys

The second key discourse we wish to discuss is that of the 'failing school' which, in turn, fails the boys who attend it. This is a discourse which has permeated much of education policy in a number of different countries over the past decade. In the British context, it forms the linchpin of much educational policy under New Labour, building on the policies of the previous Conservative government. This globalized discourse takes different forms and proffers different solutions in different countries: in the United Kingdom and Canada it has been linked mainly with the 'school effectiveness' and 'school improvement' movements (Sammons *et al.* 1994; Stoll and Fink 1996); Australia and New Zealand have been more likely to turn to 'outcomes-based' (sometimes called 'standards-based') education (Crittenden 1994; Hearn 1996) – though both versions have been applied in all these places with somewhat different stresses. They have been picked up by governments, particularly in low- to middle-income countries, and, indeed imposed on them by supranational organizations like the World Bank (Unterhalter 1996), inevitably transmuted by local conditions, but often applied without reference to local histories and social structures. The new education policy of South Africa, for example, looks to the antipodean model of outcomes-based education, while its neighbour, Botswana, has been heavily influenced by UK versions of 'school effectiveness'. The two models are somewhat different, but share some important characteristics: they are both undertheorized in relation to issues of inequalities (of, for example, class, gender and 'race'); they are technicist and managerialist in their approaches to schooling; their primary reference point is competitiveness in the global economy; and their primary method is constant testing, often associated with league tables of successful and unsuccessful schools.[2]

As such, these models constitute a key element in the marketization of education, and represent the educational aspect of the 'New Managerialism'. Indeed, it could be argued that 'school effectiveness', while not pursued by the 'Lads' Movement', is the grail of the New Managerialists in education. Michael Apple (1997) has argued that the New Managerialists within the public services come 'under the hegemonic umbrella of the New Right', while, as individuals, not necessarily agreeing with many of the ideas of New Right politicians like Margaret Thatcher, Ronald Reagan or John Howard.[3] Unlike the 'Lads' Movement', it is rare for proponents of the 'failing schools' discourse to make overt and direct attacks on feminism. Nevertheless, much of their language is, as Lynn Raphael Reed and Pat Mahony point out in their chapters, unrelievedly masculinist in style, relying heavily on military metaphors with 'targets', strategies', 'hit squads' and 'action zones' forming the basis of their approaches to improving 'standards' and thus the attainment of boys at school. Raphael Reed's account shows how the closing ('targetting') of Hackney Downs School not only set up a self-fulfilling prophecy in the case of this particular school, but also damaged, irretrievably, work with boys which challenged hegemonic and complicit masculinities (see Connell 1995 and Jackson this volume, on 'hegemonic' and 'complicit' masculinities). It is interesting, in this respect, to note the reports in the press (e.g. *Guardian, The Independent*) on 7 January 1998 that the so-called 'Education Action Zones' will be controlled by private companies. Since these Education Action Zones will, invariably, be in the poorest areas, the New Managerialism in education, thus privatized and at its most ferocious, will bear most heavily on the most disadvantaged populations and their schools.

Boys will be boys

The final key discourse which has achieved a globalized common-sense status is that of 'boys will be boys'. This essentialist, usually biologically based discourse, shares many of the characteristics of the 'poor boys' discourse – indeed, 'poor boys' is often situated within biological discourses. What is particularly interesting about the 'boys will be boys' discourse is the way it manages, at one and the same time, to posit an unchanging and unchangeable 'boyness', which involves aggression, fighting and delayed (some might say indefinitely!) maturity and yet situates poor achievement at school as extrinsic to boys themselves. Indeed, as we have shown above, there is a tradition which claims that boys' very lack of attainment at school is evidence of their superior powers of intellect (Cohen this volume; Walkerdine 1989).

It is, perhaps, unsurprising that the 'solutions' offered by proponents of the 'boys will be boys' discourse resemble those of the 'Lads' Movement'. This is particularly the case in relation to ideas about shifting classroom practice in order to engage boys' interests more strongly and to work with their perceived strengths and to correct their perceived weaknesses (see Raphael Reed and Swann in this volume). Another feature of 'boys will be boys' approaches is the utilization of girls to police, teach, control and civilize boys. This should not surprise us, for it draws on well-established notions of women as responsible for controlling men across a range of activities, but especially in relation to sexuality (Jackson and Scott 1996; Richardson 1996). Furthermore, as Hey *et al.* show in their contribution to this volume, the exploitation of girls in the classroom interacts with notions about special educational needs, with boys' general unwillingness to ask for or accept help from each other, and with racialized perceptions of both boys and girls. This approach rests firmly on the determined and unrelenting heterosexualization of schools (Epstein and Johnson 1998; Hey 1997). Boys will not only be boys, it seems, they will be heterosexual boys; and it is because they are (assumed to be) heterosexual boys that the presumption is made that the civilizing influence of girls will work.

Boys, which boys?

Pat Mahony, in her contribution to this volume, warns that 'We could commit the rest of our lives in trying to find out which boys are underachieving in relation to whom, in what areas, when, in which countries and why.' (p. 39) Her note of caution needs to be taken seriously, but, it is nevertheless important to pause to consider the question, 'Which boys?'. Most of the coverage of education in the popular media would lead one to believe that all girls are doing better than all boys in measured attainment at school. However, as Jannette Elwood has pointed out elsewhere, (Elwood 1998) and as Patricia Murphy and Jannette Elwood show in Chapter 10,[4] the picture is far from simple. There is more overlap between the attainment of boys and of girls than there is difference; there are significant differences in the relative attainments of boys and girls in different subjects and at different levels; and, while there are many boys who are not performing well at schools, there are many others who are doing very well indeed[5] (see also, Arnot and Arizpe 1997; Power *et al.* 1998).

Furthermore, success in school examinations is not everything. For example, girls' success in gaining grade C passes in GCSE mathematics has not, generally, enabled them to go on to A levels because of the way that banding or setting of pupils is gendered. Girls are more likely than boys to be placed in the second band for mathematics GCSE, where the best available grade is a C, rather than the top band (Elwood and Comber 1996; Murphy and Elwood this volume). This enables girls to gain a grade C pass, at best, but most schools allow only those in the top band to choose mathematics at A level and thus go on to a range of mathematical and scientific courses in tertiary education. Moreover, higher achievement at school does not necessarily translate into equality in the labour market. As Pam Gilbert (1998: 28) comments with regard to literacy in Australia:

> [Achievement] does not automatically translate into economic advantage in the world of work. One telling set of figures included in an ACER [Australian Council for Educational Research] report on reading in the junior secondary school suggests that, while good literacy skills provided a clear earnings advantage for 19 year olds in employment, the earning advantage is predominantly experienced by men rather than women.[6] 19 year old women with Very High literacy skills (measured at 14) could expect to earn $335 per week – a wage that was $60 *less* per week than the wage 19 year old men with the same skills could expect. In fact, young men designated as having low and very low literacy levels were still able to earn more than young women who had very high levels of literacy achievement.

There are *particular groups* of boys/young men who are doing badly in the compulsory years of schooling, especially in those areas of the curriculum which traditionally have been seen as 'soft' subjects and therefore falling into the domain of 'girls' work'. Even in these areas, the picture is more complicated that it would appear, as Joan Swann (this volume) shows in relation to language. Patricia Murphy and Jannette Elwood, in their chapter, argue convincingly that the way attainment is measured has gendered effects and that sociocultural factors play an important part in *which* boys and *which* girls do relatively well or badly in examinations in the range of curriculum subjects. They show, furthermore, that often levels of attainment in tradition-ally boys' and traditionally girls' subjects are reversed as students move from GCSE into A level. For example, the small number of girls who decide to take physics at A level are likely to do better than boys, while in English and other languages, boys who pursue them to A level do better than girls. Moreover, as students move from school to university, the gendered effect is that men tend to get more first-class degrees than women and that more men than women undertake higher degrees.

Overall, the 'underachievement' of boys at school is a strongly classed and racialized phenomenon. Indeed, class and the associated level of education of parents (for both boys and girls) continue to be the most reliable predictors of a child's success in school examinations (Riddell 1998; Turner *et al.* 1995). This is particularly clearly demonstrated in the publication of 'league tables' of local education authorities in the United Kingdom. Notwithstanding claims made by Stephen Byers, Labour Minister for Education, that social deprivation cannot be allowed to affect school-based achievement (Smithers 1997), these league tables provide an accurate demographic map of England and Wales, with the poorest and most deprived LEAs coming lowest in the league and the wealthiest, most middle-class LEAs winning the prizes. While there *is* a school effect on achievement, with some schools doing better than others given the same kinds of intake in terms of class and social deprivation (see, for example, Mortimore and Whitty 1997), the evidence suggests that that effect is significantly less than the effect of social factors (Bernstein 1971). Furthermore, as Mortimore and Whitty (1997: 9) point out, 'if all schools performed as well as the best schools, the stratification of achievement by social class would be even more stark than it is now'.

David Gillborn and Caroline Gipps (1996) have shown the disproportion-ate disadvantage of African-Caribbean boys in British schools, both in terms of measured attainment and in terms of exclusions from schools, but this is a statistical generalization and does not mean that all African-Caribbean boys are doing equally badly at school. Tony Sewell (1997, this volume) offers an account, based on ethnographic research, of how black boys con-struct their masculinities within the school context in highly differentiated ways, responding to schooling, and the racism they experience within it, by taking up different versions of masculinity which he represents by four ideal types: the 'conformists', the 'innovators', the 'retreatists' and the 'rebels'. Similarly, Máirtín Mac an Ghaill (1988, 1994) uses his ethnographic work to delineate a range of ways in which young men/boys take up and resist the discursive possibilities offered by schools as 'masculine-making' institutions. Indeed, their work, as well as important publications by others interested in masculinity and schooling[7] including chapters by Debbie Epstein and David Jackson in this volume, show clearly how much exertion is put into achiev-ing masculinity by boys themselves and how much effort is made in schools by teachers and others (often without even realizing they are doing it) to ensure that boys become the 'right kind' of boys.

This brings us back, in some respects, to the 'Lads' Movement', for, as David Jackson and Debbie Epstein both argue in this book, it is those who would be recognized as 'natural born warriors' who are the 'right kind' of boy in the context of many schools. This does not mean that all boys are naturally aggressive, inattentive, troublesome beings, but the hegemonic masculinities of most schools are characterized in these ways and schools are particularly difficult places for boys to depart from the norm. Furthermore, Sally Power and her colleagues (Power *et al.* 1998) show the importance of effortless achievement in elite schools, while Redman and Mac an Ghaill (1997) describe the production of what they call 'intellectual muscularity' in the sixth form of a grammar school. Jackson (this volume) points out that many men and boys 'although seemingly toeing the patriarchal line, are uneasy and troubled about their sense of inner contradiction', while the chapter by Debbie Epstein shows how the harassment of 'sissies' prevails in school cultures. In this context, they argue that for a boy to work at school, or, at least, to do so in detectable ways, is likely to lead to being on the receiving end of homophobic abuse, for the misogyny and homophobia of normative, school-based masculinities regularly conflate school work with effeminacy and homosexuality (see also, Nayak and Kehily 1997).

Feminist interventions in the schooling of boys

This book does not constitute the first feminist/pro-feminist contribution to debates about the schooling of boys. Indeed, Madeleine Arnot's (1984) question 'How shall we educate our sons?', asked almost 15 years ago, has remained a pertinent one for many feminists, and many feminist educators have been involved in trying to develop anti-sexist approaches to the education of boys (e.g. Askew and Ross 1988). In general, feminists writing about education (along with many critical/pro-feminist men) have worked with a wider definition of what it means to educate than that of the current hegemonic view of education as a kind of hurdle race, with tests to leap over at every opportunity, or, to use Paulo Freire's influential metaphor, as a kind of system of banking (Freire 1972) in which more and more knowledge is deposited in the pupils, which can then be drawn out to pass (pay for?) the test.

Feminists' insistence that the personal is political has meant that they have been readier than most others to think about the affective dimensions of schooling. Jenny Shaw (1995) has shown how education can give rise to all kinds of unconscious anxieties best understood from within a psychoanalytic frame of reference. Her analysis of the current debates about boys' 'underachievement' as an expression of these anxieties draws powerfully on metaphors of feeding and the withdrawal of feeding to explain the depth of panic which has pervaded much of the coverage of boys' 'underachievement' (Shaw 1996; see also Mitchell 1986).[8] There are, however, dangers in approaching education as if it were a kind of therapy, as Hey *et al.* (this volume) show in their discussion of special educational needs. Jane Kenway and her colleagues (1996) have also demonstrated some of the dangers of education as therapy, on the one hand, and versions of what she calls 'feminist authoritarianism', on the other.

While most feminists working in education would eschew the kind of zero-sum competition set up, in particular, by supporters of the 'Lads' Movement', it can be treacherously easy to slip into the kind of binarisms, critiqued by David Jackson in his chapter, which seem to assume that the gains of one sex constitute the inevitable losses of the other. Further, almost without noticing it, one can also slip into a set of discourses which either actually blame individual boys for male power in patriarchy, or seem to boys in schools as if they are being blamed (see also Kenway *et al.* 1997). Models of equal opportunities in relation to gender which rested on assumptions that girls were completely powerless and boys all-powerful (or which seemed to say that girls were inevitably in the right and boys inevitably in the wrong) were, as Kenway (1995a: 77) says:

> not sufficiently nuanced to be read as meaningful in the context of people's experience. Often the evidence is so starkly black and white that it is readily refuted as other inequalities (race, ethnicity, sexuality and class) come into the picture.

Notwithstanding these caveats, we would argue, for a number of reasons, that it is through the work of feminists and those profoundly influenced by feminism, that the education of boys and of girls can be improved. First, equity issues, which are at the root of feminism, are of key importance in the education of all pupils/students. The complex interweaving of such issues, the ways that differences which make a difference shape and are shaped by each other, must not be forgotten, as all the contributors to this book would argue (see, especially, Mahony, Jackson, Hey *et al.*, Sewell and Raphael Reed). For, as we have shown in this chapter, experiences of schooling and school-based achievement (even narrowly defined in terms of test/ examination results) are, simultaneously classed, gendered and racialized (at the very least). Second, taking resources away from girls in order to give them to boys, who have always received more educational resources and continue to do so, is not likely to recommend itself as a solution to the problem of educating boys to those working with a feminist theoretical framework. (See Hey *et al.*, this volume for a discussion of how this works in the case of special educational needs.) This is important, not only because to shift resources in this way would be unfair, but also because it is likely to be counter-productive, especially if used to increase, rather than challenge, the hold of hegemonic masculinities in schools as suggested both by proponents of the 'poor boys' and of the 'boys will be boys' discourses. Third, feminist and other critical educators are working with traditions which are likely to resist the kind of credentialism, individualism and competition through tests put forward by proponents of the 'failing schools' discourse. In contrast to the individualized subject of this discourse, feminist and other critical frameworks invariably situate the subject socially, and are therefore better placed to analyse the complex power dynamics of schools as institutions. Fourth, feminist educators have always seen schools as being about sets of concerns over and above those which have been narrowly defined as achievement in current popular and policy debates about the boys. This recognition by feminists (and others) in the past has resulted in the examination of both hidden and taught curricula, styles of teaching and school management, and of the purposes of education beyond the vocational and economic. Without it, in the present context, we are likely to be stuck with the managerialist and technicist approaches of New Labour/Old Tory for some time to come.

A number of feminist and pro-feminist writers, building on earlier feminist work in relation to both girls and boys, suggest ways of intervening in schooling which will improve the education of boys and girls both in terms of attainment in tests/examinations and more broadly. Madeleine Arnot's work and that of her colleagues in the United Kingdom and in Europe (Arnot and Arizpe 1997) is important in that it sets up research and curriculum development projects with schools in ways which pay attention to the lessons learnt from earlier feminist interventions. Similarly, others are working (and have worked) in imaginative ways to develop appropriate, progressive policies and practices for educating boys (Kenway and Fitzclarence 1997; Raphael Reed this volume; Salisbury and Jackson 1996). The current moral panic around boys' 'underachievement' has produced a key opportunity for challenging gender inequalities in schools (see also, Jackson this volume), but it is one which is fraught with danger. As with all such moments, a reactionary recuperation of feminist insights and concerns is also possible. The task of the moment is to ensure that this does not happen.

However, readers will note that we have resisted any temptation to close this book with a chapter of 'conclusions', indicating 'solutions' or the 'way forward'. The series of ESRC seminars which was the genesis of the collection aimed to map the field of issues in the area of underachievement and to examine relevant research, not to seek out 'best practice'. Of course, readers will draw out important principles for positive action, either stated or implied in various chapters. But the issues are multi-faceted, the research complex, and it would be premature to suggest firm directions for others to follow, not least because the complexity and diversity of what is presented here indicates that much of the response needs to be site-specific, and based on a thorough, sensitive collection and analysis of local data. As the book shows, lessons can be learnt from earlier feminist interventions in schools. But even those who were active in work for gender and racial equity in the 1980s are working under new (and less favourable) conditions and, as Pat Mahony (Chapter 3) indicates, the networks and other supports underpinning such work are largely dismantled. It will be important to rebuild them. Equally important is to recognize that any response to the issues raised here would require policy and action both within schools and beyond. Under-achievement is not merely the responsibility of schools.

Acknowledgements

We would like to thank the ESRC for supporting the series of seminars held by the Centre for Research and Education on Gender at the University of London Institute of Education. This book is one of two publications arising from the series, the other being a special issue of the *International Journal of Inclusive Education* (Epstein *et al.* 1998). We would also like to acknowledge the derivation of the title of this chapter from Valerie Walkerdine's (1990) book, *Schoolgirl Fictions* and from a variation of that, 'Schoolgirl frictions', used by Mary Kehily in a chapter of her PhD, currently in progress.

Notes

1 For a survey of the international work in this field see Connell (1996).
2 Bob Lingard (1998: 6), points out that policies which attempt to improve literacy by testing, without regard to social justice, student disadvantage and socio-economic status '[forget] the wise observation that you "don't fatten the cow by weighing it"'.
3 This may, in fact, go some way to explaining why, in the United Kingdom, 'discourses of derision' (Kenway 1987) about teachers which reached a high point under the Conservative government (Ball 1990), have continued unabated during the first year of the New Labour government.
4 See, also, a longer version of the chapter in the *International Journal of Inclusive Education* (Murphy and Elwood 1998).
5 The flurry of newspaper items which appeared on 5, 6 and 7 January 1998 (in, for example, the *Observer*, the *Guardian*, the *Daily Mail* and the *Evening Standard*) focused on 'boys' underachievement'. However, an examination of the 'league tables' published in the *Observer* and some of the other papers, shows that this is not universally the case.
6 This data is available in Australian Council for Educational Research (1997: 9).
7 For example, Connell (1989, 1995), Christine Griffin's and Sue Lees' special issue of *Gender and Education* (1997), Kenway and colleagues (Kenway 1995a; Kenway *et al.* 1997) and Peter Redman and Máirtín Mac an Ghaill (1997).
8 It is a matter of great regret to the editors of this book that, because of time constraints, Jenny Shaw was unable to write up her contribution to the seminar series for us.

References

Apple, M. (1997) Educating the right way. Paper presented to the Culture, Commun-ication and Societies/Policy Studies joint seminar, University of London Institute of Education.

Arnot, M. (1984) How shall we educate our sons?, in R. Deem (ed.) *Co-education Reconsidered*. Milton Keynes: Open University Press.

Arnot, M. and Arizpe, E. (1997) The new boys of the 90s: a study of the reconstruction of masculinities in relation to economic change. Paper presented at the ESRC funded seminar series 'Gender and Education: Are Boys Now Underachieving?'. Centre for Research and Education on Gender, University of London Institute of Education, May.

Askew, S. and Ross, C. (eds) (1988) *Boys Don't Cry: Boys and Sexism in Education*. Milton Keynes: Open University Press.

Australian Council for Educational Research (1997) *Reading and Numeracy in Junior Secondary Schools: Trends, Patterns and Consequences*. Melbourne: Australian Council for Educational Research.

Ball, S. J. (1990) *Markets, Morality and Equality in Education*. London: Tufnell Press.

Bernstein, B. (1971) Education cannot compensate for society, in B. Cosin, I. R. Dale, G. M. Esland, D. Mackinnon and D. F. Swift (eds) *School and Society: A Sociological Reader*. London and Henley: Routledge and Kegan Paul in association with the Open University Press.

Biddulph, S. (1994) *Manhood: A Book about Setting Men Free*. Sydney: Finch Publishing.

Bly, R. (1990) *Iron John: A Book about Men*. Reading, MA: Addison-Wesley.

Boaler, J. (1997) *Experiencing School Mathematics: Teaching Styles, Sex and Setting*. Buckingham: Open University Press.

Boaler, J. (1998) Mathematical equity – underachieving boys or sacrificial girls?, in D. Epstein, J. Maw, J. Elwood and V. Hey (eds) *International Journal of Inclusive Education: Special Issue on Boys' 'Underachievement'*, 2(2): 19–134.

Board of Education (1923) *Report on the Differentiation of the Curricula Between the Sexes in Secondary Schools*. London: HMSO.

Connell, R. W. (1989) Cool guys, swots and wimps: the interplay of masculinity and education. *Oxford Review of Education*, 13(3): 291–303.

Connell, R. W. (1995) *Masculinities*. Cambridge: Polity.

Connell, R. W. (1996) Teaching the boys. *Teachers College Record*, 98(2): 206–35.

Crittenden, B. (ed.) (1994) *Confusion Worse Confounded: Australian Education in the 1990s: Cunningham Lecture and Annual Symposium*. Canberra: Academy of the Social Sciences in Australia.

Elium, D. and Elium, J. (1992) *Raising a Son: Parenting and the Making of a Healthy Man*. Stroud: Hawthorn Press.

Elwood, J. (1998) 'Gender and performance in the GCE A level: gender equity and the gold standard', unpublished PhD thesis. University of London Institute of Education.

Elwood, J. and Comber, C. (1996) *Gender Differences in Examinations at 18+: Final Report*, London: University of London Institute of Education.

Epstein, D. and Johnson, R. (1998) *Schooling Sexualities*. Buckingham: Open University Press.

Epstein, D., Maw, J., Elwood, J. and Hey, V. (eds) (1998) *International Journal of Inclusive Education: Special Issue on Boys' 'Underachievement'*, 2(2).

Freire, P. (1972) *Pedagogy of the Oppressed*, trans. Myra Bergman. London: Penguin, 1996.

Gilbert, P. (1998) The 1997 Radford Lecture. Gender and schooling in new times: the challenge of boys and literacy. *Australian Educational Researcher*, 25(1): 15–36.

Gillborn, D. and Gipps, C. (1996) *Recent Research on the Achievements of Ethnic Minority Pupils*. London: HMSO.

Griffin, C. and Lees, S. (eds) (1997) *Gender and Education: Special Issue on Masculinities* 9(1).

Hearn, S. (1996) *Standards-based Assessment in New Zealand and the United Kingdom: The New Zealand Qualifications Framework and GNVQ,* Associateship report. London: University of London Institute of Education.

Hey, V. (1997) *The Company She Keeps: An Ethnography of Girls' Friendship.* Buckingham: Open University Press.

Jackson, S. and Scott, S. (eds) (1996) *Feminism and Sexuality: A Reader.* Edinburgh: Edinburgh University Press.

Kenway, J. (1987) Left right out: Australian education and the politics of signification. *Journal of Education Policy,* 2(3): 189–203.

Kenway, J. (1995a) Masculinities in schools: under siege, on the defensive and under reconstruction? *Discourse: Studies in the Cultural Politics of Education,* 16(1): 59–79.

Kenway, J. (1995b) Masculinity and education. Paper presented at the Centre for Research and Education on Gender/Social Science Research Unit Seminar, University of London Institute of Education, November.

Kenway, J. and Fitzclarence, L. (1997) Masculinity, violence and schooling: challenging 'poisonous pedagogies'. *Gender and Education,* 9(1): 117–33.

Kenway, J., Blackmore, J., Willis, S. and Rennie, L. (1996) The emotional dimensions of feminist pedagogy in schools, in P. Murphy and C. V. Gipps (eds) *Equity in the Classroom: Towards Effective Pedagogy for Girls and Boys.* London/Paris: Falmer Press UNESCO.

Kenway, J., Blackmore, J., Willis, S. and Rennie, L. (1997) *Answering Back: Boys and Girls in School.* Sydney: Allen and Unwin; London and New York: Routledge, 1998.

Kruse, A.-M. (1996) Approaches to teaching girls and boys: current debates, practices and perspectives in Denmark, in P. Mahony (ed.) *Changing Schools: Some International Feminist Perspectives on Working with Girls and Boys.* Special Issue *Women's Studies International Forum,* 19: 429–45.

Lingard, B. (1998) The disadvantaged schools programme: caught between literacy and local management of schools. *International Journal of Inclusive Education,* 2(1): 1–14.

Locke, J. (1989) *Some Thoughts Concerning Education,* ed. J. S. Yolton and J. W. Yolton. Oxford: Clarendon Press (first published 1693).

Lydon, N. (1996) Man trouble. *Guardian,* 14 May.

Mac an Ghaill, M. (1988) *Young, Gifted and Black.* Milton Keynes: Open University Press.

Mac an Ghaill, M. (1994) *The Making of Men: Masculinities, Sexualities and Schooling.* Buckingham: Open University Press.

Miller, J. (1996) *School for Women.* London: Virago.

Mitchell, J. (ed.) (1986) *The Selected Melanie Klein.* Harmondsworth: Penguin.

Mortimore, P. and Whitty, G. (1997) *Can School Improvement Overcome the Effects of Disadvantage?* London: University of London Institute of Education.

Murphy, P. and Elwood, J. (1998) Gendered experiences, choices and achievement – exploring the links, in D. Epstein, J. Maw, J. Elwood and V. Hey (eds) *International Journal of Inclusive Education: Special Issue on Boys' 'Underachievement',* 2(2): 95–118.

Nayak, A. and Kehily, M. (1997) Masculinities and schooling: why are young men so homophobic?, in D. L. Steinberg, D. Epstein and R. Johnson (eds) *Border Patrols: Policing the Boundaries of Heterosexuality.* London: Cassell.

Power, S., Whitty, G. and Edwards, T. (1998) Schoolboys and schoolwork: gender identification and academic achievement, in D. Epstein, J. Maw, J. Elwood and V. Hey (eds) *International Journal of Inclusive Education: Special Issue on Boys' 'Underachievement',* 2(2): 135–53.

Redman, P. and Mac an Ghaill, M. (1997) Educating Peter: the making of a history man, in D. L. Steinberg, D. Epstein and R. Johnson (eds) *Border Patrols: Policing the Boundaries of Heterosexuality*. London: Cassell.

Richardson, D. (ed.). (1996) *Theorising Heterosexuality*. Buckingham: Open University Press.

Riddell, S. (1998) Boys and underachievement: the Scottish dimension, in D. Epstein, J. Maw, J. Elwood and V. Hey (eds) *International Journal of Inclusive Education: Special Issue on Boys' 'Underachievement'*, 2(2): 169–86.

Salisbury, J. and Jackson, D. (1996) *Challenging Macho Values: Practical Ways of Working with Adolescent Boys*. London: Falmer Press.

Sammons, P., Thomas, S., Mortimore, P., Owen, C. and Pennell, H. (1994) *Assessing School Effectiveness: Developing Measures to put School Performance in Context*, a report by the Institute of Education for the Office for Standards in Education. London: University of London Institute of Education, International School Effectiveness and Improvement Centre.

Sewell, T. (1997) *Black Masculinities and Schooling: How Black Boys Survive Modern Schooling*. Stoke-on-Trent: Trentham Books.

Shaw, J. (1995) *Education, Gender and Anxiety*. London: Taylor and Francis.

Shaw, J. (1996) Boys' underachievement and defence mechanisms: a defence against what? Paper presented at the ESRC-funded serminar series 'Gender and education: are boys now underachieving?', Centre for Research and Education on Gender, University of London Institute of Education, 15 November.

Smithers, R. (1997) Poverty row looms over literacy drive, *Guardian*, 20 October.

Stoll, L. and Fink, D. (1996) *Changing Our Schools: Linking School Effectiveness and School Improvement*. Buckingham: Open University Press.

Turner, E., Riddell, S. and Brown, S. (1995) *Gender Equality in Scottish Schools: The Impact of Recent Educational Reforms*. Manchester: Equal Opportunities Commission.

Unterhalter, E. (1996) States, households and the market in World Bank discourses 1985–1995: a feminist critique. *Discourse: Feminist Perspectives on the Marketisation of Education* (special issue ed. D. Epstein and J. Kenway), 17(3): 389–401.

Walkerdine, V. (1989) *Girls and Mathematics: New Thoughts on an Old Question*. London: Virago.

Walkerdine, V. (1990) *Schoolgirl Fictions*. London: Verso.

Willis, P. (1977) *Learning to Labour: How Working Class Kids Get Working Class Jobs*. Aldershot: Saxon House.

2

'A habit of healthy idleness': boys' underachievement in historical perspective

MICHÈLE COHEN

> As we enter the next millenium it is the under-achievement of boys that has become one of the biggest challenges facing society today.
>
> (Ted Wragg, *Times Educational Supplement*, 16 May 1997)

In the past few years, there has been an increasing amount of anxiety about 'boys' underachievement'. The underachieving boy, Chris Woodhead (Chief Inspector of Schools) is reported to have said, is 'one of the most disturbing problems facing the education system' (*Times Magazine*, 30 March 1996). The sense of crisis has been compounded by press and media headlines such as 'Girls doing well while boys feel neglected' (*Guardian*, 26 August 1995), 'Girls outclassing boys' (*Guardian*, 26 November 1997), and 'Is the future female' (*Panorama*, BBC1, May 1995), which have not only taken this anxiety into people's homes, but suggest at the same time that the world is somehow upside down.

The question all the various commentators are asking, explicitly or implicitly, is 'Why are boys now underachieving?' This question solicits a wide variety of analyses, all suggesting a 'cause' for the new problem: these causes include the lack of male role models for boys at school; schools 'abdicating their responsibilities' and frustrating boys 'to the point of frenzy by a perverse refusal to give them clear goals' (*Daily Telegraph*, 19 November 1996); economic changes affecting boys (especially working-class boys) more markedly than girls; and finally, the 'crisis of masculinity'. Despite the confusion, two interlinked strands can be discerned. The first is that girls' achievement since the 1980s has something to do with boys' failure, as if a 'backlash period' has sprung forth 'as a result of a decade of equal opportunities policy making deliberately aimed at girls and young women' (Weiner *et al.* 1997: 1). The second strand, less frequently articulated – perhaps because it seems an obvious implication of the first – is that, until recently, boys were doing better than girls, boys were best. What boys used to think about was 'beating the other chaps for top prizes . . . passing the scholarship, coming top of the class, getting the apprenticeship: whatever the most esteemed feats were in their particular social milieu' (*Daily Telegraph*, 19 November 1996). Similarly, one young unemployed man, interviewed about his and his male classmates' attitude to the school he left only 5 years before, said to the interviewer 'the boys worked only if pushed whereas the girls all had wanted to work and tried harder.' 'But', he added, 'it used to be the other way round' (BBC1 1995b).

Stories about a 'Golden Age' of boys' achievement are particularly interesting for an historical perspective on boys' underachievement, for my main argument in this chapter is that over the period I have been researching – from the late seventeenth century to the present – boys have always 'underachieved', and more importantly, this underachievement has never been seriously addressed. What I mean is that though it has been of concern, underachievement has never been treated as a problem of boys. The main reason for this is the way the discourse on achievement has been organized and deployed. Boys' achievement has been attributed to something within – the nature of their intellect – but their failure has been attributed to something external – a pedagogy, methods, texts, teachers. The full significance of this becomes clear when the subject of the discourse is girls, for in their case it is their failure which is attributed to something within – usually the nature of their intellect – and their success to something external: methods, teachers or particular conditions. Attributing boys' failure to a *method* has made it possible to explain away their poor results without implicating boys themselves. Attributing girls' success to the method has had different effects (see Cohen 1996a), the most important one for this discussion being that their performance holds the promise for *boys'* achievement.

Two examples, one from the 1980s, and one from the late seventeenth century, will illustrate my argument. *Boys, Girls and Languages in School* (1985) is a short monograph which I chose because its author, Bob Powell, claims to be addressing boys' underachievement. Powell's argument is that whereas girls' underperformance in maths and sciences has received a lot of attention since the 1970s, none has been directed at boys' underperformance in languages.[1] What Powell does not say is that for most of this century girls have been observed to outperform boys in French. However, there has always been some explanation for boys' underperformance – and for girls' superior achievement: boys did not do well at French because they considered it a "cissy" subject or at least not a boys' subject' (Dale 1974: 156), or because the teachers were female; boys underperformed in (oral) French because they were shy and 'reluctant to make an effort with French pronunciation in front of an opposite sex who on the average tend to be more at home in this aspect of the work' (Dale 1974: 135). Girls outperformed boys because they have a better ear and greater mimetic ability (Board of Education 1923), because French is a girls' subject and they like it (Dale 1974: 158), or because they have an innate verbal advantage (Hawkins 1981). The teachers in Powell's survey provide yet other explanations. Some attribute boys' poor performance to the early emphasis on 'written accuracy', others ascribe girls' superior grades to their neatness. According to one teacher 'it is all too easy to take neat, careful written work produced by girls as evidence of linguistic ability whilst boys, who are probably just as capable, tend not to pay as much attention to this area' (Powell 1985: 67). Powell's own explanation is that girls' superiority results from their accepting to do the repetitive and meaningless tasks required by current methods while boys refuse. Not surprisingly, Powell's solutions include making language learning more interesting and appealing to boys by making it more 'mathematical' and introducing more computer-based teaching and problem-solving exercises. What about the girls? Powell suggests that teachers should ensure they get 'fair access' to the computers (Powell 1985: 62–3).

In his 1693 educational treatise *Some Thoughts Concerning Education* (1989), John Locke too was addressing boys' underachievement. He was concerned by young gentlemen's failure to master Latin despite spending years studying it. Locke attributed this lack of success to the practice, current at the time, of teaching Latin by grammar rules.[2] By contrast, he noted, little girls learned French rapidly and successfully just by 'pratling' it with their governesses. It is not because Locke wanted to remark on little girls' cleverness that he mentioned their success at French. Rather, he meant his remark to show how *easy* it was to learn languages by the *conversational method*, the method he wanted to promote (against contemporary opinion) to teach boys Latin.

Highlighting the *method* as the means to success, then, holds the promise of boys' achievement. It also serves to ensure that girls are repositioned in the proper hierarchy of intellect. For Locke in the seventeenth century, this was self-evident, and he commented 'I cannot but wonder, how Gentlemen have over-seen this way [the conversational method] for their sons, and thought them more dull or incapable than their Daughters' (1989: 218). Though Powell, in the twentieth century, claims to be addressing boys' underachievement, this underachievement vanishes before our very eyes as it becomes transformed into a healthy (and long overdue) rebellion against ineffectual teaching techniques, while girls' superiority becomes just a trick of the light, a matter of their compliance, obedience, or seduction of teachers by the neat appearance of their work.

Two important points can be drawn from these examples. The first is a question. Why has it been so important, and for so long, to protect the notion of boys' potential? The second concerns gender: gender is crucial to the historical perspective I am proposing not just because of the future – the call for a focus on boys' performance must not be at the expense of girls – but because of the past. I shall be arguing that in the gendering of Englishness that emerges at the end of the eighteenth century, 'potential' was *constitutive* of the sexed mind and masculinity. It has continued to be perceived as a distinctive feature of the male intellect (see Walkerdine 1989, 1994). But because potential is gendered,[3] its relation to achievement is far from straightforward: a boy's poor performance tends to be read as a sign that he possesses what it takes to succeed – his potential intact *because* it is invisible – while a girl's good performance is read as a sign of lack. 'Potential' thus threatens to subvert the notion of achievement itself, and the tension between gendered potential and gendered achievement that has existed since (at least) Locke's day still serves to divert attention from boys' underperformance.

The problems around boys in today's schools cannot be examined simply as 'results' of present circumstances, especially when these include an alleged feminization of schooling, of achievement, of the teaching profession (see for example Cross 1982; Morris 1996) or of textbooks to explain boys' failure.[4] Unless historical considerations, and in particular the historical construction of masculinity, are brought to bear on the analysis, interventions are likely, at best, to perpetuate the current problems, and at worse, to threaten the gains made for sex equality since the 1970s. I will now turn to a consideration of performance and the historical construction of masculinity.

Conversation, taciturnity and the English gentleman

Locke was not concerned only with young gentlemen's failure to master Latin. He also criticized their English:

> There can scarce be a greater Defect in a Gentleman, than not to express himself well either in Writing or Speaking. But yet, I think, I may ask my Reader, whether he doth not know a great many, who live upon their Estates, and so, with the Name, should have the Qualities of Gentlemen, who cannot so much as tell a Story as they should; much less speak clearly and persuasively in any Business. This, I think not to be so much their Fault, as the Fault of their Education.
>
> (Locke 1989: 240–1)

Locke was unequivocal: gentlemen should 'labour to get a facility, clearness and elegancy' in their own tongue, English (p. 244). Locke was not an isolated voice. Gentlemen's expression in English was a focus of comment and criticism throughout the eighteenth century. The context for this concern was the sociability and politeness essential to eighteenth-century society, and the supreme importance of an easy and elegant conversation to the fashioning of the gentleman (Cohen 1996b). From Defoe (1712: 317) who, early in the century, complained that young men came out of academies 'perfectly ignorant . . . of their Mother Tongue, especially as to the Beauties of Style, Cadence, and Politeness of Language' to the Reverend James Fordyce (1770)

who, at the end of the century, commented on the awkwardness and grace-
lessness of men's conversation, criticism converged on gentlemen's failure to
achieve the conversational ideal required by politeness.

In the same period, from Locke in the late seventeenth century to Hannah
More 100 years later, the 'Elegancy and Politeness' (Locke 1989: 198) of
women's language was noted – an achievement all the more remarkable
since women did not learn grammar. As Hannah More (1799: II 59) would
put it

> In the faculty of speaking well, ladies have such a happy promptitude of
> turning their slender advantages to account that there are many who,
> though they have never been taught a rule of syntax, yet by a quick
> facility in profiting from the best books and the best company, hardly
> ever violate one.

My aim here is to discuss not whether there was a 'real' problem with men's
English expression and why, but rather the explanations that were adduced
for their perceived incompetence. In general, it was attributed to boys' education, as Locke claims (1989: 240–1, quoted above). The study of the classics,
James Fordyce specified, gave men 'habits of accuracy' which hampered their
'faculties' (1770: 153); it was this that hindered their fluency and made their
conversation awkward. Other factors were also held to account for the
inadequacy of men's conversation. The most significant was taciturnity –
which essayist Joseph Addison (1711) deemed a (male) national trait, contrasting it favourably with Frenchmen's 'light, talkative humour', but which
grammarian Thomas Wilson (1729: 32) denounced as the 'clog upon the
tongue' of Englishmen.[5]

It could be argued that the concern over men's expression in English was
historically specific, an attempt to discipline the social in the age of politeness. Yet, similar criticisms were voiced two centuries later. In the Newbolt
Report on *The Teaching of English* (Board of Education 1921), Rugby's headmaster complained that the English composition of a large proportion of
boys entering his school was 'clumsy and painful to the verge of illiteracy',
and that boys were 'unable to grasp a line of argument or assimilate or
criticize the contents of a book'. This, he suggested, was the result of the
neglect of English. The neglect of the mother tongue was also held to lead to
'the inhibition of the general power of thinking [of boys] between the ages
of 7–14 years' (Board of Education 1921: 87–8). At the same time, however,
Rugby's headmaster also pointed out that 'to be bad at English . . . seemed to
be regarded by both masters and boys as a natural defect' (Board of Education 1921: 105). It may be true that the emphasis on the classics at the
expense of English failed boys, preventing them from developing skills in
their mother tongue. After all it was only in the second decade of this
century that English came to be established as the core of the modern
curriculum (Doyle 1987; Shrosbree 1988). But then, how are we to read
this historical evidence in the light of present concerns about boys lagging

behind girls in English language and especially reading, in today's secondary schools. The reasons adduced for this are, again, many and varied (see Millard 1997). Boys see reading as a 'female more than male activity' (Wragg 1997: 4) because, some argue, it is mothers, not fathers, who read to young children at home; or because there are too few male teachers in primary schools. Others still claim that school books cater only to girls' interests: one newspaper article even reports that one secondary school 'discovered that in a purge of political correctness in the Eighties, its library had been stripped of adventure and action books' (*Times Magazine*, 30 March 1996).[6] Yet, the same article points out that 'boys have always lagged behind girls in language skills'. The problem is that they seem to be getting worse.

A historical perspective on this issue suggests an altogether different interpretation, one whose relevance to the overall concern of this chapter will soon become clear. I have been arguing that for most of the eighteenth century, men's conversation was seen as less accomplished than women's, which was held up as a model of elegance and politeness. In the last 20 years of the eighteenth century, however, a major shift took place: conversational skills and fluency became suspect. This 'derogation of the tongue', I have argued elsewhere (Cohen 1996b), is related to changes in English masculine identity. As long as conversation defined the English gentleman, cultivating the tongue was the main technique for fashioning the self. In the late eighteenth century, as part of the shift implied by the discourse on the sexed mind (which I discuss below) the gentleman was to be produced by the training and disciplining of his mental faculties and the tongue came to be derogated. The English gentleman's reticent tongue and inarticulateness, which had been unfavourably contrasted with the conversational fluency of English women and of the French for most of the eighteenth century, now became evidence of the depth and strength of his mind. Conversely, women's conversational skills became evidence of the shallowness and weakness of their mind. If men sound confused, argued Hannah More (1785: 54), it is because of their 'deep reflection', whereas women's 'sprightliness', their 'rash dexterity', is often the mark of their thoughtlessness. It was the strength of men's minds that provided the self-regulation and restraint on their tongues that women lacked. Taciturnity, once held to result from the 'Clog upon the tongue' of the Englishman, now became the emblem not only of his manly self-regulation but of his mental superiority over both English women and the talkative French (Cohen 1996b). For this discussion, the most important consequence of the derogation of the tongue was the forging of an obligatory connection between depth of intellect, masculinity and taciturnity.

Though Addison (1711) had remarked, in the early eighteenth century, that the English 'delight in Silence', it was only later in the century that verbal reserve came to be valued. From John Andrews (1784: 42), who commended the 'natural reserve of the English' (in contrast to the loquacious and effeminate French), to Carlyle's (1840) silent and manly heroes, taciturnity was not only associated with masculine Englishness but became the index of the 'natural' superiority of (elite) English males. Twentieth-century representations of Englishness – the 'intensely reserved' public school boy (Board of Education 1921: 122), the phrases 'stiff upper lip', 'cool', 'strong silent type' – all point to a continuing association of reserve and taciturnity with Anglo-Saxon masculinity. Is it possible to consider that the couple masculinity-taciturnity sits uneasily for boys with today's emphasis in schools on 'communication competence'?

The sexed mind and the boy's potential

Though it could still be argued in the 1780s that 'the mind has no sex' (Jardine 1788: I 324), conduct and educational literature was also beginning to be marked by a desire for a more radical differentiation between the sexes.[7] 'The mind of each sex has some kind of natural bias which constitutes a distinction of character' declared Hannah More in 1785 (p. 13), and at the end of the decade educationists were actively constructing sets of mental traits distinctive to each sex. In this new discourse of difference, male and female bodies were believed to be homologous with their minds, so that the female's greater weakness of body and mind formed a continuity, as did the male's physical and mental strengths. 'Woman's outward frame is marked with a physical inferiority. It appears not to be calculated for such efforts of thinking as the more abstracted sciences require' asserted John Bennett (1787: 104).[8] More significantly for this discussion, difference was also constructed by taking specific female qualities such as vivacity and quickness as distinctive evidence of the inferiority of the female mind. Vivacity, declared Bennett (p. 107), is 'unfavourable to profound thinking'. Woman has scarcely a thought she can call her own, 'except what is fugitive and transient as lightning' (Chirol 1809: 8). Thus, if little girls were quicker and generally more advanced than boys of the same age, this was not, Bennett (1787: 105–6) argued, because they were cleverer. On the contrary, it was because boys were thoughtful and deep that they were slow and appeared dull: 'gold sparkles less than tinsel'. Thus, as the eighteenth century came to a close, girls' brightness, construed as inferiority, and boys' dullness construed as potential, were woven into the fabric of gender difference. Vicesimus Knox (1784: 30), for example, warned parents against the 'common mistake' of thinking that 'early vivacity and loquacity [were] marks of genius . . . I would sooner despair of a remarkably vivacious child, than of one whose reserve and silence wear the appearance of dulness'.

By the closing decades of the nineteenth century, conspicuous dullness, the sign of the upper-class boy's incommensurable *potential*, placed him at the apex of evolution, and distinguished him not just from all girls but from bright and expressive lower-class boys. Thus, physician Sir James Crichton-Browne (1883: 343–4) declared that

The premature sharpness . . . of our street Arabs [is] proverbial, and contrast[s] with the obtuseness . . . of well-to-do . . . children; but the street Arabs finally fall far short of the latter in intelligence. Girls are in all countries more precocious than boys, but they stop at a lower point in mental evolution . . . Forwardness of intellect . . . is only a sign of inferior organisation.[9]

Before I consider the impact of the discourses around 'potential' on education today, I want to turn briefly to another aspect of the history of boys' underachievement, the discourse of 'overstrain'.

Overstrain and boys' achievement

Overstrain makes sense only in the context of the belief, prevalent in the late nineteenth century, that the body's energy is finite and that its resources have to be carefully managed. 'Nature is a strict accountant', wrote Herbert Spencer in 1873 (1905: 217) 'and if you demand of her in one direction more than she is prepared to lay out, she balances the account by making a deduction elsewhere . . . Let it never be forgotten that the amount of vital energy which the body at any moment possesses, is limited.' Though Spencer's warnings about overstrain did not focus specifically on girls, it was girls who became the main object of physicians' concern because, the argument went, girls were 'overconscientious'. To explain the way girls' 'overconscientiousness' came into the discourse on education and related to boys' underachievement, we must first go back to the Schools' Inquiry Commission (1868), the first systematic and public assessment of boys' and girls' performance.[10] Comparing girls and boys, the Assistant Commissioners found, again and again, evidence that girls outperformed boys. Assistant Commissioner Bryce, for example, found that they were better in reading, spelling, geography and history. Though girls were found less 'quick and accurate in arithmetic, algebra and Euclid', when they had been prepared for the same maths exam as boys, they did better than the boys (Taunton Commission 1868: I 549, 550). Assessing girls' capacity to follow the same curriculum as boys, the assistant commissioners noted in particular girls' greater eagerness to learn and the female mind's tendency to develop more rapidly than the male's (vol. V 952). This soon became ground for concern not about how boys would keep up with the girls, but about the danger of overstrain for girls.

This concern grew, fuelled by Edward Clarke's *Sex in Education* (1873) and was immediately taken up in England by the eminent British psychiatrist Henry Maudsley (1874).[11] Although women physicians such as Mary Putnam Jacobi (1877) in the United States and Elizabeth Garrett Anderson (1874) in the United Kingdom[12] cleverly rebutted Clarke's and Maudsley's arguments, the discourse of overstrain took on increasing importance, 'every attempt to broaden the syllabus in girls' schools produced its crop of portentous threats' (Manton 1965: 237), and culminated in eugenic anxieties at the turn of the century. 'Woman's eager nature and greater conscientiousness during adolescence lead her on to take too much out of herself when she is being educated' asserted Dr Clouston, Vice President of the Royal College of Physicians in Edinburgh (1906: 157). Doctors and physiologists, the 'priests of the body and the special guardians of the physical and mental qualities of the race' (Clouston 1906: 156), were especially concerned with the stress intellectual endeavours might put upon women's capacity for healthy maternity and the additional risk of 'atrophied maternal instincts' (Clouston 1911: 111). The question is: why was there so little concern about overstrain in boys?[13]

'Girls come to you to learn; boys have to be driven', noted one of the witnesses to the Schools Inquiry Commission (Taunton Commission 1868: V 952, Q.11874). Comparing boys and girls in their review of the advantages and disadvantages of coeducation, C. Grant and N. Hodgson (1913: 272) declared that the boy's 'breezy attitude to life . . . successfully secures him from morbid concentration on the acquisition of knowledge'. By contrast, the girl 'broods over her tasks and reproaches herself her imperfections'. The eager and achieving girl had become pathologized, while boys' underperformance was an expression of their 'traditionally "boyish" ways'. Accounting for girls' superior performance as a pathology ensured that boys' underachievement needed no theorizing, leaving their potential intact.

In its *Report on the Differentiation of the Curricula Between the Sexes in Secondary Schools* (1923), the Board of Education institutionalized these differences. It asserted that girls were just as able as boys from the point of view of intellect, and there was thus no reason to differentiate the curriculum according to sex. But because girls were more industrious and conscientious, they were susceptible to overstrain. This became 'a determining factor in the differentiation of the curriculum according to sex' and became an integral element in educational discourse (Cohen 1996a: 132). Boys were safe from overuse of (mental) energy because, 'it is well known that most boys, especially at the period of adolescence, have a habit of "healthy idleness"' (Board of Education 1923: 120). 'Overstrain' is thus a crucial construct for a history of boys' underachievement, because it contributed to producing the underperformance of boys as an index of their mental health.

The figure of the overconscientious or even 'morbidly' diligent girl and that of the 'healthily' unconcerned boy became a commonplace in educational writing – echoed by the teacher in Powell's survey cited earlier (Powell 1985). Nothing is more telling of the pervasiveness of the stereotypes than casual, offhand, remarks like that in a book about language teaching published in 1930, where the author writes 'girls on the whole are more conscientious in their attitude toward their work. Many girls will work at a subject they dislike. No healthy boy ever does!' (Brereton 1930: 94–5).

Public schools, masculinity and the myth of effortless achievement

I argued earlier that in the nineteenth century the English elite male was distinguished by his 'natural' mental superiority. This superiority required exercising and disciplining, a task best accomplished in the public schools which had increasingly been favoured by the aristocracy since the late eighteenth century (Cannon 1984). Cultivating the mental faculties may thus have been 'the single most important educational learning theory of the nineteenth century' (Rothblatt 1976: 129–30), but what the public school system aimed to produce was 'manly gentlemen' (Vance 1975: 23) not 'effeminate, enfeebled bookworms' (Mangan 1981: 189). As old Etonian John Walter put it in his testimony to the Clarendon Commission (1864: 301, Q.9413), 'you want a strong healthy race of men, both in mind and body, and not a number of finely grown plants'.[14] It was not academic achievement but 'character' that was at the heart of education in the Victorian public schools, what Stefan Collini (1985: 47) calls 'those great ateliers for turning out well-made characters'.

The crucial point here is not just that character had a 'mystical', ineffable quality which, like the aristocratic *je ne sais quoi*, was incommensurable, but that it was counterposed to scholarly achievement.[15] Even while a school like Eton had 'the worst record of classical scholarship' (Shrosbree 1988: 28), it could claim to train the mind better than any other school. 'The true object of education' declared John Walter (Clarendon Commission 1864, Eton evidence III Q.9412), who had three sons at Eton at the time of the Clarendon Commission, 'is to train the mind to overcome difficulties, and to get it into shape'. Too much knowledge will 'confuse the mind' and though you 'gain amounts of knowledge . . . you lose power. The great object is to gain power.' Indeed, 'the attempt to teach anything well, even the classics, lowered the tone of the school, for it meant that the aristocracy were judged by what they could do rather than by who they were' (Shrosbree 1988: 28). Nevertheless, the mental superiority of the public school boy was always assumed. It was the premiss upon which the whole edifice was built. Ultimately, the product of the public school fits John Barrell's definition of the eighteenth-century gentleman as one who is 'in, so to speak, a condition of empty potential, one who is imagined as being able to comprehend everything, and yet who may give no evidence of having comprehended anything' (Barrell 1983: 203).

The relevance of what may seem to be a digression into public schools is that these schools, especially Eton, were the models for twentieth-century secondary education (Shrosbree 1988; Wiener 1981). One consequence is that the illusion of excellence (Shrosbree 1988) fostered by public schools became a real standard of attainment for all. Thus, as late as 1974, in the introduction to the third volume of his *magnum opus* on coeducation, R. R. Dale (1971: III 3) was still maintaining that 'high academic attainment is not the most important aim of a school. We are all agreed that good character, right attitudes and a healthy emotional development are of far more value.' Similarly, most of the headmasters and teachers surveyed in the Schools Council (1968) *Enquiry* No. 1, *Young School Leavers* – who were mostly working-class children – maintained that personality and character were the most important school objectives for school-leavers of both sexes, and examination achievement the least. For parents, these priorities were reversed.

Examination achievement has become much more important in the past few years, but while it is important to understand why things have changed, I would want to argue that it is also necessary to ask what has remained the same. In *The Making of Men* (1994) Máirtín Mac an Ghaill discusses groups of boys' negotiations of a masculine identity within a school setting. The group of interest to my discussion is the group of white middle-class boys who called themselves the 'Real Englishmen'. Mac an Ghaill (1994: 59, 64–70) describes the features constituting their peer-group identity: they saw themselves as 'arbiters of culture'; they made 'highly public display of a contradictory "effortless achievement"'; they 'rejected the school's work ethic assuming that intellectual talent was "naturally" inscribed within their peer group'; and they were 'critical of "hard-working" students' in the school, especially the 'Academic Achievers', a group of Asian and white young men from skilled working-class backgrounds, whom they dismissed as 'sloggers'. For Mac an Ghaill, these traits constitute part of these boys' challenge to the authority relations of the classroom. In particular, because he sees 'effortless achievement' as a contradiction, he explains: these boys have 'inverted the taken-for-granted relationship between academic success and a positive response to mental labour' (p. 67).

Without a historical perspective, the 'Real Englishmen's' stance seems indeed contradictory and paradoxical. My point, however, is that in English culture this is not a paradox. 'Effortless achievement' contructs the 'Real Englishmen's' 'natural' intellectual talent as it has the mental superiority of the aristocrat or gentleman. 'Effortless achievement' is a key concept in the English aristocratic attitude to education (Power *et al.* 1998: 143)[16] and constructs not only the superior mental power of the English gentleman but his 'other', the swot, whose hard work is the very evidence of his lack of 'natural' intellect: the 'scholarship boy',[17] academic achievers such as the working-class boys in Mac an Ghaill's study, and all females. As Power *et al.* (1998: 140) point out, the public school ethos of manliness is one where academic achievement is not important – in fact, it threatens masculinity. It is not surprising then that boys who have a 'positive orientation to the academic curriculum' and seek academic credentials (Mac an Ghaill 1994: 59) are deemed 'effeminate'. By contrast, not only is study not seen as bad for girls' image (*Guardian*, 26 August 1995), but Power *et al.* found that girls felt 'it was cool to be working'. It could be the case that academic achievement, far from becoming feminized, has actually been feminine for a long time.[18] It is beyond the scope of this chapter to explore this issue in greater depth. Nevertheless, it should be noted that one of the main reasons for promoting coeducation since the early years of this century, was that girls would provide incentive and 'emulation' for boys to work harder (Dale 1974; Grant and Hodgson 1913; Woods 1919).

The myth of effortlessness, on the other hand, can be sustained by public school boys and by boys like the 'Real Englishmen' for whom, Mac an Ghaill (1994: 70) notes, 'qualifications are insignificant in terms of predicting employment destinies'. It fails all the others. The point is not so much that there is no taken-for-granted relationship between academic success and a positive response to mental labour, but that academic achievement has been irrelevant to success for a particular social class. This is where the contradiction lies, and its lie is at the heart of the English educational system. Nor is it the case that working-class boys alone are underachieving – the underachievement of the others can be, and has always been, masked by cultural constructs like 'gentleman', 'character', 'potential' which have been essential to the construction of English masculinity since the turn of the nineteenth century.

The question that needs to be asked, then, is not 'Why are boys now underachieving?', but rather that of why boys' underachievement has now become an object of concern. Boys' underachievement is not just the result of the destruction of the industrial base, though this may have helped its visibility. Nor is it 'caused' by the pressures put on men by feminism or by girls' superior achievement in recent years. If, as I have been arguing, the discourse on achievement is structured so that practices have the achievement of boys as their main object, then the call for a new focus on boys not only is not 'new', but is likely to perpetuate the historical process which has worked for so long to produce the fiction of boys' potential and has protected boys' underachievement from scrutiny, processes which, as can be seen today, have not served them well. Focusing on boys' underachievement requires first rethinking the terms of the debate. The first step is to problematize boys, not girls, and the construction of masculinities. This process has begun and the essays in this collection are a testimony to the opening of the debate.

Acknowledgements

I wish to thank Phil Bevis, Jos Hackforth-Jones, Tim Hitchcock and John Tosh for their comments and helpful suggestions on earlier drafts of this paper.

Notes

1 The Assessment of Performance Unit [APU] survey of foreign language performance in schools (APU 1985: 335) showed that the performance of girls was higher

than that of boys in French, German and Spanish. The differences were smaller in French than in German and Spanish. French has the highest number of takers in English secondary schools.

2 Not only was Latin taught by grammar rules, but these rules were often in Latin, the language the boys had not yet mastered (see Clarke 1720).

3 Walkerdine (1994: 58) notes that teachers did not ascribe 'potential' to girls.

4 The headmaster interviewed in the *Panorama* programme cited above (BBC1 1995b) said that he wanted to encourage boys to achieve but one problem was that 'all set texts favour girls'. He wanted to find books that 'gripped boys'.

5 Throughout the eighteenth century, Englishmen's taciturnity was the object of comments by Englishmen and foreign visitors alike (see Cohen 1996b).

6 The reverse situation never prevented girls from achieving. Indeed it seems to have been expected that girls would thrive on material aimed at boys. As one educator put it, 'what schoolgirl will not confess, in private at least, to a definite predilection for boys' school and adventure yarns' (Mallinson 1953: v).

7 The following section is based on my discussion of the sexed mind in Cohen (1996b).

8 The term 'science' at the time included the study of Latin grammar and classical literature.

9 Street Arabs were homeless children, or children of the street (*Oxford English Dictionary*). Sir James Crichton-Browne was an eminent physician who wrote on the nervous system and the brain and on education. See also n. 11 below.

10 A Royal Commission set up initially to investigate boys' secondary schools, the Schools Inquiry Commission eventually consented to include girls' schools in its investigation, thanks to pressure from women who sought and fought to improve girls' education, Emily Davies in particular. See Josephine Kamm (1965).

11 Edward Clarke had been a medical professor at Harvard, and was a member of the Massachusetts medical society. His views were also taken up by Crichton-Browne (1892).

12 Mary Putnam Jacobi was then the leading woman physician in America, and Elizabeth Garrett Anderson was a pioneer in the struggle to get women admitted to medical school in England (Sayers 1982). See J. Manton's (1965) biography of Elizabeth Garrett Anderson; see also K. K. Sklar (1995: ch. 4) for a discussion of Jacobi's study.

13 There is evidence of some concern, in the late nineteenth and early twentieth century about the effects of overstrain and overpressure on boys (see, for example, Roberton 1972). However, this evidence is often confused and contradictory and certainly requires further research. The important point for this chapter is that in 1906, Clement Dukes MD could claim that the boy who is lazy is just 'suffering from brain fatigue' due to overstrain (Dukes 1906: 179), while barely twenty years later, the boy's laziness had become an indication of his mental health (Board of Education 1923).

14 The Clarendon Commission (1861–4) was a Royal Commission set up to invest-igate the nine public schools. See Shrosbree (1988) for a brilliant analysis of the impact of this commission on subsequent educational policy.

15 Sir Michael Sadler, though a supporter of public schools, remarked that a 'keen intellectual interest about school work is not the distinguishing mark of the rank and file in the English Public School for boys' (Sadler, quoted in Rosenthal 1986: 94).

16 It might be interesting to explain it by reference to Bourdieu's concept of *habitus*: 'the residual effect of *older cultural practices* on current social routines' – as Millard (1997: 43–4) has done, to explain why reading is identified as more appropriate to female members of families.
17 In his recent television series *The History of the Tory Party*, Alan Clark MP could not resist referring to former Prime Minister Macmillan, a middle-class boy who went to Eton, as a 'scholarship boy' (Clark 1997, 28 September).
18 I do not wish to imply that the issue is simple and straightforward. It must not be forgotten that the complexity of female achievement led to the postulation and study of a female 'motive to avoid success' from the late 1960s to the late 1970s (see for example, Hartnett *et al.* 1979; Mednick *et al.* 1975; see also Cohen 1996a).

References

Addison, J. (1711) *Spectator*, 135.
Anderson, E. G. (1874) Sex in mind and education: a reply. *Fortnightly Review*, 15: 582–94.
Andrews, J. (1784) *Letters to a Young Gentleman on his Setting out for France*. London.
Assessment of Performance Unit [APU] (1985) *Report on 1983 Survey of French, German and Spanish*. London: HMSO.
Badley, J. H. (1920) *Co-education and its Part in a Complete Education*. Cambridge: Heffer.
Barrell, J. (1983) *English Literature in History 1730–1780: An Equal, Wide Survey*. London: Hutchinson.
BBC1 (1995a) Is the future female? *Panorama*, May n.d.
BBC1 (1995b) Men aren't working, *Panorama*, 16 October.
Bennett, J. (1787) *Strictures on Female Education*. London.
Board of Education (1921) *The Teaching of English in England* [Newbolt Report]. London: HMSO.
Board of Education (1923) *Report on the Differentiation of the Curricula Between the Sexes in Secondary Schools*. London: HMSO.
Bourdieu, P. (1990) *The Logic of Practice*. Cambridge: Polity Press.
Brereton, C. (1930) *Modern Language Teaching in Day and Evening Schools*. London: University of London.
Cannon, J. (1984) *Aristocratic Century: The Peerage of Eighteenth-Century England*. Cambridge: Cambridge University Press.
Carlyle T. (1840) *On Heroes, Hero Worship, and the Heroic in History*. London.
Chirol, J. L. (1809) *An Enquiry into the Best System of Female Education*. London.
Clark, A. (1997) *The History of the Tory Party*, BBC2.
Clarke, E. (1873) *Sex in Education: Or, A Fair Chance for Girls*. Boston: J. R. Osgood.
Clarke, J. (1720) *An Essay Upon the Education of Youth in Grammar Schools*. London.
Clouston, T. S. (1906) *The Hygiene of Mind*. London: Methuen and Co.
Clouston, T. S. (1911) *The Position of Woman: Actual and Ideal*. London: James Nisbet and Co.
Cohen, M. (1996a) Is there a space for the achieving girl? in P. F. Murphy and C. V. Gipps (eds) *Equity in the Classroom: Towards Effective Pedagogy for Girls and Boys*. London/Paris: Falmer Press/UNESCO.
Cohen, M. (1996b) *Fashioning Masculinity: National Identity and Language in the Eighteenth Century*. London: Routledge.

Collini, S. (1985) The idea of 'character' in Victorian political thought. *Transactions of the Royal Historical Society*, 35: 29–50.

Crichton-Browne, Sir J. (1883) Education and the nervous system, in M. Morris (ed.) *The Book of Health*. London: Cassell and Co.

Crichton-Browne, Sir J. (1892) Education in foreign periodicals. *Education Review*, 4: 164–78.

Cross, D. (1982) Sex differences in achievement. *System*, 11 (2): 159–62.

Dale, R. R. (1971–4) *Mixed or Single-Sex School*. 3 vols. London: Routledge and Kegan Paul.

Defoe, D. (1712) *The Present State of Parties in Great Britain*. London.

Doyle, B. (1987) The invention of English, in R. Colls and P. Dodd (eds) *Englishness: Politics and Culture 1880–1920*. London: Croom Helm.

Dukes, C. (1906) Health, in *Public Schools from Within: A Collection of Essays on Public School Education*, written chiefly by schoolmasters. London: Sampson Low, Marston and Co.

Fordyce, J. (1770) *Sermons to Young Women*. London.

Grant, C. and Hodgson, N. (1913) *The Case for Co-Education*. London: Grant Richards.

Hartnett, O., Boden, G. and Fuller, M. (eds) (1979) *Sex-Role Stereotyping*. London: Tavistock.

Hawkins, E. (1981) *Modern Languages in the Curriculum*. Cambridge: Cambridge University Press.

Jacobi, M. P. (1877) *The Question of Rest for Women During Menstruation*. New York: McGraw-Hill.

Jardine, A. (1788) *Letters from Barbary, France, Portugal, etc.*, 2 vols. London.

Kamm, J. (1965) *Hope Deferred: Girls' Education in English History*. London: Methuen.

Knox, V. (1784) *Liberal Education*. London.

Locke, J. (1989) *Some Thoughts Concerning Education*, J. S. Yolton and J. W. Yolton (eds). Oxford: Clarendon Press (first published 1693).

Mac an Ghaill, M. (1994) *The Making of Men: Masculinities, Sexualities and Schooling*. Buckingham: Open University Press.

Mallinson, V. (1953) *Teaching a Foreign Language*. London: Heinemann.

Mangan, J. A. (1981) *Athleticism and the Victorian and Edwardian Public School: The Emergence and Consolidation of Educational Ideology*. Cambridge: Cambridge University Press.

Manton, J. (1965) *Elizabeth Garrett Anderson*. London: Methuen and Co.

Maudsley, H. (1874) Sex in mind and education. *Fortnightly Review*, 15 (Jan.–June): 582–94.

Mednick, M. T. S., Tangri, S. S. and Hoffman, L. W. (1975) *Women and Achievement: Social and Motivational Analyses*. London: John Wiley and Sons.

Millard, E. (1997) Differently literate: gender identity and the construction of the developing reader. *Gender and Education*, 9 (1): 31–48.

More, H. (1785) *Essays on Various Subjects Principally Designed for Young Ladies*. London.

More, H. (1799) *Strictures on Female Education*. 2 vols. London.

Morris, E. (1996) *Boys Will Be Boys? Closing the Gender Gap*. Labour Party consultation paper, November. London: The Labour Party.

Powell, B. (1985) *Boys, Girls and Languages in School*. London: CILT.

Power, S., Whitty, G., Edwards, T. and Wigfall, V. (1998) Schoolboys and schoolwork: gender identification and academic achievement, *International Journal of Inclusive Education*: Special Issue on Boys' 'Underachievement', 2 (2): 135–53.

Report from the Commissioners, Schools Inquiry Commission [Taunton Commission] (1868) 23 vols. London.

Report of Her Majesty's Commissioners Appointed to Inquire into Revenues and Management of Certain Colleges and Schools [Clarendon Commission] (1864) 4 vols. London.

Roberton, A. B. (1972) Children, teachers and society: the overpressure controversy, 1880–1886. *British Journal of Educational Studies*, 20: 315–23.

Rosenthal, M. (1986) *The Character Factory: Baden Powell and the Origins of the Boy Scout Movement*. London: Collins.

Rothblatt, S. (1976) *Tradition and Change in English Liberal Education: An Essay in History and Culture*. London: Faber.

Sayers, J. (1982) *Biological Politics*. London: Tavistock.

Schools Council (1968) *Enquiry No. 1, Young School Leavers*. London: HMSO.

Shrosbree, C. (1988) *Public Schools and Private Education*. Manchester: Manchester University Press.

Sklar, K. K. (1995) *Florence Kelley and the Nation's Work*. London: Yale University Press.

Spencer, H. (1905) *Education: Intellectual, Moral and Physical*. London: Williams and Norgate, first published 1873.

Vance, N. (1975) Tom Brown's universe, in B. Simon and I. Bradley (eds) *The Victorian Public School: Studies in the Development of an Educational Institution*. Dublin: Gill and Macmillan.

Walkerdine, V. (1989) *Counting Girls Out*. London: Virago.

Walkerdine, V. (1994) Femininity as performance, in L. Stone (ed.) *The Education Feminism Reader*. London: Routledge.

Weiner, G. M., Arnot, M. and David, M. (1997) Is the future female? Female success, male disadvantage and changing gender patterns in education, in A. H. Halsey, P. Brown, H. Lauder and A. Stuart-Wells (eds) *Education: Culture, Economy and Society*. Oxford: Oxford University Press.

Wiener, M. J. (1981) *English Culture and the Decline of the Industrial Spirit 1850–1980*. Harmondsworth: Penguin Books.

Wilson, T. (1729) *The Many Advantages of a Good Language to Any Nation*. London.

Woods, A. (ed.) (1919) *Advance in Co-education*. London: Sidgwick and Jackson.

Wragg, T. (1997) Oh boy!, *Times Educational Supplement*, 16 May.

PART II

Different constructions of the debate and its undercurrents

3

Girls will be girls and boys will be first

PAT MAHONY

In this chapter I explore some of the underlying themes and negative consequences of the ways that the 'underachievement of boys' are currently being expressed. My argument is not that the education of boys is unimportant but that the assumptions and purposes underpinning the current obsession with their academic performance are misconceived. As a consequence, key questions concerning the role of schools in the social construction of masculinities are omitted; the practices and consequences of different masculinities in relation to women become invisible; and the effects on different groups of boys of the internal orderings of masculinities are obscured. In relation to the last and sensitized by recent work on women and social class (Mahony and Zmroczek 1997), there is, for example, a great deal of work to be done in identifying how boys from working-class backgrounds are subordinated by the practices, values and conceits of white, middle-class modes of masculinity. This chapter is critical of the way that the debates about boys are currently being expressed while welcoming the fact that after generations of breaking their bodies by providing fodder for coal mines, factories and battlefields, serious questions are being forced on us about the education of working-class boys.

At the present time, a number of interdependent issues and themes tumble over each other, coalesce around and find expression in current concerns about boys. The 'problem' emerges differently in different countries depending on how issues inherent in the restructurings of patriarchal capitalism are being perceived, experienced and responded to. In order to trace such themes, I look first at the different and sometimes contradictory claims made in relation to the 'evidence' on the underachievement of boys. Next, I place the concern with academic achievement within the wider context of the changing global economy which is framing the education and social policies of national governments. In this I consider the effects of the restructuring of capitalism and some patriarchal investments in and anxieties about these. I move on to explore some of the negative consequences of the English response to these wider changes before moving on to draw out some of the dilemmas involved both in current policy and in proposals for change.

Noisy data

First, it is important to note that Michèle Cohen's work (1996: 8–9), demonstrates that the preoccupation with masculinity is not new:

> The question then, is not why there was an anxiety about masculinity at a specific time, say the eighteenth century, but how the anxiety about masculinity is articulated at any particular historical moment – or geographical space.

Second, it is interesting to note that the current preoccupation with the 'what about the boys' debate is not confined to the United Kingdom. Heard from an international perspective, there is din of anxiety but with enough variations on a theme to alert us to the possibility that a number of concerns are gathering round this one issue. Only in some countries, is the examination performance of boys being played in a major key and even here, there are conflicting claims about which groups of boys are underachieving, in which curriculum areas, at what level of qualification, according to which definitions of underachievement and according to what evidence.

In Australia, Martin Mills and Bob Lingard (1997: 278) describe the debate as developing in response to the claim that girls were outperforming boys in the public exam held at the end of secondary schooling. They suggest that closer analysis of the data revealed that:

> a small group of mainly middle class girls are now performing as well as, and thus challenging, the dominance of middle class boys in the high status, 'masculinist' subjects such as Maths, Chemistry and to a lesser extent Physics.

In another article they alert us to the existence of 'a particular version of masculinity politics' which is 'a recuperative, reactionary politics which seeks to reassert male dominance and traditional sex roles and in some manifestations is explicitly anti-feminist, even misogynist' (Lingard and Mills 1997: 4).

In England, the problem has been defined by the Chief Inspector of Schools as 'the failure of boys and in particular white working class boys' (Pyke 1996: 2). In this case the evidence does not support the claim that boys *per se* are underachieving once we move beyond the public examinations at 16 plus. In relation to A level, for example, Patricia Murphy and Jannette

Elwood (1998: 19) point out that, 'whilst males continue to outperform females in mathematics, males now outperform females in English'. In fact, as Arnot, David and Weiner (1996) demonstrate, male students continue to achieve higher performances in relation to their entry than female students in nearly all subjects.

Odette Parry's discussion of Caribbean examination results adds a further dimension to the debate. She cites evidence from the World Bank claiming that 'females do better than males at both primary and secondary levels of schooling' (Parry 1996: 2–3). She goes on to note that 'subject choices follow the traditional pattern with girls highly visible in arts and boys in science'. When she compares English grade results with physics we find that '81.4% of the grade one (English) results were taken by females and 60.7% of the grade one physics went to males'. These figures bear a striking resemblance to patterns of gender-segregated achievement identified in the United Kingdom in the 1980s (Mahony 1985). However, at the time, such data was taken as signifying the 'underachievement of girls'. Seen in its historical context, similar evidence is being used across time and place to signify opposite conclusions. This raises a separate but related issue.

When the focus was on the alleged underachievement of girls, it took a good deal of persuasion by (mainly) feminists before policy makers would look beyond the innate capacities of girls themselves for explanations of 'failure' in maths and science. Such responses have not figured highly in relation to the 'underachievement of boys' though, inflamed by racist accounts of intelligence, they may lurk behind some teachers' explanations of the achievement gap 'between the Black and white boys in this school' (MA student's statement in class). By and large what was once evidence of the problem *of* girls has now become, not even the problem *of* boys but the problem *for* boys. The first casualty is that many of the gains made for girls, such as sensitivity to the messages contained in course materials, are increasingly being eroded as the belief takes hold that 'girls have had it too good for too long' (Barber 1994: 2). Some educationists argued in the 1980s that these messages matter, not because of any causal relationship between girls' achievement and images in textbooks (if this had been the case girls would never have succeeded in anything), but because the images were degrading and distorting in portraying boys as adventurous and active while girls dripped around waiting for the first opportunity to serve them (Moys 1980). I will return to this point later but for the moment we need only to note that 'achievement' and 'underachievement' like other relational concepts, drift into finer and finer specificity the more data becomes available. We could commit the rest of our lives in trying to find out which boys are underachieving, in relation to whom, in what areas, when, in which countries and why. Or we could ask another question. Why is there such a concern, even an obsession with academic achievement in the first place? I shall now go on to locate this obsession within the rise of the 'competition state'. This in turn has generated a whole variety of education policy reforms within which the 'underachievement of boys' can be partly (but not entirely) understood.

Education and the global economy

The 'underachievement of boys' has to be seen in part within a broader context of change.

> As the world is characterised by increasing interpenetration and the crystallisation of transnational markets and structures, the state itself is having to act more and more like a market player, that shapes its policies to promote, control, and maximise returns from market forces in an international setting.
>
> (Cerny 1990: 230)

In the United Kingdom (as elsewhere) the preoccupation with increasing the competitiveness of the nation state plc in the global economy is pervasive and although the precise contribution of schooling to such competitiveness is controversial, the belief that national prosperity depends on high levels of knowledge and skill (one of the principles of microeconomic reform) is clearly presumed in the major educational policy documents of governments as far apart as Australia or New Zealand and the United Kingdom (Grace 1991; Knight *et al.* 1994).

In England it is a belief which is evident in the education policies of the Labour government (albeit set alongside a new concern with inequality):

> The Government's policy decisions, and the framework within which the DfEE [Department for Education and Employment] operates, will be shaped by powerful economic, social and technological forces. We believe the most important are:
> • globalisation – new opportunities and risks in an increasingly global economy where goods, services, capital and information are highly mobile and success depends more and more on the skills of the workforce.
>
> (DfEE 1997a)

Within this and in the words of David Blunkett, the Secretary of State for Education:

> We are talking about investing in human capital in the age of knowledge. To compete in the global economy, to live in a civilised society and to develop the talents of each and every one of us, we will have to unlock the potential of every young person.
>
> (DfEE 1997b: 3)

In this respect there has been little change in government policy from the former Conservative government in which competition in the global economy clearly underpinned the school effectiveness movement and defined the priorities of schooling. As the Chief Executive of the Teacher Training Agency (the body responsible for teacher training in England) put it:

> everyone is now agreed that the top priority in education is the need to raise pupils' standards of learning. . . . And there is a widespread aware-ness that, in a competitive world, constant progress is necessary just to maintain parity with other nations.
>
> (Millett 1996)

Finally, as has been argued elsewhere (Hextall and Mahony 1998), it has provided a dominant theme within the Teacher Training Agency's (TTA) reconstruction of what it means to teach and of what constitutes career progression in teaching.[1]

At the time of writing, it is too early to identify the continuities and discontinuities in the recently elected Labour government's policies but the former Conservative government's strategy for levering up standards of achievement in school is well known. In pursuit of global competitiveness, the drive to school effectiveness was directly tied to the National Curriculum and judged in accordance with criteria derived from it, mediated through performance indicators of published league tables of examination results and inspection reports. In a context of competition between schools for students, academic achievement becomes highly visible and even heightened through such mechanisms as parental choice and 'measures' of individual teacher effectivity while explanations of, and solutions to, underachieve-ment proliferate. Individual students or groups of students (such as boys) thus become crucial in determining the overall academic performance of schools, geared to the demands of the competition state. Since the demands of the global economy have become one of the major new plausibilities in Britain, it is worth noting (Mahony and Moos 1997: 12) that the Danish Minister for Education, Ole Vig Jensen has been very direct in rejecting a model of education based on the economic rationalism underpinning so much of recent education policy in the United Kingdom: 'Our educational system shall not be a product of a global educational race without thinking of the goals and ideals we want in Denmark.' But the 'global race' is not the end of the story.

Lean, mean and flexible

If one driving force in policy reform has been the need to increase 'effect-iveness' then the other two of the 'virtuous three Es of economy, efficiency and effectiveness' (Pollitt 1993: 59), have involved the need to reduce public expenditure. To this end new public management (NPM) or New

Managerialism has been introduced across all parts of the UK public sector, in most OECD countries (Shand 1996) and may even be having an impact further afield in countries such as Pakistan and Kenya (Davies 1994). There is increasing evidence that different countries and sectors have introduced NPM in different ways according to their diverse historical and cultural traditions (Ferlie *et al.* 1996). For example, changes in the United Kingdom have been marked in particular ways by the influence of the New Right and their nostalgia for a fictitious age when 'traditional values' were beyond question and by a particularly hard version of market liberalism. Broadly conceived, NPM in the United Kingdom is viewed as a way of dispersing the management, reporting and accounting approaches of the public sector and modelling them by different degrees along the lines of 'best', i.e. 'efficient', commercial practice.

The imperative to reduce public expenditure marks a change of view in which public spending, for example, on unemployment benefit, is no longer seen as an entitlement of citizens or as a social investment but as an unproductive cost. Such expenditure becomes identified as a drain on the public purse along with those who 'consume' it. Here the call for a highly skilled labour force connects with the demonization of the 'work shy' in the need for an increased inculcation of the work ethic. The slide from 'unemployment' to an assumption of 'unemployability' easily passes unnoticed giving rise to the assumption that the conditions creating both are the same. Today's underachieving boy stands at the brink of tomorrow's unemployed youth in the form of public burden number one. I shall return later to say more about the labour market, but for the moment I want to pick up another strand of the argument.

Me Tarzan, you Jane

One of the issues in the movement towards various forms of NPM is how the values and motivations of particular powerful groups of white, male elites (Hutton 1995) have connected with the 'efficiency fetish' (Lingard 1995). Such men are powerful within the transnational organizations such as the World Bank as well as influencing policy in or behind national governments and their departments.

Within a restructuring of capitalism the patriarchal cage seems to have been rattled by a belief that men are losing economic ground to women. There is indeed an issue emerging in some areas of the labour market which, as I shall suggest later, forms a significant element in the concerns about 'underachieving' boys. But for white male elites the 'natural order' is not about to be overturned and any panic in that direction is unfortunately unwarranted with women constituting fewer than 5 per cent of senior management in the United Kingdom and United States (2 per cent in Australia), 5 per cent of UK Institute of Directors and less than 1 per cent of chief executives (Collinson and Hearn 1996).

Weiner *et al.* (1997: 13) note that when it was newly formed in 1995, appointments to the Department for Education and Employment were 'overwhelmingly male at all senior levels despite the fact that the Secretary of State was a woman'. In an age of the calculative frameworks of managerialism, it would be pertinent to know whether these DfEE officials mirror the new generation of economics graduates described in Pusey's study of government restructuring in Canberra (1991), for as Prue Hyman (1994: 33–4) argues:

> free rider behaviour (selfish unwillingness to pay for public goods) was more prevalent in economics graduates . . . selfish behaviour in an experimental game was more common both among economics majors than others and among men than women.

It would also be interesting to know how far they reject offensive modes of management-speak 'full of lurid gender terminology: thrusting entrepreneurs, opening up virgin territory, aggressive lending, etc.' (Connell 1993: 614) and how far the sexualized discourse of management has connected for male managers in education with the 'pre-pubescent boy's fantasy of being "big", one's potency being judged according to the size of one's budget' (Hoggett 1996: 15).

Collinson and Hearn (1996: 3–4) suggest that the 1990s has brought an increased evaluation of managers and their performance, one criterion being 'the masculinist concern with personal power and the ability to control others and self'. They too argue that conventional managerial discourse has become redolent with highly (hetero)sexualized talk of 'penetrating markets' and 'getting into bed with suppliers/customers/competitors'.

Given the restructuring of the public sector in line with 'best commercial practice', it is not surprising to find similar versions of masculinism in evidence. According to Clarke and Newman (1997: 70):

> many public sector organisations have taken on images of competitive behaviour as requiring hard, macho or 'cowboy' styles of working. It is as if the unlocking of the shackles of bureaucratic constraints has at last allowed public sector managers to become 'real men', released from the second-class status of public functionaries by their exposure to the 'real world' of the market place.

There are other indications that while capitalism has fiddled, patriarchy has burned, even without the help of the efficiency fetish or its first cousin, the achievement fetish. This provides further evidence that the economic argument is not the only or indeed a sufficient explanatory framework for understanding the current concern about boys. In Denmark anxieties have been expressed about the demise of the 'Real Man':

> The newest tendencies in Denmark support the statement that: 'Real men are a scarce commodity', and that boys ought to be allowed to be

more 'macho' . . . Projects aimed at and for boys are being initiated in kindergartens at a rate unheard of up to now, because the predominantly women staff have been exposed to a good deal of male criticism. This criticism has made the women preschool teachers battle with their own insecurity and many of them now allow 'boys' anxiety-based aggression' to run free by buying weapons and war toys and encouraging boys to let loose their wild ideas. Furthermore there is a call for more men teachers. In Viborg the head of a preschool teachers training college in the media has advertised not only for men or for qualified men, but for 'Real Men' . . .

(Kruse 1996: 438–9)

Kruse goes on to describe the arguments of a number of prominent men among whom is former teacher and author Bertill Nordahl:

school is a terrible place for boys. In school they are trapped by 'The Matriarchy' and are dominated by women who cannot accept boys as they are. The women teachers mainly wish to control and to suppress boys. According to him, men teachers are not a lot better off, over-run as they are by women and female values, which undermine their masculinity and self-esteem. In order to survive in the workplace dominated by women, they submit themselves to female values – thereby becoming *vatpikke* (cotton wool pricks).

(Kruse 1996: 439)

As I have suggested, what is interesting about this version of the 'what about the boys?' movement is its independence from any statistics on achievement.

I now move on to discuss some of the negative effects of NPM on schools. I have written elsewhere about the negative effects of NPM on feminist work in teacher education (Mahony 1997) so I shall limit my comments to the school context.

The problem with basics

The blinkered preoccupation with achievement, defined narrowly as subject knowledge, literacy and numeracy has been the subject of some criticism both within the United Kingdom and elsewhere. Commenting on issues which arose from a school effectiveness research project McGraw *et al.* (1992: 174) concluded that:

School effectiveness is about a great deal more than maximising academic achievement. Learning and the love of learning; personal development and self-esteem; life skills, problem solving and learning how to learn; the development of independent thinkers and well rounded confident individuals; all rank as highly or more highly as the outcomes of effective schooling as success in a narrow range of academic disciplines.

Even within the school effectiveness 'movement', a major figure in the United Kingdom has argued that:

> In Britain and internationally, there is a sense in which the entire enterprise of school effectiveness appears in a 'time warp'. The studies that have been conducted are all ageing rapidly and are of less and less use in the educational world of the 1990's. This world has new needs at the level of pupil outcomes from schools – the skills to access information and to work collaboratively in groups, and the social outcomes of being able to cope in a highly complex world are just three new educational goals which are never used as outcomes in the school effectiveness literature.
>
> (Reynolds 1994: 23)

The effects of current UK plc definitions of what it means to 'become educated' are highlighted when one works with teachers in other countries, many of whom cite UK research and development from the 1980s (derided by our own Government) as inspiring their current initiatives. Much of that work was undertaken by classroom teachers, yet such is the degree of centralization of educational policy in this country that teachers' voices have increasingly been removed from policy-making circles, their professionalism undermined and their creativity stifled (Mahony and Hextall 1997a).

In addition, teacher 'efficiency' is in the process of being reconstructed through a revised appraisal system, performance-related pay, inspection reports on individual teachers, development of teaching standards and the restructuring of the profession into four stages.

None of this is likely to foster a climate in which teachers will find it easy to be creative about developing different ways of working with different groups of young people. Nor will they be thoroughly prepared or motivated to engage in the kind of progressive work which I suggest later is necessary if we are seriously asking 'What about the boys?' Such work which may well 'rock the boat' will require a fresh look at gender relations in a context where over the last few years, we have witnessed a full frontal *attack* on such work in schools. Many new teachers in the United Kingdom have never known a time when the purposes of schooling went beyond the pursuit of higher academic standards. They do not remember that in the run-up to the 1987 general election 'equal opportunities' were derided as the invention of the 'loony Left' and our alleged intention to deprive children of a good education. They probably do not remember that one book in one teachers' centre in one London borough which told the story of a girl visiting her father and his male lover, became a *cause célèbre*; that lies abounded in the tabloid press which told of gay sex being taught to 5-year-olds and of traditional children's stories being rewritten by teachers obsessed with sex equality (Cooper 1989). They may believe along with a first-year undergraduate student teacher that 'being OK about gays in school is against the law' or that 'teachers in the old days' (defined as the 1980s!) 'were too political'. Thus when John Major (Chitty and Simon 1993) dismissed the politics of 'gender, race and class' as diverting schools from their 'true purposes', his words probably fell on uncritical ears. It will take time and considerable political will to put issues of social justice back on the agenda for schools and there is no guarantee that our first-year student will ever come to understand the following quotation as located precisely within the politics of gender (and class).

> In 1995 the proportion of men receiving 1st class honours degrees in History at Cambridge was three times that of women . . . men fare better because they adopt a punchy, aggressive and adversarial approach in their essays.
>
> (Targett 1996: 3)

There are further problems with our obsession with narrow definitions of academic achievement. It leads to a 'sex war' mentality in which our ever increasing preoccupation with who is doing better than whom leads each year to a media panic expressed in such headlines in the *Times Educational Supplement* as 'Male brain rattled by curriculum oestrogen' (15 March 1996), 'Perils of ignoring our lost boys' (28 June 1996) and in the *Guardian* 'Girls on top of the learning curve' (19 October 1996). It is a short step from this kind of headline to the conclusion expressed by our Chief Inspector for Schools in *The Times* and repeated in the *Times Educational Supplement* that 'the failure of boys and in particular white working class boys is one of the most disturbing problems we face within the whole education system'. It fuels the claim made the year before that 'girls have had their way for long enough, now it's time for the boys' and the call for 'reverse discrimination' (Smith 1995). And it heightens the pressure to pour resources into researching the causes of the 'underachievement of boys', and to change classroom practice in ways which benefit boys (Klein 1995).

Furthermore, it is not clear where the contexts exist in which different value positions about the purposes of schooling or the different needs of young people, positioned differently by class, 'race', gender, sexuality or ability, could even be debated.

We have seen so far that the concern about boys fits into a wider set of issues about the relationship of the nation state to the global economy and into a range of anxieties concerned with reasserting patriarchal dominance. Having outlined some of the negative responses in the United Kingdom, I now move on to a consideration of the terrain between schools and the global economy constituted by the world of paid work. This forms the immediate context into which young people move and to which the achievement effort is partly directed. Here again we see an interweaving of the issues I have raised so far as we reflect on what it means to be prepared for, and positioned within, a changing labour market.

The world of McWork

> A quiet revolution is going on which is transforming the lives of millions
> of workers in Britain. The world of full-time pensionable employment
> is retreating before their eyes; and in its stead is emerging an insecure
> world of contract work, part-time jobs and casualised labour.
>
> (Hutton 1995: 20)

This 'quiet revolution' has had dramatic effects on economic inequality in
the United Kingdom. Lean and Ball (1996: 1) note that according to the
Human Development Report published by the UN Development Programme:

> Britain is now the most unequal country in the Western world . . . The
> report shows that the poorest 40 per cent of Britons share a lower
> proportion of the national wealth – 14.6 per cent – than any other
> Western country. The richest fifth of Britons enjoy on average, incomes
> 10 times as high as the poorest fifth.

The gendered effects of poverty within these statistics are not mentioned
nor, conversely, have the effects on children's educational potential featured
highly within the school-effectiveness movement. The displacement of the
'masculine' manufacturing base by the 'feminine' service sector has meant
that an increasing proportion of casualized work is being carried out by
white and black working class women (EOC 1997). It would seem that since
1977 when Paul Willis wrote *Learning to Labour: How Working Class Kids Get
Working Class Jobs*, it is the world which has changed, not the boys and there
is no longer a fit between large areas of it and many of the boys. This raises
the spectre of the 'traditional' heterosexual nuclear family being made
unstable by the 'underachievement of boys'.

If such employment as is available for groups of young working-class
people exists largely in the service industries, then it has to be recognized
that these require high levels of expertise in the expressive aspects of customer service. Qualities such as 'warmth, empathy, sensitivity to unspoken
needs and high levels of interpersonal skills to build an effective relationship
with customers' (Devereux 1996: 13) would seem to be at odds with masculinities encouraged in, and adopted by, some adolescent boys. The latter poses
a really difficult challenge for, on the one hand, in terms of the demands
of the labour market, the problem for some boys seems to be that they are
not more like girls. It would follow that some masculinities need to change.
On the other hand any attempt to critique or transform such masculinities
strikes at the heart of the gender regime from which men earn the 'patriarchal
dividend' (Connell 1995: 41). How far there really is a need for everyone to
achieve high levels of academic knowledge in order to ensure UK plc's
competitiveness in the global economy and how far the real problem lies in
the threat to the 'natural order' of the working class male breadwinner
would be a question worthy of further pursuit.

Evidence from one region in the south-east of England indicates that the reconstruction of masculinities will be hard to achieve. In a project undertaken with 130 14-year-olds, about their attitudes to school subjects and their ambitions for the future (Mahony and Frith 1995), it emerged that for many boys, biological accounts of gender were alive and kicking. Being good at (or bad at) different subjects was a matter beyond their control – 'It's in yer brain' as one boy said and there was nothing to be done for some boys for whom it was not 'in yer brain' but to 'f— about'. Girls on the other hand tended to think that if 'you work harder maybe you get to like it and get better at it'.

Students of both sexes, thought that some subjects were easier for girls or boys though their reasons differed; boys again tended to blame the gendered nature of 'natural ability' whereas girls cited 'what you're used to since you were little'.

Whether the boys really did believe in 'nature' rather than 'nurture' is a moot point. In one report: 'Staff felt that boys appeared more concerned with preserving an image of reluctant involvement or disengagement; for many boys, it is not acceptable for them to be seen to be interested or stimulated by academic work' (Hofkins 1995: 5). Two points need to be interjected here about the ways in which biological determinism rolls on and off the explanatory stage. First, biological determinism is not the quaint prerogative of 14-year-old boys in south-east England but pervasive across other sites. One recent example occurred during my recent period of jury service on a case involving violent assault, when a barrister said, 'you may think there is a little too much testosterone in this case, but unfortunately that is natural'. It remains unclear what would have been the point of punishing the accused, if found guilty, but then perhaps it is a mistake to seek logical argument in the legitimating discourses of male violence.

In an opposite tendency, anecdotal evidence from teachers suggests that girls are increasingly acting in ways conventionally associated with particular forms of masculinity (for example, in their increased tendency to resort to physical violence). Here, femininities and masculinities are not regarded as biologically fixed but as fluid and (in the case of the girls) as both amenable to, and in need of, reconstruction. That such a strategy (to eliminate masculinist behaviour) should not have occurred to our money conscious policy makers as a way of cutting the cost of policing, prosecuting and imprisoning men (and a few women) is perhaps no surprise. It would after all undercut one of the major props in the maintenance of patriarchal power.

To return to the study, it was predominantly the male students who wanted to get a job at 16 rather than continuing into further education and mostly the boys who were unclear about the future. They also tended to be less informed than the girls about relevant pathways to different occupations, despite the fact that all the students had spent a considerable amount of time studying 'careers'. For example, one student who wanted to be a PE teacher said he would either go to college to study English, media and art or get a job.

Where they had them, the ambitions of the white working-class boys clustered simultaneously round two poles of the male labour market. On the one hand they aspired to enter the middle-class professions even though 40 per cent of them could not accurately spell their chosen 'career'. Given what is known about the widening social class divisions in access to higher education and the social class backgrounds and exclusionary networking practices of members of the legal and medical professions, it is highly unlikely that the opportunity will really exist for these boys to become a 'barraster', 'solister' 'docter' or 'arcatec'. Perhaps knowing this, they nearly always proposed alternatives to their preferred futures such as 'getting a practical job', 'a physical job', 'a job using my body', 'being a courier' or 'driving a big lorry'. Not one of them wanted to work in the service industries, a common aspiration for the girls and none predicted that he would find employment there. This raises a further set of complexities. Does the future lie in the reskilling (and 'feminization'?) of working-class boys so that they can displace working-class women at the edge of the labour market or does it reside in encouraging them into modes of perceived middle-class masculinity so that they can enter the more stable ranks of the managerial classes? These dilemmas are further cross-cut by the recognition that masculinities are neither fixed nor framed solely by social class but by sexuality, region, age, ability and by ethnicity as well as by the availability and nature of work, being shaped in part by economic policies geared to the needs of multinational companies, operating across national borders. In any event, there are real problems in the 1990s around the claim that some masculinities need to be reconstructed. Let us briefly explore these.

From pen to practice

First, a perspective favouring the reconstruction of particular masculinities will not be easy to introduce, even if the grounds on which it is advanced were reframed in terms of the employability of boys. The attack on the equity work of the 1980s at least in the United Kingdom has probably left too much detritus in the popular imagination for the arguments to be taken seriously and the anti-feminist backlash inherent in some forms of masculinity politics seem set to exploit this (Connell 1997). Second, though recent literature has stressed the transformational potential of 'variety, difference and plurality, both between men and men and within individual boys and men' (Jackson and Salisbury 1996: 109) and though these particular authors make a rare and much welcome foray into suggesting practical strategies for working with boys (Salisbury and Jackson 1996), it is not clear how the cracks and fissures in the constructions of masculinities could be systematically exploited in school to produce new gender regimes. How would this much needed work stand alongside the competition to achieve higher academic results, defined within 'Blairjorism' as the true purposes of schooling? How could the attempt to soften the hard competitive edges of some forms of masculinity sit comfortably within a context where *increased* competitiveness (in the global economy) has all but become the national anthem for the millennium? Within the increasingly managerialist restructuring of schools (Mahony and Hextall 1997b), it may even be that masculinist values are on the increase:

> Organisations clearly reproduce themselves. People in power (who are mostly men) mentor, encourage, and advance people who are most like themselves . . . a number of studies have shown that as women move up the organizational hierarchy, their identification with the masculine model of managerial success becomes so important that they end up rejecting even the few valued feminine managerial traits they may have endorsed.
>
> (Kanter 1993: 72)

The second problem in the United Kingdom is that few are now qualified to do such work. Nor is it clear how teachers could become qualified in the current climate. The priorities for continuing professional development for teachers are being centrally defined around the need to increase teachers' subject knowledge and their 'leadership' skills and the spaces for thinking about the wider purposes of schooling are not evident within the framework of national standards for teaching currently being developed by the TTA.

The increasing gap between research and practice in the education of teachers does not help matters. As teachers work longer and harder to ensure that theirs is an 'effective school' so, in parallel, researchers are striving to meet the demands of the academy for the publication of yet more academically orientated texts. Theory and practice become progressively estranged, to the detriment of both.

Within the academy there is a further problem. Just as it is easy for researchers to get lost in the detailed data on underachievement, so the temptation is to be drawn into the increasingly detailed exploration of masculinities, femininities, ethnicities, sexualities or class identities. This is an attractive option, to be sure, easier than trying to change the world and allowing a sensitive subject to be avoided. This is that masculinities, for all their variety and internal jockeying, coalesce around a main axis of power relations with women. This awareness and its implications for action are low on both the research and practice agenda, not helped in either case by the way that the 'underachievement of boys' debate has been framed. Responsibility for this cannot be laid at the door of the pressing demands of the global economy. Other countries inhabit the same globe without feeling the need to deny that expressions of male power in the form of sexual violence are issues which have to be dealt with in school.

The European dimension

A European workshop on in-school 'prevention' of sexual violence against girls and boys was recently held in Germany. The workshop grew out of the joint local government/European Union financed PETZE project, set up in Schleswig Holstein to develop a teachers' INSET programme on sexual violence against girls and boys (Schmidt and Peter 1996). Sixty men and women (of whom I was one) from thirteen countries participated in the workshop including doctors, government officials, academics and youth workers. In preparation, a survey was conducted on the activities of the fifteen member states in relation to 'prevention work' in school, how questions of sexual violence were discussed and how teachers were supported in this work. The questionnaire from the United Kingdom was not filled in though a note was attached explaining that it was 'impossible to fill it in because such work is the responsibility of the LEAs [local education authorities]' (Kavemann 1996). *The Leeds Inter-Agency School Project* (1996: 1), however, suggests that 'LMS has made it difficult to promote and resource such work across the LEA'. Delegates from various countries reported that 'we are very worried that we will go the same way as the English – obsessed with exams' and the question 'How have you in your country let this happen?' was one I could not answer, even in my own language.

Astounding, was the similarity of the evidence of sexual violence quoted from many of the countries. As definitions of sexual violence vary and research methods change, so the findings of prevalence studies vary. However, bearing this difficulty in mind, much of the evidence presented at the workshop confirmed the findings of Kelly *et al.* (1991) that if unwanted sexual events or interactions are included then one in two women and one in four men will have experienced at least one event before the age of 18. If 'abuse attempts successfully resisted' and 'less serious' forms of abuse are excluded then one in five women and one in fourteen men experienced at least one event before the age of 18.

The outcome of the workshop was that agreement on a five-page resolution was reached and sent off 'to Europe'. Read out of the context in which it was produced and from a perspective which theorizes the continuum of sexual violence as functioning to maintain patriarchal domination, the first paragraph of the resolution is less than perfect:

> The most far-reaching aim of prevention is to change social structures of power and violence between the sexes and the generations which produce sexual abuse of children, particularly of girls, to abolish the myths around sexual violence and the denial of its devastating consequences.
>
> (European workshop 1996: 81)

On the other hand, as the culmination of the participants' work over 3 days, in which the predominant theme had been men's sexual violence and its functioning in the social control of women, it provided evidence that perhaps we need to look outside England for examples of broader and more equitable views of the 'true purposes of schooling' and of what it means to take a wider view of gender relations. Masculinities form only part of this wider perspective and the 'underachievement of boys' an even smaller part.

Conclusion

I have argued that the 'underachievement of boys' debate is part of a much bigger bundle of anxieties around 'What about the boys?' and that these cannot be understood outside various forms of patriarchal capitalist restructurings occurring within different sites. There is an untidy heap of issues around what it means to engage with the problem which range from the diversionary through to the radical. Even from a radical perspective which explores the potential for transforming masculinities, the danger is that the wider spectrum of gender relations and the positionings of women within it, will be overlooked. In particular, sexual violence, its devastating effects on individuals and its functioning in the social control of women are not high on the agenda in some of the theorizing around masculinities and the difficulties of educating women and men teachers to undertake transformational work in this country should not be underestimated within the purposes of schooling as defined by Blairjorism.

As a way forward we might explore the potential for exploiting at a national level the contradictions between education policy in the United Kingdom and what is currently being recommended as best practice by transnational organizations such as the OECD (Townshend 1996). We might also consider the possibilities afforded by forging alliances with other groups expressing dissatisfaction with current definitions of the purposes of schooling (Gardiner 1997). Finally, we need to question whether there are spaces in which it might be possible to overcome some of the difficulties I have highlighted in order to engage in radical work at the level of the 'local'. Some of the work currently being conducted under the banner of 'underachieving boys' would be an obvious starting point notwithstanding the fact that teachers willing and able to do it will need time, acknowledgement and support.

Evidence which gives cause for optimism at the level of the local suggests that parents' views on the purposes of schooling are rather wider than those pursued over recent years (Mahony and Moos 1997). There are also practical examples where such views are being accessed and developed to legitimate a broader view of the purposes of the individual school (MacBeath *et al.* 1996).

Even though these local spaces may provide opportunities for radical work, such possibilities mark the beginning, not the end of current debates. They raise but do not resolve wide-ranging concerns evident throughout the whole area of public-sector reorganization over patterns of centralization/decentralization and questions of accountability and representation (Mahony and Hextall 1997a). We are led ultimately to questions about forms of social participation and control, the nature of society itself in the late 1990s and the representation of different voices and value positions within it. As is often the case, issues of gender lead ultimately to questions concerned with what kind of society we want, who the 'we' is who wants it and the nature of our powers to achieve it.

Note

1 The data on the Teacher Training Agency was gathered during an ESRC funded project 'The Policy Context and Impact of the Teacher Training Agency' undertaken with Ian Hextall from September 1995 to November 1996.

References

Arnot, M., David, M. and Weiner, G. (1996) *Educational Reforms and Gender Equality in Schools*. Manchester: Equal Opportunities Commission.

Barber, M. (1994) Report into school students' attitudes, *Guardian*, 23 August.

Cerny, P. (1990) *The Changing Architecture of Politics: Structure, Agency and the Future of the State*. London: Sage Publications.

Chitty, C. and Simon, B. (eds) (1993) Extract from John Major's speech to the 1992 Conservative Party conference, in *Education Answers Back: Critical Responses to Government Policy*. London: Wishart.

Clarke, J. and Newman, J. (1997) *The Managerial State*. London: Sage Publications.

Cohen, M. (1996) *Fashioning Masculinity: National Identity and Language in the Eighteenth Century*. London: Routledge.

Collinson, D. and Hearn J. (eds) (1996) *Men as Managers, Managers as Men*. London: Sage Publications.

Connell, R. W. (1993) The big picture: masculinities in recent world history. *Theory and Society*, 22: 597–624.

Connell, R. W. (1995) *Masculinities*. Sydney: Allen and Unwin.

Connell, R. W. (1997) Men, masculinities and feminism. *Social Alternatives*, 16: 7–10.

Cooper, D. (1989) Positive images in Haringey: a struggle for identity, in C. Jones and P. Mahony (eds) *Learning our Lines: Sexuality and Social Control in Education*. London: The Women's Press.

Davies, L. (1994) *Beyond Authoritarian School Management: The Challenge for Transparency*. Derbyshire: Education Now Publishing Co-operative.

Department for Education and Employment [DfEE] (1997a) *Learning and Working Together for the Future*. London: HMSO.

Department for Education and Employment [DfEE] (1997b) *Excellence in Schools*. London: HMSO.

Devereux, C. (1996) *Cross Cultural Standards of Competence in Customer Service*. Cheam: W. A. Consultants.

Equal Opportunities Commission [EOC] (1997) 'Briefings on Women and Men in Britain: The Labour Market', Manchester: Equal Opportunities Commission.

European Workshop (1996) Prevention of sexual violence against girls and boys in school. Documentation. Ministry of Education, Science, Research and Cultural Affairs of the Land of Schleswig-Holstein, Germany.

Ferlie, E., Pettigrew, A., Ashburner, L. and Fitzgerald, L. (1996) *The New Public Management in Action*. Oxford: Oxford University Press.

Gardiner, J. (1997) Editors back new progressivism, *Times Educational Supplement*, 24 January.

Grace, G. (1991) Welfare Labourism versus the New Right: the struggle in New Zealand's educational policy. *International Studies in the Sociology of Education,* 1: 25–41.

Hextall, I. and Mahony, P. (1998) Effective teachers for effective schools, in R. Slee, S. Tomlinson and G. Weiner (eds) *Effective for Whom?* London: Falmer Press.

Hofkins, D. (1995) Why teenage boys think success is sad, *Times Educational Supplement,* 18 August.

Hoggett, P. (1996) New modes of control in the public service. *Public Administration,* 74: 9–31.

Hutton, W. (1995) *The State We're In.* London: Jonathan Cape.

Hyman, P. (1994) *Women and Economics: A New Zealand Feminist Perspective.* Wellington, New Zealand: Bridget Williams Books Ltd.

Jackson, D. and Salisbury J. (1996) Why should secondary schools take working with boys seriously? *Gender and Education,* 8: 103–15.

Kanter, R. M. (1993) *Men and Women of the Corporation,* 2nd edn. New York: Basic Books.

Kavemann, B. (1996) Verbal comment made during presentation of *Evaluation of a Survey of the European Union Member States Concerning Prevention of Sexual Violence against Girls and Boys.* Schleswig-Holstein: Ministry of Education, Science, Research and Culture.

Kelly, L., Regan, L. and Burton, S. (1991) *An Exploratory Study of the Prevalence of Sexual Abuse in a Sample of 16–21 Year Olds.* London: Child Abuse Studies Unit, University of North London.

Klein, R. (1995) Tails of snips and snails, *Times Educational Supplement,* 9 June.

Knight, J., Lingard, B. and Bartlett, L. (1994) Reforming teacher education policy under Labor Governments in Australia 1983–93. *British Journal of Sociology of Education,* 15: 451–66.

Kruse, A.-M. (1996) Approaches to teaching girls and boys: current debates, practices and perspectives in Denmark, in P. Mahony (ed.) *Changing Schools: Some International Feminist Perspectives on Working with Girls and Boys.* Special Issue, *Women's Studies International Forum,* 19: 429–45.

Lean, G. and Ball, G. (1996) UK most unequal Country in the West, *Independent on Sunday,* 21 July.

Leeds Inter-Agency School Project (1996) *Summary, Key Issues and Recommendations.* Leeds: Leeds City Council.

Lingard, B. (1995) Re-articulating relevant voices in reconstructing teacher education. The Annual Harry Penny Lecture, University of South Australia.

Lingard, B. and Mills, M. (1997) Masculinity politics: an introduction. *Social Alternatives,* 16: 4–6.

MacBeath, J., Boyd, J., Rand, B. and Bell, S. (1996) *Schools Speak for Themselves: Towards a Framework for Self-Evaluation.* Strathclyde Quality in Education Centre, University of Strathclyde.

McGraw, B., Piper, K., Banks, D. and Evans, B. (1992) *Making Schools More Effective.* Victoria: Australian Council for Educational Research (ACER).

Mahony, P. (1985) *Schools for the Boys?* London: Hutchinson.

Mahony, P. (1997) Talking heads: feminist perspectives on public sector reform in teacher education. *Discourse,* 18: 87–102.

Mahony, P. and Frith, R. (1995) *Factors Influencing Girls' and Boys' Option Choices in Year 9.* Report to Essex Careers and Business Partnership. London: Roehampton Institute.

Mahony, P. and Hextall, I. (1997a) Problems of accountability in reinvented government: a case study of the Teacher Training Agency. *Journal of Education Policy*, 12: 267–78.

Mahony, P. and Hextall, I. (1997b) Sounds of silence: the social justice agenda of the Teacher Training Agency. *International Studies in Sociology of Education*, 7: 137–56.

Mahony, P. and Moos, L. (1997) Facts and fictions of school leadership. Paper presented at European Conference on Educational Research, Frankfurt, Germany, 24–26 September.

Mahony, P. and Zmroczek, C. (1997) *Class Matters: 'Working Class' Women's Perspectives on Social Class*. London: Taylor and Francis.

Millett, A. (1996) *Chief Executive's Annual Lecture*. London: Teacher Training Agency.

Mills, M. and Lingard, B. (1997) Masculinity politics, myths and boys' schooling. *British Journal of Educational Studies*, 45: 276–92.

Moys, A. (1980) *Modern Languages Examinations at 16+*. London: Centre for Information on Language Teaching Research.

Murphy, P. and Elwood, J. (1998) Gendered experiences, choices and achievement: exploring the links, in D. Epstein, J. Maw, J. Elwood and V. Hey (eds) *International Journal of Inclusive Education: Special Issue on Boys' 'Underachievement'*, 2(2): 95–118.

Parry, O. (1996) Cultural contexts and school failure: underachievement of Caribbean males in Jamaica, Barbados and St Vincent and the Grenadines. Paper presented to ESRC seminar series 'Gender and Schooling: Are Boys Now Underachieving?', University of London Institute of Education.

Pollitt, C. (1993) *Managerialism and the Public Services*, 2nd edn. Oxford: Blackwell Publishers.

Pusey, M. (1991) *Economic Rationalism in Canberra: A Nation-Building State Changes its Mind*. New York: Cambridge University Press.

Pyke, N. (1996) Boys 'read less than girls', *Times Educational Supplement*, 15 March.

Reynolds, D. (1994) School effectiveness and quality in education, in P. Ribnew and E. Burridge (eds) *Improving Education: Promoting Quality in Schools*. London: Cassell.

Salisbury, J. and Jackson, D. (1996) *Challenging Macho Values: Practical Ways of Working with Adolescent Boys*. London: Falmer Press.

Schmidt, B. and Peter, A. (1996) The Petze Project: working with teachers on the prevention of sexual violence against girls and boys in Germany, in P. Mahony (ed.) *Changing Schools: Some International Feminist Perspectives on Working with Girls and Boys*. Special issue *Women's Studies International Forum*, 19: 395–407.

Shand, D. (1996) The new public management: an international perspective. Paper presented to Public Services Management 2000 Conference, University of Glamorgan, 11 October.

Smith, M. J. (1995) Silence of the lads, *Times Educational Supplement*, 24 March.

Targett, S. (1996) Women told to take risks to get a first, *Times Higher Educational Supplement*, 1 November.

Townshend, J. (1996) An overview of OECD work on teachers, their pay and conditions, teaching quality and the continuing professional development of teachers. Paper presented at UNESCO International Conference on Education, Geneva, October.

Weiner, G., Arnot, M. and David, M. (1997) Is the future female? Female success, male disadvantage and changing gender patterns in education, in A. H. Halsey, P. Brown, H. Lauder and A. Stuart-Wells (eds) *Education: Culture, Economy and Society*. Oxford: Oxford University Press.

Willis, P. (1977) *Learning to Labour: How Working Class Kids Get Working Class Jobs*. Aldershot: Saxon House.

4

'Zero tolerance': gender performance and school failure

LYNN RAPHAEL REED

Introduction

Two powerful signifiers shape our current educational landscape; the 'under-achieving boy' and the 'failing school'. Each define liminality: markers of the boundary between that which is acceptable/safe/desired in dominant educational policies and practices, and that which is unacceptable/unsafe/feared. Both are perceived of as a threat to the achievement of an established order of 'excellence' and 'standards', yet each is essential to the articulation of that vision and the strategies by which it might be pursued. Indeed, deconstruction of the dominant discourses around both boys' underachievement and school failure reveal their productive power; in particular, in reformulating and recasting the relationship in education between gender, equity and social justice.

This chapter considers the positioning of concerns about gender performance in the late 1990s within the discourses of school failure and school improvement. The term 'gender performance' here is used in two senses: both the measurable academic outcomes for pupils differentiated by gender; and the gendered actions and performances of staff, pupils, parents and governors in the context of having been identified as a 'failing school' i.e. gender as a performative act within a specific social context. Case-study material is drawn from Hackney Downs School for boys, the first and only school to have been taken over by an Educational Association and subsequently closed (O'Connor et al. 1997).

En-gendering school failure and success

The influence of school effectiveness and school improvement perspectives on post-Conservative education policy is widely acknowledged and increasingly critiqued (Angus 1993; Brown, Duffield and Riddell 1995; Hatcher and Jones 1996). In relation to issues of racial equity and social justice, Hatcher (1997a) highlights how current accounts of 'effective schools' are frequently deracialized, assimilationist and technicist, indicating an important shift in Labour Party perspectives on racial in/equality and education over the last two decades:

> The contrast between Labour's perspectives today and the earlier multicultural phase of Labour policy is striking. Then, the key to problems of achievement among ethnic minority pupils was seen to lie in reforming the curriculum to bridge the cultural gap. Its weakness was its all too often superficial notion of ethnic cultures and its reluctance to explicitly address racism. Now, ethnic differences in achievement are assimilated into a universal discourse of raising standards, in which the curriculum is seen as unproblematic and pupil cultures as irrelevant.
>
> (Hatcher 1997a: 123)

While there is a similar tendency for current school effectiveness and school improvement discourses to undertheorize gender and gender in/equality, one cannot say that gender issues *per se* have become assimilated or made invisible in quite the same way. Indeed, one might argue, that a specific form of gender analysis within these discourses (which focus on male underachievement) is overdetermining attention to certain education processes, policies and practices, and repositioning the significance of 'race' and class. The defining parameters of the 'underachieving boy' phenomenon within the broader discourse of school effectiveness and school improvement do, however, indicate the loss of a critical sociological perspective on the issues involved. Weiner *et al.* (1997) in describing the influencing paradigms in Britain since the 1940s around gender and education, point to the situated nature of the concern with boys within a broader shift away from earlier articulations of equal opportunities (see Table 4.1).

Despite the clarion call from the Chief Inspector of Schools that 'the failure of boys and in particular white working class boys is one of the most disturbing problems we face, within the whole education system' (Woodhead, quoted in *Times Educational Supplement*, 15 March 1996), full data on the intersection of 'race', social class and gender in national patterns of achievement remains unavailable, concealing sound markers of social differentiation, and undermining the apparent validity of a more radical critique of gender performance in specific social contexts. While Gillborn and Gipps provide useful evidence that the pattern of girls outperforming boys may only hold uniformly for white pupils across all social class backgrounds (Gillborn and Gipps 1996: 17) and that specific concerns remain about the levels of achievement of African-Caribbean boys, they admit to the frailty of the data sources available. Yates (1997) reviewing parallel concerns about boys' underachievement in the Australian context, argues that one critical factor influencing recent reform agendas is the growing concern of middle-class parents and families that their sons should not be outclassed. At the

Table 4.1   Parallel educational discourses

Historical period	Prevalent discourses of education	Prevalent discourses of gender and education
1940s and 1950s	Equality of opportunity – IQ testing (focus on access)	Weak (emphasis on equality according to 'intelligence')
1960s and 1970s	Equality of opportunity Progressivism/mixed ability	Weak (emphasis on working-class male disadvantage)
1970s to early 1980s	Equality of opportunity – gender, race, disability, sexuality etc. (focus on outcome)	Equal opportunities/ anti-sexism (emphasis on female disadvantage)
Late 1980s and early 1990s	Choice, vocationalism and marketization (focus on competition)	Identity politics and feminisms (emphasis on femininities and masculinities)
Mid-1990s	School effectiveness and improvement (focus on standards)	Performance and achievement (emphasis on male disadvantage)

Source: Weiner *et al.* (1997: 622).

same time, Teese *et al.* (1995) remind us that working-class girls continue to have a rough deal from schooling, and that the key question is 'not whether girls as a group or boys as a group are more disadvantaged but which girls and which boys' (Teese *et al.* 1995: 109).

Despite the continuing need to sensitize our understandings of pupil experiences of current schooling and their educational outcomes across the diversities of 'race', class and gender, the association of girls with educational success and boys with educational failure has increasing potency. Ball and Gewirtz (1997) in their study of the marketing, selection and recruitment practices of schools, parents and pupils in 14 case study schools, point to the accretive value of female pupils in a competitive education market:

In the 'structured' education market, where school examination performance and behavioural regimes are increasingly tied to reputation and recruitment, girls are a valuable and sought after resource. Their performance in public examinations outstrips that of boys and their presence in school normally conveys positive impressions to parents about ethos and discipline.

(Ball and Gewirtz 1997: 214)

While acknowledging that 'not all girls are of equal value in the education market' (p. 220), and that the choice of single-sex education for girls is also often founded on contradictory desires to expand female opportunity but at the same time to reinforce traditional and limiting notions of femininity, what is striking about recent studies of gender and school choice, is the frequent articulation by girls and their parents that boys in school are depressing girls' achievements and damaging their educational experience. The relationality between female and male experience and situation, identified so cogently in earlier feminist writing (Arnot and Weiner 1987; Lees 1986; Stanworth 1981; Weiner and Arnot 1987) is thereby being rearticulated within the dominant discourses of the 1990s around achievement and success. Girls across social classes in Watson's study (1997), all gave as a major reason for choosing single-sex schools, the desire to escape boys' non-work/ failing behaviours and influence.

The permeation of this perspective that girls are 'successful' and boys are 'failing', is reinforced by statistics on girls' achievements in all-female settings, across school type and social class. Arnot et al. (1996), producing snapshot data from 1994 of the proportion of pupils achieving five or more A–C grades in GCSE in seven specified categories of school (LEA comprehensive; LEA secondary modern; grant-maintained comprehensive; grant-maintained selective; independent selective; independent no fixed admissions policy; voluntary-aided comprehensive), show that all-girls' schools obtained higher ratings than all-boys' schools in all seven categories and were the highest performing schools in six categories. Benn and Chitty (1996) in their survey of the current state of comprehensive education, found that girls' comprehensive schools achieved better exam results than equivalent boys' or mixed schools, despite scoring higher on average on indices of social deprivation. None of this is surprising given the national discrepancy in achievement between girls and boys, particularly at the higher grades, where in 1997 50 per cent of girls achieved at least 5 A*–C grades or the GNVQ (General National Vocational Qualification) equivalent, compared with 40.5 per cent of boys (DfEE 1997b), but it broadens the perception that the higher achievements of all-girls' schools can be explained as a function of social privilege. It becomes essentially associated as a feature of the female.

The other side of this equation is the profile of a 'failing school'. The origins of legislation to identify and intervene in schools deemed to be failing and in need of 'special measures', lie in the market-driven policies of the neo-liberal Conservative Right. *Choice and Diversity – A New Framework for Schools* (DfE 1992) linked recovery programmes for schools at risk to the faltering project of extending grant-maintained school status. However, the use of Section 10 inspections to advance the new Labour government's 'zero-tolerance of failure' agenda is marked. Between September 1993 and July 1996, just over 200 schools (including primary, secondary and special) had been identified as failing; by September 1997 that number had increased to 402 schools. Of these 402 to date, 25 schools have been deemed to have improved sufficiently to remove them from the list, and a further 20 have been closed (Ofsted 1997a).

In a recently produced Ofsted booklet *From Failure to Success: How Special Measures are Helping Schools Improve* (Ofsted 1997b), the defining characteristics of schools on the list include descriptive features closely associated with the wider underachievement of boys:

> standards of literacy . . . are too low; . . . behaviour seriously affects learning; . . . attendance is unsatisfactory and punctuality is often poor; . . . exclusion rates are high and for boys from ethnic minorities very high; . . . there are many more boys than girls in schools that are not providing an acceptable standard of education.
>
> (Ofsted 1997b: 9)

Indeed, of the 402 schools which have been identified, 70 are special schools with high proportions of boys on roll, and while 2 per cent of all primary and secondary schools have been placed under special measures, as a proportion of all boys' schools, the percentage of boys' schools is closer to 6 per cent. The message is clear: the 'underachieving boy' and the 'failing school' are intimately linked. While social deprivation, social class and poverty are acknowledged as constitutive features of failing school profiles, the significance of these structural and cultural features are denied in preference to an account that condemns teacher/school inefficiency and ineffectiveness:

> The schools in special measures range from inner-city secondary and primary schools to rural village schools. Many serve pupils from areas with high levels of social deprivation. This is not an excuse for failing to educate pupils properly because there can be no valid reason for not providing all young people with an acceptable quality of education. Ofsted inspections show clearly that schools serving similar areas often perform very differently; some well and some poorly.
>
> (Ofsted 1997b: 4)

No such refutation exists in relation to the issue of gender. The representation of unmet needs associated with the discursive composition of the underachieving boy ensures that unassuaged masculinity becomes a defining force behind the reshaping of educational discourses on learning, school practices and wider educational policies. It is this to which I now want to turn.

The 'masculinization' of educational policies and practices

The determination of the underachieving boy

As I have argued elsewhere (Raphael Reed 1997a), deconstructing the subject of the underachieving boy is not to engage in an argument about whether male underachievement exists: its 'reality' is a measure of its productivity in shaping educational policies and practices and there is considerable evidence of its current effects (Arnold 1997; Ofsted/EOC 1996; Morris

1996). Rather, it is an attempt to understand the significance of how the issues are presented and understood, accepting that 'the reality represented does not determine the representation or the means of representation. Instead, the process of signification itself gives shape to the reality it implicates' (Henriques *et al.* 1984: 99). Key elements of this subject include: a boy's underachievement in measurable assessments at Key Stages 1–4 with his performance eclipsed by girls, even in subjects he could once take as his own; his alienation and disarticulation from society and social norms, represented by poor levels of behaviour, exclusion, truancy, criminality and increasing depression and suicide. High profile examples of boys 'at risk' cement popular perceptions about the nature of the problem (for example, the white, working-class 13-year-old Nottingham boy who was the focus of intense media scrutiny when his teachers threatened to strike if he was not permanently excluded, and whose picture appeared on the front page of national newspapers with headlines such as 'Boys will be boys, or is he the worst pupil in Britain?').

Two dominant explanatory paradigms are drawn upon in practitioner and popular accounts to explain these indices of concern. The first rests on a crude version of cognitive psychology and theories of innate difference, often advanced with little reference to sound or published research data (Head 1996). This claims that the male brain is structured and operates differently from the female, finding it hard to deal with reflective emotional-centred tasks and preferring speculative thinking and action (Hannan 1996). The argument then is that predominant classroom practices favour the reflective and language rich approach to learning of girls and seriously disadvantage boys, with boys naturally poorer on things which require reflection and carefully thought-through organization and sequential planning. Nicholas Tate as Chief Executive of the School Curriculum and Assessment Authority urged schools to use more structured teaching methods to stop boys falling further behind in school subjects (Macleod 1995).

While some of the classroom management techniques suggested to 'compensate' for this particular learning orientation make good sense as sound, differentiated classroom teaching strategies, there are other implications to identify. To some extent, it represents part of a shift in the dominant individualist pedagogic perspective, building on Piagetian preoccupations with the emergence and activation of innate developmental stages, and heavily influenced by the work of Howard Gardner on multiple intelligences (Gardner 1993). The related interest in 'accelerated learning strategies', reflected again in popular in-service courses and LEA and school development plans of the moment (Smith 1995) provides a rearticulation of child-centred pedagogy, where the teacher is responsible for identifying and matching individual pupil learning needs by preferred learning style, and by failing to do so, becomes responsible for pupil failure (Walkerdine 1984). This way of looking at classroom experience is fundamentally apolitical and asocial; gender as a social practice is replaced by idiographic descriptions of learner orientations, with gendered preference embedded in the brain. It is also of significance that the subject areas and teachers linked most closely with the problem of boys' underachievement are predominantly female: English teachers, primary teachers, and special educational needs teachers.

Combined with a call to make the curriculum more relevant in content to boys' interests (e.g. using football scores to teach mathematics), this discursive element is already leading to a further masculinization of teaching styles and classroom environments. This is particularly evident in secondary schools, although it is also found in primary classrooms where teaching is required to be more didactic and structured (through, for example, phonics-based approaches to literacy, whole-class inculcation of mathematical rules, etc.).

The implications for gender equity are worrying. A recent newspaper report on the implementation of the National Numeracy Project, heralded as a huge success, with 40 per cent of schools involved reporting improvement in mathematics standards through the use of 'whole-class teaching and rigorous learning of the times tables' ('"Real Maths" wins praise: a Government numeracy project has achieved "staggering" results': *Times Educational Supplement*), also acknowledged: 'One of the report's more surprising findings was that girls did not do as well as boys, bucking the trend. Co-ordinators say they need to keep a check that girls play as active a role as boys in lessons' (*Times Education Supplement*, 12 December 1997).

Boaler (1997a) indicates that girls more than boys are switched off mathematics when it is delivered in a procedural and rule-bound way, and that they tend to become anxious in settings that are competitive and where the pace of the lesson is fast or fixed. Such a pedagogic shift nests within a trend in school organization at both primary and secondary level towards an increase in setting according to perceived ability. While no convincing evidence exists that such a strategy improves achievement overall (Slavin 1996), there is evidence that the students who are disadvantaged by this system are predominantly, working class, female, from a minority ethnic group or the very able (Boaler 1997b; Hatcher 1997b).

This combines with a shifting balance of subjects in the primary National Curriculum. The literacy and numeracy hours are producing increasing demands for a more narrowly focused curriculum (Macleod 1997) and the recent Teacher Training Agency frameworks on Initial Teacher Training mean that an increasing number of teacher training establishments are likely to shift their curriculum to prepare newly qualified teachers to teach only the core curriculum (English, mathematics and science) plus information technology and possibly one other subject. Outline details in the School Standards and Framework Bill of the Education Action Zones (EAZs) planned for areas of social deprivation indicate schools in EAZs will be able to suspend entitlement to the full National Curriculum, to encourage concentration on basic skills. Inevitably, pupils will have an increasingly masculinized curriculum experience. One could see this as a reinforcement of hegemonic masculinity through curriculum content and the form of pedagogy; privileging rationality and the 'mastery of reason' as individual power, over emotional and intuitive connectedness through social and linguistic practices (Walkerdine 1988) but legitimated through concerns with 'standards'.

One consequence of these ideas around boys and their learning is to construct all boys as if each had by virtue of being a boy a special educational need. This will exacerbate the tendency already noted in schools for boys to be 'seen' more visibly in school than girls, and for them to absorb the larger proportion of additional support and resources (Daniels *et al.* 1996; Riddell 1996) while suggesting that the issues affecting girls are all resolved. As Weiner *et al.* note: 'What is evident is that new educational discourses have silenced demands for increased social justice for girls and women, characterised by increasing resistance to policies and practices focusing specifically on them' (1997: 15).

The second explanatory paradigm rests upon simplistic notions of the significance of social role. Commonly, accounts tend to emphasize the significance of material and ideological changes to men's position and role in society and anxiety about the lack of positive male role models for boys. This is articulated most clearly in relation to African-Caribbean boys where deficit models still predominate through a crude sociological proposition that absent black fathers in the home must be substituted for by positive black role models in the classroom and that African-Caribbean boys suffer from overdomination by the black matriarch in the family. Overall, most reports assume that boys consider it 'uncool' to be successful at school with schoolboy cultures unmediated by work-orientated male models or unsupported by family aspirations and standards. Engaging the support of Premier club footballers in after-school study centres is supposed to help.

Such a perspective on the 'problem' leads to particular educational solutions, themselves potentially problematic. The intervention of black male mentors into primary schools has been criticized by some for diverting attention away from institutionalized racism, and for undermining the integrity of female teachers (Hutchinson and John 1995); and the whole construction of 'black underachievement' and gender relations in African-Caribbean families has been critiqued by Mirza (1993), as has a tendency to oversimplify and over-essentialize black male student identities and experiences in school (Sewell 1997).

Furthermore, unproblematized notions of masculinity are embedded in certain 'positive' role models. One school in Rochdale (Greater Manchester) established a mentoring scheme for boys to shadow business people in industry, so that 'boys will see what being busy and organised at work really means' (Haigh 1995). This included being picked up by a male manager at 6.45 a.m. to attend a business meeting over breakfast: a questionable and highly gendered practice to emulate and one which reasserts traditional hegemonic notions of masculinity. A recent whole-page British Telecom advertisement in the *Times Educational Supplement* promoting education business partnerships, shows a white primary-aged boy dressed as a city financier, with the *Financial Times* tucked confidently under his arm. The idea of returning to a 'self-discipline through authoritative male practices' is equally evidenced in recent suggestions that what badly behaved and unmotivated boys need is a compulsory period of military discipline in the cadet corps (Harding and Fairhall 1997). Hegemonic masculinity itself is not seen as part of the problem.

This articulation of regulation and surveillance with a gender dimension has wider significance when put together with current criminal-justice legislation and social-welfare reforms, and when we consider the permeation of specific values within recent national education-policy agendas. Apple (1994: 356) reminds us: 'Gender and its regulation is not just an afterthought in state policy. Rather, it is a constitutive part of it. Nearly all of the state's activity is involved in it.' What we need to do is analyse the 'assumptive worlds' of policy actors (Marshall 1997: 5) in the new Labour government from a gender-critical perspective.

Penetrative policies, punishment and 'zero tolerance'

Under the rubric of the newly launched Social Exclusion Unit, policies designed to ensure 'social cohesion and not social division' (Tony Blair, at the launch of the Social Exclusion Unit, 8 December 1997) are targetted on 'anti-social elements' of the population, predominantly male. This 'anti-social' population includes excluded and truanting schoolchildren, drug dependants who refuse rehabilitation courses, and anti-social tenants on housing estates (Wintour and Cohen 1997). The criminal justice White Paper, *No More Excuses: A New Approach to Tackling Youth Crime in England and Wales* (Home Office 1997) proposes local curfews to keep unsupervised under-10s off the streets after 9 p.m.; wider powers to detain in secure accommodation those between 12 and 14; the abolition of the rule of *doli incapax*, that presumes a child under 14 does not know the difference between right and wrong; and parenting orders for parents of young offenders requiring them to take responsibility for their children or face penalties. Parallel to this is the reform of the welfare benefits system through the welfare-to-work programme which has extended from a New Deal for the young unemployed, to policies attempting to move any welfare recipient into work if it can, including single parents and the disabled, with increasing elements of compulsion including loss of benefits.

All of this points to the discursive repositioning of family and state responsibilities, but what is of real significance to my argument is the placing of gender at the heart of state actions: the 'out of control' and uneducable boy is in need of reigning in; the parent at home, oftentimes the single parent/mother, is made responsible for and penalized for his actions; at the same time she is culpable in the production and sustenance of family poverty by not having a real job, and will be further penalized by changes to tax and benefit support.

The same masculinization and regulation of the female can be detected in recent education policy texts and associated debates, in particular, the first education White Paper of the Labour government's term of office, *Excellence in Schools* (DfEE 1997a), partially legislated in the School Standards and Framework Bill currently before Parliament. Commitments such as extra resourcing to reduce class size and improve the quantity of pre-school provision, the establishment of a form of General Teaching Council, new professional qualifications for teachers and termly scholarships, the establishment of Education Action Zones in 25 urban areas in the next 3 years are combined with a range of other more interventionist and regulative measures. These include increased intervention in the school curriculum especially around basic skills; increased testing of children with base-line testing for all 4-year-olds and tests in English and mathematics for 9-year-olds; increased differentiation and stratification in secondary schools encouraging further limitation of mixed ability teaching, fast tracking for successful pupils and the establishment of specialist schools; increased vocational and work-related education; school performance tables to continue and school improvement targets to be set by individual schools with quicker procedures for dismissing teachers deemed incompetent as a result of inspection and mechanisms for closing and reopening 'failing schools'; mechanisms for inspecting and penalizing LEAs who fail to deliver improving standards on a regional basis and materially rewarding those schools and LEAs which do well; home–school contracts to boost homework and address truancy, with fines for persistent non-attendance; compulsory homework and additional study centres; and increased control of the teacher training curriculum.

What is most striking in the policy text and discourses surrounding these debates is the specificity of political rhetoric used in attempting to cohere fealty around the standard of 'standards', particularly the permeation of masculinist and bellicose language and imagery. We are asked to join the government 'crusade', to use 'tough love', send in 'hit squads', 'name and shame', have 'zero tolerance of failure' and silence the 'doubts of cynics and the corrosion of the perpetual sceptics'.

Furthermore, the positioning of teachers in this discourse is problematic, with stated support for teacher professionalism undermined by a disempowering tendency to overregulate, inspect and penalize teacher practices. Kenway, writing recently on the influence and effects of technical rationality on gender reform policies in Australia, identifies the consequences of privileging teacher accountability over teacher professionalism:

Indeed ideas about teacher professionalism have now almost entirely given way to those about teacher accountability. Clearly, accountability mechanisms produce a very different emotional dynamic. They position teachers in a non-dialogical relationship to policy makers in what

Foucault (1977) might call a confessional mode of self-regulation and self-monitoring. And as such, they implicitly infantilise teachers and imply they do not understand, cannot be trusted, must be shamed into good practice and will be blamed if change does not occur. It is predictable that emotional responses to this will not be positive, particularly if one takes into account the broader political context of recent times involving major educational restructuring, a 'mean and lean' approach to supporting teacher development for change, and reform fatigue on the part of teachers.

(Kenway 1997: 335)

There is an important gender dimension to acknowledge in this. Jeffrey and Woods (1996) in their study of the effects on primary teachers of an Ofsted inspection, point to the damage caused by the combination of 'persecutory guilt' and 'depressive guilt' to use Hargreaves' terms (1994) experienced by teachers involved, and the challenge posed to their sense of 'self' (Nias 1989) in a professional context. The model of education implied by and tested through the inspection process, which moves practices away from humanistic, holistic and child-centred versions of pedagogy, is experienced as especially traumatic. The teachers they observed, who in the main were women, showed strong emotional reactions akin to that experienced in sexual harassment, assault and abuse, and closely associated with powerlessness:

The teachers experienced fear, anguish, anger, despair, depression, humiliation, grief and guilt – emotions produced by the mismatch between the power of the critical event they were experiencing and the cultural resources provided by their beliefs and past experiences.

(Jeffrey and Woods 1996: 340)

The continuation of the 'double burden' for female teachers, still taking principal responsibility for domestic work including childcare in the home alongside their paid employment, was evidenced with specific consequences when teaching work became intensified:

'Sometimes I get home and it's really late, you know, and I just feel guilty. There I am in school, telling these children to read, making sure someone reads to them, and telling them to make somebody listen to them and I'm not listening to my children.'

(Jeffrey and Woods 1996: 337)

'I did 13 hours at the weekend, from Friday night right the way through to Sunday night. Sunday afternoon I burst out crying. The sun was streaming through the window, I'd been sat there since 11 and it was half past 4 in the afternoon and I had to cook the dinner and waiting for me was a pile of ironing and I just sat down and cried.'

(p. 329)

Equally, the types of management practices and school cultures affirmed and supported by the current quality assurance procedures in school have significant gender dimensions. Ball (1997) in his analysis of the practices invoked by total quality management, school development plans and Ofsted inspection, identifies from one case study in an all-girls' school a 'heady mix of feminism, surveillance, initiative, competition and corporate culture' (1997: 334). In part though, his data evidences further masculinization of values and actions in the school culture, if one takes increasing competition, corporate efficiency, regulation of the body and symbolic forms, like the erection of a school flagpole, as gendered practices. The possibility within the School Standards and Framework Bill that failing schools or failing authorities could be taken over by a private sector business organization, will only increase this tendency further.

What seems increasingly possible is that 'poisonous pedagogies' (Kenway and Fitzclarence 1997) and phallocentric school cultures may well be supported and advanced as a consequence of the penetrative policies of the new Labour government, proposing 'zero tolerance' of failing schools and the underachieving boy. In this sense 'gender performance' becomes the spur for gender as a performative act.

Lessons from the past: the case of Hackney Downs School

I want to extend my argument by presenting some case-study material from the experience of Hackney Downs School for boys (HDS) in London, illustrating the 'gender performances' elicited as a consequence of its identification as a 'failing school'. This inner-city all-boys' comprehensive school was closed in December 1995 on the advice of the first Educational Association set up under Section 218 of the 1993 Education Act. Closure followed a long and acrimonious battle between on the one hand staff, parents and governors in the school, and on the other officers of the LEA, with political instability in the local council exacerbating the conflict. The unfolding of this story in the 1990s, in the political context of the last few years of Conservative government – with explicit policies of marketization and school stratification and failure as a consequence – has been analysed and presented elsewhere (O'Connor et al. 1997; Slee, Tomlinson and Weiner 1997; Tomlinson 1997). My intention here is to look to the lessons we might learn from an earlier period in the history of that school, and in particular from its experience in the 1980s under the Labour-led Inner London Education Authority (ILEA). I am drawing here upon observations as a participant since I was a teacher in the school from 1983 to 1990, and also from reflections of a number of staff interviewed by me retrospectively as part of a project recording life histories of teachers committed to social justice (Raphael Reed 1995).

Hackney Downs School was a very early and interesting example of Labour politicians using 'naming and shaming' as a mechanism for social regulation and control. In 1989 the ILEA moved to identify publicly ten schools as being a 'cause for concern' and they were subsequently vilified in the press as being 'problem' or 'dunce' schools. David Mallen, Chief Education Officer at that time, reported that the ILEA had been monitoring schools since 1985, although in the only league tables made public from this monitoring process in March 1986 (adjusted using indices of social deprivation by the ILEA Research and Statistics Department) HDS ranked fifty-ninth out of 152 schools. It was a school included in a major school effectiveness study in the 1980s (Smith and Tomlinson 1989), in which in 1986 it achieved examination passes on a par with other London schools studied and higher than five Midlands schools in the research.

In a letter to the head teacher in 1989, Mallen argued that: 'the school became a source of real concern following the publication of an ILEA Inspectors Report back in 1985', yet, looking back, that last full inspection report by the ILEA reveals a different assessment:

> The school has much to recommend it . . . there has been considerable curricular development in many areas of the curriculum. Much of the teaching is distinguished, a variety of appropriate styles being used. The school has played a leading role in implementing the Authority's initiatives . . . The school is to be congratulated upon developing highly positive relationships between pupils and staff and also within the staff. This is a school with a most civilised and humane working environment that is a credit to the whole staff.
>
> (David Hargreaves, Chief Inspector, July 1985)

In particular, since the late 1970s, it was in the forefront of advancing equal-opportunities strategies; mixed ability teaching, integrated humanities, anti-racist teaching and anti-sexist work with boys. For the last of these it was being applauded by the ILEA at the very moment that it was supposedly being identified as a 'problem':

> Hackney Downs is the first of the Authority's all boys' schools to make the issue of gender explicit in the curriculum. It is essential for schools to find ways to challenge sexist attitudes and values. Hackney Downs sets an example of attitudinal education which, while raising issues, is not coercive but which extends very positively the range of choices that pupils have not only in curriculum content but also in the formation of their attitudes and values. It is, in our opinion, a valuable example of real education for a better society.
>
> (Morrell 1985)

The experience and perspectives on anti-sexist work developed in the school found expression in publication (Askew and Ross 1988) and in the wider educational community; far from being perceived as a 'dunce' school, HDS had a well earned international reputation for much of its work:

> I have talked to groups of teachers about the achievements of your

school in New York, Washington, San Francisco, Tuscon Arizona and
Wellington New Zealand, as well as to seminars in this Institute and all
over Britain.

(McLeod 1985)

What was true was that the school had a continual drop in roll from 1985 to
1988 for a number of reasons. First, reorganization of secondary schooling in
the borough had meant the opening of a large mixed comprehensive nearby,
and given the tendency for boys to opt for mixed places in greater numbers
than girls, this had consequences for recruitment (London Borough of
Hackney 1989).

Second, and probably more significantly, the school had a well-organized
and militant staff, active in the teachers' union, who took industrial action
throughout the 1980s to defend teachers' pay and conditions as well as
pupils' rights to learn in safety. HDS teachers resisted the imposition of the
teachers' contract; took action against compulsory redeployment of teachers
across the ILEA; and initiated the fight to have asbestos removed from
school buildings which led to dozens of other schools following suit, costing
the authority a considerable amount of money at a time when it was des-
perately attempting to implement cuts.

The final straw perhaps was over the school's stance on exposing the
authority on its lack of commitment to challenge racism (Troyna 1993). In
1986, after ILEA officers refused to provide additional security for pupils and
staff in a school in Tower Hamlets where right-wing youths had used knives
to attack pupils on the school premises, 12 teachers were arrested and
prosecuted for demonstrating outside the divisional offices. It provoked an
all-out strike of London teachers. Two of the teachers arrested came from HDS.

Throughout this period, the school received consistently bad press in the
London and Hackney newspapers, and recruitment continued to suffer. As
the roll continued to fall, the intake became skewed towards an increasingly
vulnerable population, with some of the most disadvantaged children in
London in the school. Statistics from 1988 indicate this clearly (see Table 4.2).
The context for this action by the authority of course was the 1988 Education Reform Act which legislated for the abolition of the ILEA by 1990. In
retrospect, this period in the history of the school seems to represent an
early example of Labour proving its conservative credentials and distancing
itself from a more militant or radical face of labour activism, by invoking the
charge of school failure. It also represents a shift in ideological and political
perspective on what constitutes priorities and expectations around school
policies and practices in the inner city, with a firm retreat from any commitment to anti-racist and anti-sexist school strategies as central to that agenda.
One governor of that time, reflected later:

Well, I thought it was entirely cynical, I have to say. It was at the time
of the breakup of the ILEA. There was a battle going on between the
ILEA hierarchy of officers and the union, and I think it was a kind of

Table 4.2   Measures of disadvantage

	Hackney Downs School	Hackney	London
% of pupils awarded free school meals	61.2	57.2	46.2
% of pupils in large families (4+)	34.1	33.2	26.4
% of pupils in families with no wage earner	40.3	29.7	22.7
% of pupils using English as a 2nd Language	45.2	33.8	23.2

Source: ILEA Research and Statistics Department 1988.

response to the union strength in the school . . . I think that they fingered the school. I think that they wanted the union out and the union weakened in that school . . . That was what amazed me because it was never a, well . . . I was amazed to ever think of it as an 'at risk' school.

(Interview 1993)

Throughout this period the school in question was being drawn further and further into 'sink school' status and as one might have expected, the degenerative forces began polarizing the staff into apparently irreconcilable oppositions. One very striking opposition that emerged was that between white feminists who were characterized as 'soft' and 'liberal', and black anti-racists, characterized as 'macho' and 'traditionalist'. A vitriolic attack was launched by a small group of black parents, governors and staff on the anti-sexist programme with boys, Skills for Living, and what was called 'approaches around doing work on gender that fail our male youth'. At the same time there was an increase in the sexual harassment of female staff, and an increase in violent and authoritarian practices in some classrooms, under the adage that 'what black boys need is strict discipline and stern teaching of the subject'. This situation was mirrored in the furore in the national press over the 'Jane Brown' affair in 1994, when a white lesbian Hackney primary head teacher was alleged to have turned down subsidized tickets to the ballet *Romeo and Juliet* on the grounds of its romantic representation of heterosexuality and was publicly disciplined by the black male Director of Education, Gus John, despite evidence of her efficacy as a teacher and a head teacher, and support from the school community (Young 1995).

In HDS conflict between what had been previously seen as radically aligned interests was seized upon by critics of the school as further evidence of decay. Meanwhile, the behaviour and achievement of many of the boys in the school deteriorated further, and several experienced and committed staff – both black and white, male and female – unwilling to be pigeon-holed into either point of the polarization, left in distress and despair:

Well, for a start it was absolutely wrong to characterize female staff as 'soft'. I was totally clear about the importance of standards and used a whole range of strategies to raise the achievement of boys in the school . . . and my department had very good results from across the ability range . . . look at them and you'll see . . . in fact I did better than those teachers going on about discipline and the needs of black boys. They just had the brightest and toughest ones doing well and the rest just sinking and failing, or failing and frightened, which is more to the point. But what I couldn't accept was the suggestion that there was something wrong in looking at boys' emotions and feelings, both show-ing compassion and also helping them to see where parts of how they seemed to think they had to be as a boy . . . all the posturing and run-ning each other down . . . was actually stopping them doing well, and was actually oppressive.

The thing that did me though was when some people tried to make this an issue of race. I really believe in the importance of black people taking control of and asserting their needs in the education system, but in this case I think it feels like a group of manipulative and aggressive men using the 'race' card completely unjustly and using it as a cover to oppress pupils in the school. But I didn't feel I could say that because it just got put down as racism.

(Interview 1993)

In some senses this is a classic example of increasing anxiety, here as a consequence of being identified as a failing school, increasing wider gender anxiety and gender-oppressive actions, with projection, fear and fantasies about the 'other' at work (Shaw 1995). The case of Hackney Downs reveals dislocations between positions assumed on gender equality and on racial equality, and the unresolved issues that remain for us as educationists com-mitted to gender equity on how to articulate a position on education and social justice for boys, that can challenge both racism and sexism. Further-more, it exemplifies the potency of the intersection of discourses around the underachievement of boys, school failure and school improvement, when wider issues of values and social justice are subsumed under a narrower focus on improving assessment results alone, by whatever means necessary. Finally, it raises questions about the wider projection and displacement of fear of social disorder onto Hackney as a local authority over a continuing period; currently it faces retribution from a central government determined to prove its extra tough credentials by taking over the entire LEA on the basis of failure, despite recent evidence that in a value-added context Hackney schools are doing rather well (Bright 1997).

Towards a social justice perspective on the education of boys

I want to conclude this chapter with some brief discussion of a social justice perspective on education, developed further elsewhere (Raphael Reed 1997b) indicating its relevance to our concerns around the underachievement of boys. One set of difficulties with the dominant frameworks informing current educational policies and practices are the limitations of a distributive theory of social justice, with the focus solely on who gets what, and seeing the fair distribution of goods (including educational credentials) as a super-ordinate goal. I. M. Young's critique of this (1990) highlights two things. First, that by focusing on the distribution of goods we fail to notice the other relevant factors influencing this pattern of distribution, including structural inequalities, institutional processes and the separation of the private from the public sphere. Second, that by broadening distribution to cover not only material goods but also goods such as self-respect, opportunity, power, honour and so on, we reify these things, suggesting they are fixed and static, and we thereby avoid looking at social processes.

Seeing social justice as more than just a matter of distribution of material goods, and identifying the centrality of relational and diverse dynamics and actions, allows us to identify a more meaningful framework for defining and evaluating the macro- and micro-political conditions of social in/equality. Young stresses that: 'The concept of distribution should be limited to material goods and that other aspects of justice include decision-making procedures, the social division of labour, and culture' (1990: 8). And

> I wish . . . to displace talk of justice that regards persons as primarily possessors and consumers of goods to a wider context that also includes actions, decisions about actions, and provision of the means to develop and exercise capabilities.
>
> (1990: 8)

Looking at these elements in the educational experiences of boys in school rather than narrowly concentrating on just their access to academic credentials, immediately opens up a richer vein of enquiry. It points us towards examining the importance of context, behaviours and values as well as the social practices of power. In particular, her emphasis that 'Oppression and domination . . . should be the primary terms for conceptualising injustice' (p. 9) allows us to consider the complexity and reality of experience of pupils and teachers across 'race', class and gender on the same plane of analysis, since oppression and domination may be experienced by each or all of them in different ways at different times and in different contexts.[1]

The key challenge of our times is to develop a powerful and empowering counter-discourse to the dominant discourses perpetuated through the school effectiveness and school improvement literature and its associated demonization of the underachieving boy and the failing school. Such a counter-discourse must centralize a reformulated social justice perspective on schooling which can encompass both a commitment to expanding access to educational opportunities and credentials and a commitment to educational values and principles in practice, showing the interconnection between the two. This needs to include, following Young, a critical focus on gendered actions and school cultures alongside a continuing debate on the nature of the curriculum. Connell argues that: 'education is a social process in which the "how much" cannot be separated from the "what"' (1993: 18), and Salisbury and Jackson (1996) suggest a range of curricular approaches to working with adolescent boys that fulfil in many senses the criteria specified by Connell, while addressing boys' fears, anxieties and displacements which may be expressed in violent or prejudicial ways. In part, it is about challenging the increasingly rational curriculum content, as much as acknowledging the support that teachers need, to engage with such difficult issues (Kenway 1997).

Beyond this, we also need to research how particular pedagogic and policy contexts while raising examination performance, may be either promoting or undermining a social justice perspective on the education of boys. To quote Hatcher (1997b: 9): 'it should be emphasised that raising levels of pupil achievement does not necessarily entail reducing educational inequalities – in fact, standards can rise while the equality gaps widens'. Recent evidence on the relentless rise of school exclusions, particularly for African-Caribbean and working-class boys as schools focus on improving examination results, is a good example of this dynamic. However, what we must also challenge are the ways in which 'improving schools' and 'improving boys' performance' may be predicated on the restitution of hegemonic forms of masculinity and gender-oppressive practices.

Note

1 This includes powerlessness and violence – two of the five 'faces of oppression' identified by Young where 'the presence of any of these five conditions is sufficient for calling a group oppressed' (1995: 64).

References

Angus, L. (1993) The sociology of school effectiveness. *British Journal of Sociology of Education*, 14(3): 333–45.

Apple, M. (1994) Texts and contexts: the state and gender in educational policy. *Curriculum Inquiry* 24(4): 349–59.

Arnold, R. (1997) *Raising Levels of Achievement in Boys*. Slough: EMIE/NFER.

Arnot, M. and Weiner, G. (eds) (1987) *Gender and the Politics of Schooling*. London: Hutchinson.

Arnot, M., David, M. and Weiner, G. (1996) *Educational Reforms and Gender Equality in Schools*. Manchester: Equal Opportunities Commission.

Askew, S. and Ross, C. (1988) *Boys Don't Cry: Boys and Sexism in Education*. Milton Keynes: Open University Press.

Ball, S. J. (1997) Good school/bad school: paradox and fabrication. *British Journal of Sociology of Education*, 18(3): 317–36.

Ball, S. J. and Gerwirtz, S. (1997) Girls in the education market: choice, competition and complexity. *Gender and Education*, 19(2): 207–22.

Benn, C. and Chitty, C. (1996) *Thirty Years On: Is Comprehensive Education Alive and Well, or Struggling to Survive?* London: David Fulton.

Boaler, J. (1997a) *Experiencing School Mathematics: Teaching Styles, Sex and Setting.* Buckingham: Open University Press.

Boaler, J. (1997b) Setting, social class and the survival of the quickest. *British Educational Research Journal*, 23(5): 575–95.

Bright, M. (1997) Where to find real value for your children, *Observer*, 23 November.

Brown, S., Duffield, J. and Riddell, S. (1995) School effectiveness research: the policy makers' tool for school improvement? *European Educational Research Association Bulletin*, March: 6–15.

Connell, R. W. (1993) *Schools and Social Justice*. Toronto: Our Schools/Our Selves Education Foundation.

Daniels, H., Hey V., Leonard, D. and Smith, M. (1996) 'Underachievement' and 'Special Educational Needs': the gendering of special educational needs practices. Paper presented at Gender and Schooling: Are Boys Now Underachieving? (ESRC funded seminar series) Centre for Research and Education on Gender, University of London Institute of Education, 17 May.

Department for Education [DFE] (1992) *Choice and Diversity – A New Framework for Schools*. London: DfE.

Department for Education and Employment [DfEE] (1997a) *Excellence in Schools*. London: HMSO.

Foucault, M. (1977) *Discipline and Punish: The Birth of the Prison*. Harmondsworth: Penguin.

Gardner, H. (1993) *Frames of Mind: The Theory of Multiple Intelligences*, 2nd edn. London: Falmer Press.

Gillborn, D. and Gipps, C. (1996) *Recent Research on the Achievements of Ethnic Minority Pupils*. London: HMSO.

Haigh, G. (1995) Not for wimps, *Times Educational Supplement*, 6 October.

Hannan, G. (1996) Improving boys' performance. INSET materials. Much Welcome: private publication.

Harding, L. and Fairhall, D. (1997) Labour repels lads' army, *Guardian*, 3 February.

Hargreaves, D. (1985) *Inspection Report on Hackney Downs School for Boys*. London: ILEA.

Hargreaves, A. (1994) *Changing Teachers, Changing Times: Teachers' Work and Culture in the Postmodern Age*. London: Cassell.

Hatcher, R. (1997a) Social justice in education after the Conservatives: the relevance of Barry Troyna's work, in P. Sikes and F. Rizvi (eds) *Researching Race and Social Justice in Education*. Stoke-on-Trent: Trentham Books.

Hatcher, R. (1997b) New Labour, school improvement and racial equality. *Multicultural Teaching*, 15(3): 8–13.

Hatcher, R. and Jones, K. (eds) (1996) *Education after the Conservatives*. Stoke-on-Trent: Trentham Books.

Head, J. (1996) Gender identity and cognitive style, in P. F. Murphy and C. V. Gipps (eds) *Equity in the Classroom: Towards Effective Pedagogy for Girls and Boys*. London: Falmer Press.

Henriques, J., Hollway, W., Urwin, C., Venn, C. and Walkerdine, V. (1984) *Changing the Subject: Psychology, Social Regulation and Subjectivity*. London and New York: Methuen.

Home Office (1997) *No More Excuses: A New Approach to Tackling Youth Crime in England and Wales*. London: HMSO.

Hutchinson, M. and John, G. (1995) Enter the role model, *Guardian Education*, 26 September.

ILEA Research and Statistics Department (1988) *Annual Statistical Returns*. London: ILEA.

Jeffrey, B. and Woods, P. (1996) Feeling deprofessionalised: the social construction of emotions during an OFSTED inspection. *Cambridge Journal of Education*, 26(3): 325–43.

Kenway, J. (1997) Taking stock of gender reform policies for Australian schools: past, present and future. *British Educational Research Journal*, 23(3): 329–44.

Kenway, J. and Fitzclarence, L. (1997) Masculinity, violence and schooling: challenging 'poisonous pedagogies'. *Gender and Education*, 9(1): 117–33.

Lees, S. (1986) *Losing Out: Sexuality and Adolescent Girls*. London: Hutchinson.

London Borough of Hackney (1989) *Hackney Borough Plan*. London: LBH.

MacLeod, A. (1985) Letter of support to staff at Hackney Downs School for Boys (personal correspondence).

Macleod, D. (1995) Schools told to stop boys' slide, *Guardian*, 20 February.

Macleod, D. (1997) NUT calls for rapid switch to flexible national curriculum, *Guardian*, 12 July.

Marshall, C. (1997) Dismantling and reconstructing policy analysis, in C. Marshall (ed.) *Feminist Critical Policy Analysis I: A Perspective from Primary and Secondary Schooling*. London: Falmer Press.

Mirza, H. (1993) The social construction of black womanhood in British educational research: towards a new understanding, in M. Arnot and K. Weiler (eds) *Feminism and Social Justice in Education*. London: Falmer Press.

Morrell, F. (Chair) (1985) *Report to the Schools Sub-Committee on Gender in ILEA Schools*. London: ILEA.

Morris, E. (1996) *Boys Will Be Boys? Closing the Gender Gap*. Labour Party Consultation Document. London: The Labour Party.

Nias, J. (1989) *Primary Teachers Talking*. London: Routledge.

O'Connor, M., Hales, E., Davies, J. and Tomlinson, S. (1997) *Hackney Downs: The School that Dared to Fight*. Lewes: Falmer Press.

Office for Standards in Education [Ofsted] (1997a) Schools requiring special measures. doc wp/fl240997.chr, 24 September.

Office for Standards in Education [Ofsted] (1997b) *From Failure to Success: How Special Measures are Helping Schools Improve*. London: Ofsted.

Office for Standards in Education and Equal Opportunities Commission [Ofsted/EOC] (1996) *The Gender Divide: Performance Differences between Boys and Girls at School*. London: HMSO.

Raphael Reed, L. (1995) Reconceptualising equal opportunities in the 1990s: a study of radical teacher culture in transition, in M. Griffiths and B. Troyna (eds) *Antiracism, Culture and Social Justice in Education*. Stoke-on-Trent: Trentham Books.

Raphael Reed, L. (1997a) Troubling boys and disturbing discourses on masculinity and schooling: a feminist exploration of current debates and interventions around boys in school. Paper given at Transitions: Gender and Education Conference, University of Warwick, April.

Raphael Reed, L. (1997b) Power, pedagogy and persuasion: schooling masculinities in the secondary school classroom. Paper given at British Educational Research

Association Conference, 'Symposium on Social Justice in Education', University of York, September.

Riddell, S. (1996) Gender and special educational needs, in G. Lloyd (ed.) *Knitting Progress Unsatisfactory: Gender and Special Needs Issues in Education*. Edinburgh: Moray House Institute of Education.

Salisbury, J. and Jackson, D. (1996) *Challenging Macho Values: Practical Ways of Working with Adolescent Boys*. London: Falmer Press.

Sewell, T. (1997) *Black Masculinities and Schooling: How Black Boys Survive Modern Schooling*. Stoke-on-Trent: Trentham Books.

Shaw, J. (1995) *Education, Gender and Anxiety*. London: Taylor and Francis.

Slavin, R. E. (1996) *Education for All*. Lisse: Swets en Zeitlinger.

Slee, R., Tomlinson, S. and Weiner, G. (1997) *Effective for Whom?* Lewes: Falmer Press.

Smith, A. (1995) *Accelerated Learning in the Classroom*. Stafford: Network Educational Press.

Smith, D. J. and Tomlinson, S. (1989) *The School Effect: A Study of Multiracial Comprehensives*. London: Policy Studies Institute.

Stanworth, M. (1981) *Gender and Schooling: A Study of Sexual Division in the Classroom*. London: Hutchinson.

Teese, R., Davies, M., Charlton, M. and Polesel, J. (1995) *Who Wins at School? Girls and Boys in Australian Secondary Education*. Melbourne: Melbourne University Department of Education Policy and Management.

Tomlinson, S. (1997) Sociological perspectives on failing schools. Paper given at International Sociology of Education Conference, University of Sheffield, January.

Troyna, B. (1993) *Racism and Education*. Buckingham: Open University Press.

Walkerdine, V. (1984) Developmental psychology and the child-centred pedagogy; the insertion of Piaget into early education, in J. Henriques *et al. Changing the Subject: Psychology, Social Regulation and Subjectivity*. London and New York: Methuen.

Walkerdine, V. (1988) *The Mastery of Reason: Cognitive Development and the Production of Rationality*. London: Routledge.

Watson, S. (1997) Single-sex education for girls: heterosexuality, gendered subjectivity and school choice. *British Journal of Sociology of Education*, 18(3): 371–83.

Weiner, G. and Arnot, M. (eds) (1987) *Gender Under Scrutiny*. London: Hutchinson.

Weiner, G., Arnot, M. and David, M. (1997) Is the future female? Female success, male disadvantage and changing gender patterns in education, in A. H. Halsey, P. Brown, H. Lauder and A. Stuart-Wells (eds) *Education: Culture, Economy and Society*. Oxford: Oxford University Press.

Wintour, P. and Cohen, N. (1997) Poverty unit to target truants, *Observer*, 7 December.

Yates, L. (1997) Gender equity and the boys debate: what sort of challenge is it? *British Journal of Sociology of Education*, 18(3): 337–47.

Young, I. M. (1990) *Justice and the Politics of Difference*. Princeton: Princeton University Press.

Young, S. (1995) Head's tragic tale rebounds on council, *Times Educational Supplement*, 16 June.

5

Breaking out of the binary trap: boys' underachievement, schooling and gender relations

DAVID JACKSON

The Gender Divide: Performance differences between boys and girls at school, was published by the Office for Standards in Education (Ofsted) and the Equal Opportunities Commission (EOC) in 1996. Although the booklet's foreword stressed that, 'Any national debate about education and gender must take continual account of both sexes', most responses to the booklet put the spotlight on boys' performance.

The media representation of what the booklet was saying was largely framed within the dominant discourse of boys' underachievement and male disadvantage. For example, the *Guardian*'s headline (11 July 1996) selectively prioritized, 'Schools urged to focus on low achieving boys'. The booklet warned against a too literal reading of girls' examination success, saying:

> While girls are now achieving better academic results than boys at age 16, there is little evidence to indicate that this is leading to improved post-school opportunities in the form of training, employment, career development and economic independence for the majority of young women.
>
> (Ofsted 1996: 22)

However the *Guardian*'s report decided to ignore those warnings and concentrate on the point that, 'School inspectors yesterday called for a programme of positive action to combat the persistent under-achievement of boys at almost every level of the education system.'

As we can see from these examples, the language of educational inequality has dramatically shifted over the last 20 years. From the mid-1970s in Britain, when the dominant discourse was girls' disadvantage, to the mid-1990s when boys' disadvantage began to take centre stage, complex reframings have been taking place. Some of these shifts and reframings are closely associated with the seismic upheavals of the 1988 Education Reform Act and the other policy changes since 1985. They are also influenced by the increasing visibility of boys' educational failure. The old language of equal opportunity in schools, with its emphases on social justice and inequality, has been partly displaced by the language of school effectiveness, standards and performance (Arnot *et al.* 1996). The real, power inequalities between boys and girls, and between dominant, white, heterosexual boys and sub-ordinated/complicit masculinities have been masked through this process of reframing.[1]

The old language of educational inequality has been replaced then by the language of boys' underachievement and male disadvantage. Some feminist educationists have interpreted these shifts as part of an anti-feminist backlash (Weiner *et al.* 1997). They say that the boys' underachievement discourse can be seen as a diversionary tactic, deflecting attention away from girls' interests and successes and prioritizing issues of boys' performance and behaviour. They fear that in doing so traditional, gender relations might be restored that favour male interests.

Certainly there is some truth in this analysis. The politically reactionary men's rights movement (e.g. 'Families need fathers', the groups set up to oppose the Child Support Agency, and the UK Men's Movement) often use the rhetoric of 'Men are victims of oppression too', to turn the tables on feminism's analysis of male power. It is a way of muzzling the bite of pro-feminist initiatives, and more particularly, the active challenge of feminism in education. It is also a covert way of reintroducing unequal gender relations between boys/girls and men/women. Men (including myself) need to acknowledge the force of this feminist analysis. There has been an attempt to minimize girls' success and to approach that achievement as a threat to boys. Girls' success needs to be acknowledged, celebrated and defended against some men's resistances and deflections. As shown in a *Guardian* article (1996) the reality of their academic achievement is clear to see:

- girls out perform boys at ages 7, 11 and 14 in National Curriculum assessments in English; achievements in maths and science are broadly similar.
- girls are more successful than boys at every level in GCSE, with more achieving at least one grade G and more passing in at least five subjects at grade C or above.
- girls are succeeding at GCSE in 'boys' subjects' such as technology, maths and chemistry.

However this is not the whole story. The subject of boys' underachievement is much more ambivalent and contradictory than this.

Unsettling traditional models of white, heterosexual masculinities

It is important to recognize that crises of men and masculinities are not new. Some critics (e.g. Brod 1987) have argued that traditional masculinities exist in a continuing state of contradiction and crisis, in which every new generation rediscovers the problem of young men. Others have argued that, although models of masculinity are always characterized by conflict and instability, there are specific, historical junctures, like gender relations in England, 1688–1714, and the 1890s in the United States (see Kimmel 1987), when gender certainties are particularly threatened. At these times, structural and cultural changes undermine the institutions of personal life such as marriage and the family and throw conventional, gender relations into panic and confusion. It can be argued that Britain, in the late 1990s, is experiencing one of these disorientating, historical junctures. The social upheavals of the last 25 years – feminist challenges, unemployment, the collapse of the male breadwinner and the traditional father as head of the household, the emergence of HIV/AIDS and de-industrialization – have unsettled the traditional models of dominant, white, heterosexual masculinities.

The old incentives, for many boys, to become respectable, working men – status, pride, security – are now breaking apart. What some boys are left with is a bitter sense of the pointlessness of labour and an aggressive culture of heterosexual masculinity to fill in their despairing gaps. But this sense of personal pointlessness has also been exacerbated by the widening class inequalities, the increasing privatization of education and institutional racism, encountered in British schools over the last ten years. As the Conservatives intensified the selection process, established the National Curriculum and encouraged greater segregation by ability, so a limited, exclusive definition of academic, school knowledge has gained dominance. This has undermined the abilities and destroyed the confidence and motivation of many working-class girls, members of ethnic and cultural minorities and some working-class boys. Many boys have felt brushed aside by this dominant definition of school knowledge – their home and community languages, their often raw but direct insights and their everyday, street knowledges have all been experienced as invalid.

This sorting and sifting of male students into an academic hierarchy has increased the gap between 'failed' students (especially white, working-class boys and African-Caribbean boys) and successful students (largely, middle-class, white boys). As Connell remarks, 'By institutionalising academic failure via competitive grading and streaming, the school forces [a differentiation of masculinities] on the boys' (Connell 1989: 295).

Mainly middle-class boys, the academic successes, construct their masculinities through an emphasis on rationality and responsibility and are rewarded by a social power that gives them 'access to higher education, entry to professions, command of communication', while the 'reaction of the "failed" is likely to be a claim to other sources of power, even other definitions of masculinity. Sporting prowess, physical aggression, sexual conquest may do' (Connell 1989). So we see that social exclusion and academic rejection often entice 'failed' boys into a compensatory culture of aggressive laddism. And as we shall see below, an integral part of that culture is to view school learning as effeminized. Class and racial inequalities often erect barriers to learning but some boys also actively participate in their own underachievement by defiantly rejecting the school-approved, middle-class culture of hard work by ironically associating it with an inferior wimpishness.

The ambivalence of boys' underachievement comes from the extent to which conventional, gender certainties in schools have been destabilized by these wider, social movements. The discourse of boys' underachievement certainly masks gender inequalities. But it also has a more constructive side to it. Feminism, Britain's decline as a major power in a post-colonial context, unemployment and so on have disrupted dominant, white, heterosexual masculinity as a taken for granted norm – supposedly natural, unexamined, centre stage – and have begun to interrogate it. As conventional, heterosexual masculinity has become a more explicit and visible object of enquiry, a more nuanced, critical focus has emerged on the gendering, heterosexualizing and masculinizing of boys and men.

As debates about men and masculinities have deepened in complexity, a more precise targeting of the ruling, most damaging forms of masculinity has developed. It has begun to be seen that traditional, macho culture in schools gains its power over the lives of many boys and girls through the sticky web of overlapping, social forces that go into its making. These forces are hierarchical heterosexuality; English, white nationalism; and traditional, masculine behaviours. In reality, it is impossible to separate out these deeply interwoven elements (and for that reason two of them will be bracketed together) but some brief notes about the different elements might be useful here.

Hierarchical heterosexuality: traditional, masculine behaviour

Dominant heterosexuality is a constitutive part of conventional, masculine identities. If we want to change traditional, macho cultures in schools, then we have to do something about the taken-for-granted supremacy of hierarchical heterosexuality. Heterosexual masculinity is predominantly defined through the exclusion and oppression of those actors by whom it feels threatened (mainly women and homosexuals). It strengthens and buttresses its internally cracked condition through jeering at what it most fears, and takes refuge in the apparent solidarity and support of other heterosexual men in groups and organizations. As Jonathan Dollimore has pointed out (1991), gay men and gay boys are constructed as 'the demonised abnormal other' to reinforce the normality and supposed 'natural' rightness of heterosexual men's behaviour (see especially Part 7).

English white nationalism

It is impossible to consider the subject of traditional manhood in England without having to take on, simultaneously, the nationalistic and racialized meanings of that manhood. The erosion of English, imperial power and authority has led to a deep crisis of English, white, masculine identities in boys and men. For some white, working-class boys, in humiliating economic and social circumstances, there has been an attempt to forge a new meaning to their lives by reasserting manly, English pride through violent racism and xenophobia. For many of them, the true English nation has always been naturally white. This has led to defensive, neo-fascist reassertions of white, English masculinities.

The fantasy assumption behind these actions has been that the true, English nation has an essential core of pure, uncontaminated whiteness which needs to be defended against outside invasion from an anti-English, black menace. The passionate desires of some lost, hopeless, white English boys are based around the desperate need to see themselves as vigorous, manly and powerfully English again.

Training the searchlight onto the social construction of dominant, white, heterosexual boys and masculinities is different from giving boys more attention when they already have too much. On one level, boys make themselves known in classrooms through their loud and raucous presences. But on another level, boys have never been given attention as gendered beings in schools. Historically, boys have always been invisible in schools (Cohen this volume). It is only now, after 25 years of the second wave of feminism and gay liberation movements, that the gendered myths of boys' silent competence and occasional brilliance can be taken apart. Traditionally, boys' competence and brilliance have been defined in opposition to the sexist myths of girls' hard work and diligence. But now it is time to unpick those unequal, binary fictions. Girls' solid, academic success should not be trivialized. Tied into that must go a critical deconstruction of those 'fictions of masculine genius upon which versions of male success have rested' (Walkerdine 1994).

Many boys have always underperformed at school. So boys' underachievement is not a new problem (Cohen this volume). With traditional, gender certainties being undermined has come the exposure that some boys have always adapted badly to secondary schools. What is new is the combination of unemployment/economic recession and a breakdown of conventional, gender relations. It is this complex mixture that has given a pressing urgency to the problem of boys in schools and on the street. The present destabilization of 'natural' and 'normal' assumptions about boys in schools is highly contradictory. Either it can lead to a violent reassertion of heterosexual, macho culture to cover up its increasing vulnerability, or it can be seen positively as a historically unique moment to take action about boys. That action could be about making boys' behaviours in schools an explicitly visible object of equal opportunity work, with men and women working together on the interrelated issues of girls' continuing empowerment and challenging and changing boys' macho cultures.

Clearing away the competitive binary divisions

At the moment we seem to be locked into a dichotomized, confrontational model of the girls' disadvantage discourse versus the boys' disadvantage discourse. These competitive, binary divisions are getting in the way of a more open dialogue emerging between men and women working in the field.

To be concerned about what is happening to boys today does not mean that one is automatically anti-woman. Also to be concerned about some boys' distress at school (distress about physical violence from other boys, fears about being bullied and intimidated, fears about being savagely mocked as effeminate or a 'poof', fears about stepping out of line) does not mean that one is wanting to betray the feminist agenda in schools. To acknowledge that white, heterosexual men, collectively, possess power over women and subordinated men, does not mean that some men cannot oppose patriarchy for the collective interests of women and men.

Many men, who have backgrounds in social-justice campaigns, have learnt a great deal from feminism and gay liberation movements. These men often want to do something about moving towards a more gender-fair culture in Britain. But they frequently feel defensive and wary around some of these issues. They often feel anxious about their own muddled sense of being 'unright-on'. And often their own messy contradictoriness seems to inhibit them from action. However there is also a greater sense of theoretical confusion which comes from the meanings and legacies of a framework of gender absolutism and essentialism.

The discourse of gender absolutism and essentialism

In his book *Small Acts* (1993) Paul Gilroy criticizes the notion of 'ethnic absolutism'. He comments that, '[Ethnic absolutism] says that in the operation of racisms there are only two great camps: the victims and the perpetrators, as if the fixity and coherence of these complex terms and positions can be readily and permanently established' (p. 68).

Gender absolutism works in roughly the same way. It rigidly polarizes victims and perpetrators. The essentialized purity of the woman as victim (often seen as powerless, oppressed, downtrodden and passive) is defined in relation to the biological fixity of the male perpetrator (often seen as undifferentiatedly powerful, violent and controlling). Instead of a dynamic and relational view of gender that stresses the complex and contradictory relations between diverse forms of masculinity and diverse forms of femininity, all men are lumped together in a very determinist and reductive way (see Jefferson 1996; Messerschmidt 1993). What is lost in these vague generalizations about men is the actual, complex realities of men's lives. And what is blocked and denied is men's active agency to do anything constructive about all this. It is important to hang on to the real power inequalities between men and women but it is also crucial not to buy into a universalistic conception of patriarchy that flattens out all the individual creases in women's and men's lives, and which refuses men the practical and theoretical tools to do anything about it.

These theoretical contradictions have been clearly recognized within feminism itself. Challenges from socialist feminists and feminists of colour have deliberately contested the one-dimensional representations of women and men offered by some early, radical feminists. These debates around women's differences and the complex nature of their resistances and active agency, have energized fresh approaches to theorizing men and masculinities in the late 1990s in Britain. The one-dimensional model of gender relations, critiqued by some feminists, ignores new approaches to the problems of boys and men that stress variety, difference and plurality. Because there is not a mechanical one-to-one correspondence between the prevailing system of male power and all boys and men, it allows us to see how some men and boys can actively work against conventional, patriarchal power. Although most boys benefit from the institutional privileges of being a boy in a school system that is organized in the interests of male power, there are many fissures and cracks in boys' relationships to that system that come out of this new emphasis on variety and contradictoriness. The tensions between the ruling models and images of manliness and the real conditions of boys' lives gives rise to doubts, mismatches and confusions even within the lives of the peer group's 'top lads'.

The problem with gender absolutism is that it promotes a simplistic, monolithic stereotyping of boys' and men's lives. This means that many boys and men do not see their inner doubts, mismatches and confusions being talked about when confronted by the absolutist label of 'fixed oppressor'. Teaching approaches to gender work in schools that are based on a rigid polarization between victims and perpetrators simplify boys' lives and often discredit the importance of a gendered awareness of boys' schooling. This has led to a great deal of frustration, fear and defensive hostility from both male teachers and many boys when encountering a gender work approach that has addressed boys in this fixed oppressor way. Some of that hostility comes from insecure men trying to cling on to gender certainties. But many are just confused about their own contradictoriness, particularly when having to confront a representation of their gender that is simplistic and deterministic.

Many boys have turned away from gender work that seemed to be just about girls' and women's issues instead of something that was of vital importance to their own lives as well. As one boy student has commented,

'Gender work is against boys – everyone's trying to tell me I'm wrong' (Askew and Ross 1988: 91). This populist assumption that gender work is solely about doing something about the girls is still influential even in the late 1990s. *Educational Reforms and Gender Equality in Schools* reports that, 'In the case of a female equal opportunities' coordinator working in a boys' comprehensive school, a male teacher was reported as saying, "An equal opportunities' coordinator in a boys' school is daft – we don't need it"' (Arnot *et al.* 1996: 108).

The discourse of gender absolutism is a major stumbling block to men's pro-feminist/anti-sexist men's activism. It closes down the possibilities of theorizing and practising alternative masculinities that are opposed to patriarchy. Men are still often bundled together as fixed, unified oppressors and the actual range and variety of shifting and contradictory forms of masculinity are ignored. As Dawson comments, 'There was no possibility, here, of distinguishing men sympathetic to feminist concerns from those hostile to them' (Dawson 1994: 17).

What we need, then, is a more complex way of thinking about boys' and men's lives that does justice to varied and shifting forms of masculinity, and also a way of reconceptualizing boys and men that supports men in opposing patriarchy and helps them to take active responsibility for their own changes.

The old language of 1970s gender, work and equal opportunity needs to be changed, not so that men and boys can escape from the fact that they have power over women, but because there is an urgent need to break out of the stifling dualism produced by frameworks which see only girls' disadvantage and boys' advantage. First, what we need to recognize is how much excluded 'others' (for example, women victims) depend on perpetrators (for example, male oppressors) for their own meaning, and vice versa. What this means, in practice, is that the protected purity of women as victims (which some feminist theorists, for example Kelly *et al.* 1996 are now criticising as too passive and one-dimensional has depended for its internal coherence and permanence on a static, unified oppressor role for men. The fixity of both terms now needs to be dismantled and opened up to the more fluid, contested worlds of contradictory gender relations.

We must start this process by acknowledging, firmly and clearly, the social power of men and boys; of power over girls and women but also of hierarchies of power among different groups of men and between different masculinities. Materially, men and boys still benefit from their power over women. Men are much more likely than women to hold state power. In the West, 'men's average incomes are approximately double women's average incomes' (Connell 1995: 82), and the senior positions in management are still largely male-dominated. But there is also a need to move beyond simple, fixed models of power.

To Michael Kaufman, men's experiences of exercising power is always contradictory. There is, he says, 'a strange combination of power and powerlessness, privilege and pain' in the lives of boys and men. What is crucial in the perpetuation of male power is the relationship between male privilege and male pain. Male pain and fear can be either an incitement to collude in men's power or 'an impetus for change', in the sense that this contradictory combination can be the 'basis for men's embrace of feminism'. Many men actively buy into patriarchal power as a way of countering their anxieties and fears. 'Men exercise patriarchal power not only because they reap tangible benefits from it' (Kaufman 1994: 149). Men's assertion of power is also a compulsive response to their terrors of self-annihilation and alienation from their feelings, longings and need for closeness. Kaufman uses this approach to point out the complexity of gender identity, gender formation and gender relations. He comments, 'It appears that we need forms of analysis that allow for contradictory relationships between individuals and the power structures from which they benefit' (p. 151).

These observations are also supported by the work of the Women Risk and Aids Project/Men Risk and Aids Project (WRAP/MRAP) team exploring contradictions in acquiring masculine sexuality (Holland *et al.* 1993). In their conclusion, they comment on the close interrelationship between power and vulnerability in the process that reproduces and reinforces male sexual power over young women.

> Young men were clearly aware that in entering into the negotiation of sexual encounters they were laying themselves open to the possibility of failure. Their strategies for dealing with their potential vulnerability reproduce and reinforce the exercise of male power over women. Young men do not need to have any intention, nor even any awareness, of subordinating women in order to exercise power over them.
>
> (Holland *et al.* 1993: 32)

Therefore, we now need new ways of theorizing these gender differences and contradictions. Also we need to acknowledge the present, changing, social conditions of boys' and girls' lives. This fresh, theoretical approach can, I believe, be found in a more social version of post-structuralist theories which focus on gender subjectivities, discourses and power, and is supported by a critical and feminist psychoanalysis that believes in a complex interaction between society and the self. I shall now focus selectively on some of the key aspects of this theoretical approach.

The discourse of contradictory gender relations and subjectivities

Masculine subjectivities and feminine subjectivities are not singular, static and polarized 'sex roles' mechanically reproduced within the binary logic of female victims and male perpetrators. Instead boys' masculinities are actively negotiated in schools, families, peer groups and so on, through dynamic, relational processes that are constantly shifting, historically (Messner 1993). These relational processes are mainly between masculine/feminine; heterosexual/homosexual; and white Englishness/black foreigners. So traditional, heterosexual masculinities are defensively constructed by defining themselves in opposition to an excluded and subordinated 'other'.

Within social contexts of unequal but changing power relations, a varied range of subject positions are offered for boys to take up in contradictory discourses. For example, Daniel Wight (1996) has shown the shifting clashes and collisions in white, heterosexual boys' sex lives. In his study of 58 manual, white working-class, 19-year-old men in Glasgow, Wight (1996) has demonstrated how some of the young men understood their sexual selves and sexual relationships through these different, contested discourses, and how these understandings shifted at different times of their lives and according to whom they were speaking.

Many of these young men, in social contexts where they wanted to gain the approval and acceptance of other dominant, male peers, wanted to become active subjects in the predatory discourse. This governing framework of meaning is mainly concerned with building and maintaining a masculine, gender identity through heterosexual intercourse, objectified sexual activities, and impressing one's mates. So, for example, Danny (one of the men interviewed by Wight) says: 'I think guys like to have respect off their pals, and if (for example) I go out and get a different girlfriend every week my pals respect it' (Wight 1996: 154). But, some other boys felt divided between this ruling, predatory discourse and the more emotionally connected subject positions offered by the have/hold, romantic discourse – 'the set of ideas and practices associated with monogamy, partnership and family life' (p. 159).

Wendy Hollway (1984, 1989), in her work on gender difference and subjectivity, has already pointed out how many women take up positions as subjects within the have/hold discourse, actively attracting and trying to keep their men. Wight's research, while deeply indebted to Hollway's innovatory work, goes on to show that some men 'can also occupy a position as subject(s) within this discourse' (Wight 1996: 159). Although, in contexts of insecurity and supposed inadequacy, some young men try to present themselves as hard-driving, sexual studs, they also experienced desperate longings for closeness and loving attachment to a woman. As Colin (one of the interviewed young men) acknowledges: 'I've been in love but I've never been sort of – I'll say that she is, she is the one I've been looking for for a long time, know what I mean?' (Wight 1996: 162).

Subjectivity politics does not see power as the fixed possession of single, unchanging individuals. Boys do not have single, set, gender identities that confer on them a predetermined position of power or powerlessness. Power is actively exercised through relational processes. Instead boys are constantly involved in the contradictory processes of resisting, colluding, accepting or reframing the ruling discourses of the dominant culture. Boys are often trying to turn themselves into more active subjects in a ruling framework of meaning rather than passively accepting an object position in a discourse that puts them down. So there is a dynamic, restless contestation of power going on between multiple subject positions within different frameworks. As Valerie Walkerdine comments: 'An individual can become powerful or powerless depending on the terms in which her/his subjectivity is constituted' (Walkerdine 1990: 5).

Critical psychoanalysis also brings up the question of boys' incentives in taking up a subject position in a discourse. Wendy Hollway (1989) has introduced the powerful notion of emotional investment in certain subject positions. These investments operate at an unconscious or conscious level and incite boys to take up certain dominant forms of masculinity to counter their perceived sense of themselves as weak, anxious or small. Each boy's subjectivity is a contested arena where conflicting discourses collide and grapple for ascendancy in a boy's life. Seductive subject positions are offered within these conflicting frameworks, particularly at moments of perceived inadequacy and insecurity in the boy's life. As a result strong, emotional investments in tempting subject positions are often made by boys as desperate attempts to reassert force, authority and domination in social contexts where the boys are feeling increasingly powerless, dependent and threatened. So we see that the masculine subjectivities of individual boys are constructed from a 'nexus of contradictory subjectivities', not as fixed, predetermined subjects (Walkerdine 1990: 9).

Gender and boys' underachievement

This is a historically important moment which can be seen as an opportunity to clear away reductive and mechanical ways of looking at men/women, boys/girls. There is an opportunity to use the present destabilization of traditional gender certainties as a partly positive development. It could lead to making boys' behaviours in school an explicitly visible object of equal opportunities' work.

We have the constrained possibility of forming new political alliances between anti-patriarchal women and anti-patriarchal men, and heterosexual and homosexual men. Some men have been confused and half-ashamed about their present, contradictory positions. Now some of them might join in the attempt to change traditional, gender cultures in schools if a gender-relations approach is adopted. We need, simultaneously, to continue and expand working with girls and women staff, and to begin exploring, challenging and changing the macho cultures of boys. From this perspective, boys' underachievement is both an area of anti-feminist backlash and an important gender issue for educationists.

There are problems, however, in approaching boys' underachievement as a gender issue. The New Right agenda in education has disguised the links between boys' underachievement and gender. The new language of school effectiveness, standards and performance has tended to mask issues of gender equality and social justice. Instead, it has played up issues of internal school organization, like the supervision of boys' homework, and the development of boys' language and reading skills. Such school management ways of improving boys' performance are important, as long as they do not reduce our understandings of boys' complex and contradictory behaviours. But they should not be allowed to cloud the gender-related problems that boys have in schools.

Another problem is about the historical invisibility in schools of boys as gendered beings. Traditional men and boys have not seen themselves as possessing a gender. Their masculinities have been so much a part of a taken for granted norm (white, heterosexual man equals human being) that it has been difficult to get beyond massive, biologically deterministic assumptions. Because of this, teachers, governors, parents and boys themselves have often turned a blind eye to boys' behaviours in schools. Many of them have preferred to view negative behaviour as the 'natural' and 'normal' activities of 'boys will be boys'. One result of that has been, 'Surprisingly little discussion of the role of education in the transformation of masculinity' (Connell 1995: 238).

If we want those discussions and anti-sexist practices to begin, then the 'boys will be boys' assumptions need to be vigorously challenged. These assumptions and behaviours need to be changed in the staffroom as well as the classroom and corridor. Schools often generate wider cultures of aggressive manliness that some male teachers condone or even actively participate in. So school institutions, from headteacher to caretaker, need to confront what hidden messages they give out about how to be a man or a boy. Of course, there is scope here for school staff-development work on gender-aware, masculinity training, particularly at a time when boys' and men's aggressive and underperforming behaviours are being increasingly exposed. If we accept that boys and men act in the ways that they do because 'it's in their hormones' then the possibility of personal and social change in boys/men is wiped out.

As a result, the continuing struggle to change girl–boy, woman–man power relations becomes a waste of effort. So it is urgently necessary to go on reminding ourselves that conventional, manly characteristics, like being strong, powerful, hard and daring, are not innate qualities that all men and boys are born with, but, alternatively, are mainly social constructions forged out of culture, ideology and history. Alternative, educational choice and change is made possible because of these social and historical processes. From this perspective, conventional manliness stops being fixed, natural and unchangeable but instead becomes temporary, constructed and something all teachers, parents, governors and students can change through their own active and collaborative efforts.

'It's not cool to be seen as a boy who works at school'

In many traditional, macho, boys' cultures (particularly between ages 10 and 16), school learning is effeminized. Some boys' hardness and adequacy as 'real lads' is deliberately formed in relation to a sissified world of school work. In a recent study of one 11–18 Walsall comprehensive school, 'an image of reluctant involvement' is cultivated among some of the boys. The negative label, 'keeno', was applied to any boy who overtly displayed his ability. As a result, some boys managed their academic careers carefully, avoiding an open commitment to work. They sometimes negotiated a 'cool' cleverness image that allowed them to work but also did not make them the butt of schoolboy banter (Bleach 1996).

In many boys' lives at school, there is a dynamic interaction between their social/economic worlds of failure, dependency and powerlessness and their deep investments in dominant forms of heterosexual masculinities. Sensing some of the despair and pointlessness of the jobless men around them and the fragility of their own lives, they counter the 'failure' of their lives by reaching out to alternative sources of power and status. Dominant, heterosexual masculinity is one of the most enticing sources of compensatory power. And that often means buying into a culture of aggressive, heterosexual manliness which deliberately rejects school learning as an unmanly activity.

Insecure boys, who are very much aware of their vulnerability, strive to display a hyper-masculine performance that will not only defend themselves from their fantasized 'weakness' but also gain the approval of the peer group. To save their own skins, some boys develop desperate longings to gain power and apparent invulnerability through peer-group acceptance. Boys like that will often go to great lengths to prove to other boys that they are not 'soft' or 'sissyish'. As a result, not working hard at school can be seen as a defensive strategy by some boys to distance themselves from an academic world that is perceived as dangerously 'weak'. Typical comments from boys on school, as researched and explored by Mac an Ghaill (1994) support this point: 'The work you do here is girls' work. It's not real work. It's just for kids' (1994: 59).

We need to target, more specifically, the chief groups of underperforming boys within these traditional, macho cultures. The recent EOC report (Arnot *et al.* 1996: 141) has already drawn attention to 'an apparent lack of motivation amongst working class and black boys'. Mac an Ghaill has examined the 'fighting, fucking and football' culture of white, heterosexual, working-class lads (Mac an Ghaill 1994). He has shown clearly that the anti-school-work culture of many of these boys was a gendered issue. He says: 'the Macho Lads at Parnell School made a similar association of academic work with an inferior effeminacy, referring to those who conformed as "dickhead achievers". Consequently, they overtly rejected much school work as inappropriate for them as men' (p. 59).

Sewell has similarly explored the macho cultures of some African-Caribbean boys in school. What he found was a complex combination of compulsory heterosexuality, homophobia and misogyny working together. He found that many of these black, macho lads used an 'idealised, phallocentric masculinity' to contest institutional conditions of 'dependency, racism and powerlessness' (Sewell 1995: 28). Some of them actively bought into their own academic failure by being coolly indifferent to school work. And this cool indifference came out of a defensive attempt to preserve what they perceived as their threatened manhood. In Sewell's words, 'They felt that the schooling process assaulted the thing that was most precious to them – their "manhood"' (p. 36). So that black boys who worked hard at school were seen as 'batty men' (gay) or 'pussies' (effeminate) (p. 36).

Broadening the context of boys' underachievement: changing gender cultures

However it would be a mistake to imagine that we can tackle boys' under-achievement by itself. The complex reasons for that underperformance are entangled with the broader, gender regimes of different schools in different parts of the country. So as well as needing a sensitivity to local features, boys' underachievement needs to be approached as an integral part of more widely coordinated, equal opportunities' work on changing traditional, gender cultures in schools. Broadening the gendered context of boys' under-achievement means, at the very least, linking together boys' underachieve-ment with boys' disruptive and often damaging behaviours. This connection is supported by one Midlands LEA comprehensive's response to boys' under-achievement. The school recommends: 'That we move away from looking at the underachievement of boys, to looking at the disruptive behaviour of a small minority of mainly white boys which affects the achievement of the majority' (school discussion paper cited in Arnot *et al.* 1996: 142).

Behavioural management techniques (e.g. homework monitoring, class-room organization etc.) that specifically target boys' underachievement can be very useful but they need to work, hand in hand, with a gendered awareness of boys', traditional, macho cultures and with an understanding that, for some boys, academic achievement is associated with fears and anxieties about effeminacy.

If gender work in schools is an attempt to improve educational standards for all pupils, then we need a wider, equal opportunities' approach across the school, across the staffroom and across departments. Men and women need to keep on addressing power inequalities but also need to learn how to work together to change the conventional, gender cultures of schools. For boys, this means dealing explicitly with their academic underachievement, and developing classroom strategies that counteract the received idea that it is not cool to work hard at school (Whyld 1996). It also means critically investigating some boys' investments in media images of heroic manliness, such as Arnold Schwarzenegger, Bruce Lee, Mel Gibson and Rambo. It means gendering the discussion and non-violent practices connected to boys' everyday aggression and bullying. Within the arena of boys' sexualities it means questioning heterosexual boys' attempts to score and feel powerful as a way of hiding their fears of failure and their inabilities to build satisfying relationships through sensual contact. It also means looking closely at the connections between diseases, young men's sexualities and gender. Safer sex practices and condom use are often rejected by young men who want to be seen as hard-driving studs rather than caring, responsive lovers.

Challenging macho cultures can also mean noticing and changing how some boys use sexual harassment (through touching up, groping, sexual teasing, sexist grafitti etc.) to gain power over girls and other, sidelined boys. In terms of language, boys' verbal insults, jeering, name-calling, sexist jokes and put-downs also need to be explored and changed. The conformist pressures of the dominant peer group need to be critically exposed, particularly in the areas of school sport and sex. We need to look closely at the social forces in many boys' lives that incite boys to strive towards becoming a competitive, goal-fixated winner in school sport. And we need to examine closely the aggressive, militaristic culture which influences many boys through their videos, computer games and street-life culture.[2]

Working with girls and boys as a way of revitalizing gender in schools

There is still a real danger, at the end of the twentieth century, of 'colluding in the current backlash against feminism by implying that boys are now the "real victims"' (Haywood and Mac an Ghaill 1996: 59). It is important to keep on saying boys are not the real victims. Many girls still lack confidence, often have low self-esteem and have limited educational and work aspirations. A positive action programme in schools still needs to work creatively on raising girls' low expectations.

But it is also important to say that the old models of equal opportunities' work in schools were not very effective in reaching a whole school population because they worked within the simplified polarities of female virtue and male vice. Jane Kenway's research on equal opportunities for girls has pointed out that 'a strong case about the hard irrefutable facts of inequality' often did not work because the account was not 'sufficiently nuanced to be read as meaningful in the context of people's experience. Often the evidence is so starkly black and white that it is readily refuted as soon as other inequalities (race, ethnicity, sexuality and class) come into the picture' (Kenway 1995: 77).

We need a contradictory, gender-relations model of equal opportunities work that can speak directly and recognizably to both girls' and boys' messy, awkward, lived experiences. And we need that fresh model urgently because the old models of equal opportunities are in danger of being discredited.

Already '[at] LEA level, equal opportunity practice is generally low key with few specific or specialist posts for gender and little evidence that gender equality constitutes a priority' (Arnot *et al.* 1996: 99).

This generally lukewarm approach to gender work suggests that the dichotomized models are in difficulties because they are finding it hard to move with the rapidly changing times. An emphasis on fixity and purity, within the gender-absolutism discourse, has blocked the development of a more shifting, historical awareness. Ros Coward has made it clear that we have to acknowledge the shifting, socio-economic conditions in our fresh approaches to pro-feminist, anti-sexist, equal opportunities practices: 'Some feminists think the ideas they formulated 20 years ago are still OK: it's just a matter of banging on until everyone is won over' (Coward 1996). The old dichotomized model will not do in a changing, social context. We now need new ways of understanding and changing shifting gender relations within shifting, socio-economic conditions.

A broader, more inclusive approach to gender work in schools (with women and men working with girls and boys) might stand a chance of re-energizing and revitalizing equal opportunities work on gender. But only if we reconceptualize what gender work is, moving it from the confining, dichotomized world of gender absolutism towards a world where more of us can personally engage in its dynamically changing, contradictory relations. In the harsher world of local management of schools and tighter financial controls, 'equal opportunities tends to become more of a luxury rather than a requirement' (Arnot *et al.* 1996: 139). But a broader definition of gender work, working with both girls and boys, has a greater chance of being seen as a matter of urgent, day-to-day survival rather than a non-affordable, luxury item. Preventative work with boys makes cost-effective sense when you consider how much of our current time, energies and resources already go into picking up the broken pieces after boys' routine acts of vandalism, violence, stealing, display and disruption.

There is also the increasing possibility of new, political alliances, mutually working towards a more gender-fair culture, within a gender-relations approach to equal opportunity. There are openings, for example, for gay/lesbian alliances with heterosexual men and women, but only if the fresh models of gender work problematize compulsory heterosexuality, as well as misogyny and violent, white manliness. Changing traditional, macho cultures in schools means, simultaneously, interrogating the taken-for-granted premiss of compulsory heterosexuality and how conventional forms of masculine identity routinely speak heterosexuality (see Redman 1996).

Conclusion

Men and boys are at a crossroads. They can either go on reasserting themselves through dominant forms of masculinity, and in the process damaging other people and themselves, or they can join in the struggle towards a more gender-fair culture; or more complexly, some subordinated boys can turn their fears about the dominant, macho culture into a public questioning of that taken-for-granted culture. There are many men and boys out there bewildered by change, lacking meaning and purpose in their everyday lives. Many of them are secretly complicit men and boys who, although seemingly toeing the patriarchal line, are uneasy and troubled about their sense of inner contradiction.

I believe we can actively use that sense of inner contradiction in many boys and men by offering them a new vision of masculinity that vigorously opposes patriarchy. In the struggles ahead we cannot afford to leave out all those troubled men and boys who want to look closely at and change their conventional gender relations.

So instead of seeing boys and men as exercising a monolithic, unchanging system of patriarchal power, we can perhaps view schools as complex arenas of power, where masculine and feminine identities are actively made, on a daily basis, through the dynamic processes of negotiation, refusal and struggle. This means that there are real social constraints and power imbalances but also that gender regimes are more fluid and complex than we supposed back in the mid-1970s. And perhaps, with more women and men working together, there will be more opportunities for changing gender inequalities.

Notes

1 See Connell 1995 for 'complicit masculinities' and Segal 1990 for 'subordinated masculinities'.
2 For more practical examples, see Salisbury and Jackson 1996.

References

Arnot, M., David, M. and Weiner, G. (1996) *Educational Reforms and Gender Equality in Schools*. Manchester: Equal Opportunities Commission.
Askew, S. and Ross, C. (1988) *Boys Don't Cry: Boys and Sexism in Education*. Milton Keynes: Open University Press.
Bleach, K. (1996) What difference does it make? An investigation of factors influencing the motivation and performance of Year 8 boys in a West Midlands comprehensive school. Wolverhampton: University of Wolverhampton, Educational Research Unit.
Brod, H. (1987) A case for men's studies, in M. Kimmel (ed.) *Changing Men*, Newbury Park, CA: Sage Publications.
Connell, R. W. (1989) Cool guys, swots and wimps: the interplay of masculinity and education. *Oxford Review of Education*, 15(3): 291–303.
Connell, R. W. (1995) *Masculinities*. Cambridge: Polity Press.
Coward, R. (1996) Do we still need feminism? *Guardian*, 9 September.

Dawson, G. (1994) *Soldier Heroes: British Adventure, Empire and the Imagining of Masculinities*. London: Routledge.

Dollimore, J. (1991) *Sexual Dissidence: Augustine to Wilde, Freud to Foucault*. Oxford: Clarendon Press.

Gilroy, P. (1993) *Small Acts*. London: Serpent's Tail.

Haywood, C. and Mac an Ghaill, M. (1996) Schooling masculinities, in M. Mac an Ghaill (ed.) *Understanding Masculinities*. Buckingham: Open University Press.

Holland, J., Ramazanoglu, C. and Sharpe, S. (1993) *Wimp or Gladiator: Contradictions in Acquiring Masculine Sexuality*. London: Tufnell Press.

Hollway, W. (1984) Gender difference and the production of subjectivity, in J. Henriques, W. Hollway, C. Urwin, C. Venn and V. Walkerdine, *Changing the Subject: Psychology, Social Regulation and Subjectivity*. London: Methuen.

Hollway, W. (1989) *Subjectivity and Method in Psychology: Gender, Meaning and Science*. London: Methuen.

Jackson, D. (1995) *Destroying the Baby in Themselves: Why did the Two Boys Kill James Bulger?* Nottingham: Five Leaves Press.

Jefferson, T. (1996) Introduction. *British Journal of Criminology*, Special Issue, x: xx.

Kaufman, M. (1994) Men, feminism and men's contradictory experiences of power, in H. Brod and M. Kaufman (eds) *Theorising Masculinities*. Newbury Park, CA: Sage.

Kelly, L., Burton, S. and Regan, L. (1996) Beyond victim or survivor: sexual violence, identity and feminist theory and practice, in L. Adkins and V. Merchant (eds) *Sexualising the Social: Power and the Organisation of Sexuality*. London: Macmillan.

Kenway, J. (1995) Masculinities in schools: under siege, on the defensive and under reconstruction? *Discourse: Studies in the Cultural Politics of Education*, 16(1): 59–79.

Kimmel, M. (1987) The contemporary 'crisis' of masculinity in historical perspective, in H. Brod (ed.) *The Making of Masculinities*. Boston: Allen and Unwin.

Mac an Ghaill, M. (1994) *The Making of Men: Masculinities, Sexualities and Schooling*. Buckingham: Open University Press.

Messerschmidt, J. (1993) *Masculinities and Crime*. Lanham, MD: Rowman and Littlefield.

Messner, M. (1993) Changing men and feminist politics in the United States, in R. W. Connell (ed.) *Theory and Society*, special issue on masculinities, 22(5): 723–37.

Office for Standards in Education and Equal Opportunities Commission [Ofsted/ EOC] (1996), *The Gender Divide: Performance Differences between Boys and Girls at School*. London: HMSO.

Redman, P. (1996) Empowering men to disempower themselves: heterosexual masculinities, HIV and the contradictions of anti-oppressive education, in M. Mac an Ghaill (ed.) *Understanding Masculinities*. Buckingham: Open University Press.

Salisbury, J. and Jackson, D. (1996) *Challenging Macho Values: Practical Ways of Working with Adolescent Boys*. London: Falmer Press.

Segal, L. (1990) *Slow Motion: Changing Masculinities, Changing Men*. London: Virago.

Sewell, T. (1995) A phallic response to schools: black masculinity and race in an inner-city comprehensive, in M. Griffiths and B. Troyna (eds) *Anti-Racism, Culture and Social Justice in Education*: Stoke-on-Trent: Trentham Books.

Walkerdine, V. (1990) Sex, power and pedagogy, in her *Schoolgirl Fictions*. London: Verso.

Walkerdine, V. (1994) What makes girls so clever?, *The Independent*, 6 September.

Weiner, G., Arnot, M. and David, M. (1997) Is the future female? Female success, male disadvantage and changing gender patterns in education, in A. Halsey,

P. Brown, H. Lauder and A. Stuart-Wells (eds) *Education: Culture, Economy and Society*. Oxford: Oxford University Press.

Whyld, J. (1996) It's cool to be a swot. Helping boys – changing the culture. Unpublished paper presented to the Labour Party 'Boys' Initiative' workshop, 26 March.

Wight, D. (1996) Beyond the predatory male: the diversity of young Glaswegian men's discourses to describe heterosexual relationships, in L. Adkins and V. Merchant (eds) *Sexualising the Social: Power and the Organisation of Sexuality*. London: Macmillan Press.

6

Real boys don't work: 'underachievement', masculinity and the harassment of 'sissies'

DEBBIE EPSTEIN

Introduction

The *Panorama* programme (BBC1 1994) entitled (with a note of panic) 'The future is female' began with a clip, shown again later in the broadcast, of a small boy (aged about 6) being interviewed by the presenter. The boy was asked 'What would you think of a boy who worked hard at school?' to which he replied, without hesitation, 'He's not a boy.' While I hold out no apology for that programme (which reached great depths of anti-feminist moral panic, included many *non sequiturs*, and was characterized by the attribution of causes where none could logically be found),[1] this one moment does strike a chord with my experience both as a classroom teacher and as a researcher. In this chapter, I draw on the research of others and some of my own research to explore this phenomenon. My research has not been specifically focused on boys' 'achievement' (however defined) or their (non-) working habits at school. One of my projects, funded by East Birmingham Health Authority, was about the experiences of gay men and lesbians within the school system (i.e. students and teachers). The main sample of interviewees was, to a large extent, self-selected, since it was obtained by advertising in the gay press and by snowballing from the people who responded to the original advertisement. In addition, one of my students, Louise Curry, did an ethnographic study of a lesbian and gay youth group, we carried out observation and interviews in three secondary schools (one single sex girls' school and two coeducational schools) and KOLA (the Birmingham Black Lesbian and Gay Group) held two focus group discussions for us, using an agenda provided by me but without the presence of an outside researcher (see Epstein and Johnson 1998). It was not one of our specific lines of enquiry to ask about attitudes to boys who work hard at school, but a large number of our white respondents raised this as an issue and this, in itself, seems worth further investigation.

Of necessity, then, the chapter is somewhat speculative and is directed more towards raising issues for further research than reporting on significant findings. Much work remains to be done in the area, even though, as Michèle Cohen (see page 21, this volume) points out, John Locke was writing in 1693 about the fact that girls learnt to speak French better than boys. The fact that Locke did not consider this to be a particular problem but rather evidence of boys' *superiority* is interesting but somewhat tangential to the point of this chapter. On the other hand, his views about the appropriateness of upper-class boys' behaviour in resisting working at their studies are very much to the point. It is interesting to note how much passion has been generated by the perceived 'underachievement' of boys which, *qua* Locke, is neither a particularly new phenomenon, nor as Murphy and Elwood (1998) point out, sustained in all subject areas or beyond the age of 16. This is in stark contrast to the relatively small amount of interest (at least on the part of policy-makers) which has been generated by the extremely well documented problems of boys' behaviour in schools, especially where it takes sexist, racist and homophobic forms. Moreover, public concern about violence and bullying in schools has tended to appear ungendered: 'children' or 'pupils' are reported as being increasingly violent, even though a more accurate reflection of events in schools would be to talk about 'boys', predominantly (and a few girls), taking part in violent activities of one kind or another.

Nevertheless, the extensive evidence of boys being troublesome in schools, does give rise to a gut feeling (yet to be tested by research) that masculinist behaviours, including those which involve avoiding academic work at least up till the sixth form, may have something to do with a relative lack of 'achievement' (however problematic the term) by many boys at GCSE level. The old argument – noted by Valerie Walkerdine in her research on girls and mathematics in schools (1989) – that girls worked harder but boys had more flair simply will not wash any more, if it ever did! This chapter will suggest that many constructions of masculinity in schools and popular culture, including dominant versions but not only dominant ones, involve engaging in 'resistance' to schooling which is not only (or even mainly) about class as Willis (1977) suggests but also deeply invested in compulsory heterosexuality. The rejection of the perceived 'feminine' of academic work is simultaneously a defence against the 'charge' of being gay. If this is true, then it follows that, along with other strategies which pay attention to, for example, differential learning styles (Daniels *et al.* 1996; see also Hey *et al.*, this volume), different kinds of assessment (Murphy and Elwood 1998), and the specifics of different subject areas, schools will need to focus on masculinity as an issue in and of itself and, in particular, on the deleterious effects of misogyny and heterosexism. Moreover, a focus on masculinities may reframe some of the other approaches to boys' schooling in ways which give them a very different nuance.

Who's queer?

Pat Mahony (1989) argues that:

> When a boy gets 'pushed around' it is not, I would suggest, in virtue of being a boy but because he is not the right sort of boy. Perhaps he is perceived as possessing qualities which run counter to dominant notions of masculinity. In this case he may also be subject to verbal abuse, 'poof', 'queer' and 'you've got AIDS'.
> ... For him the lesson to be learnt is how to become a *real* man, dominant and not subordinate.
>
> (1989: 162–3, original emphasis)

From my research with lesbian and gay young people who had been school students during the late 1980s and early 1990s, it seems that one of the 'dominant notions of masculinity' in many schools is, indeed, the avoidance of academic work (or of the appearance of working). As stated above, I was not investigating the question of boys' academic achievement at the time, so did not specifically ask about this, but it is very noticeable, reading the interview transcripts, how often being a boy who was scholastic was given as the identifying marker for being the subject of bullying and of homophobic abuse.

This did not seem to be dependent on the kind of school attended (although there would be different inflections according to class). For example, one man who had attended a major public (i.e. elite private) school and was a particularly high achiever (he went on to gain a first-class degree at Cambridge and to undertake a PhD) spoke about taking his books up a tree in order to study and avoid the homophobic bullying that arose when he was seen to be working academically. In his case, the bullying and name-calling centred around what (he thinks) other boys saw as his 'letting down the side'. The culture of the school, in his account, was one in which achievement was not considered a problem in and of itself, but working to achieve definitely was. There seems, in this case, to be a direct development from the notion of the 'gentlemanly amateur' who manages to be good at whatever he does with the minimum of effort (see, also Cohen this volume; Power *et al.* 1998).

Teresa, on the other hand, had been at a school which she described as a very working-class, local comprehensive. In a focus group discussion including herself, Dave and some others,[2] and with some embarrassment, she told a story about having been part of a 'gang' of girls who used to bully other students and, in particular, a boy whom her gang had constantly made fun of for being 'queer':

Teresa: We used to have one boy that we used to call [laughs] and abuse [laughs]. I was horrible, I was part of a horrible gang of girls that used to go round bullying everyone [laughter] and one [laughter]. No, really, like one boy was, like some of the terms of abuse we used like poof and queer and things like that. I mean, I don't, at the time, I don't really know if I knew what they meant. In fact, I didn't know what they meant really. It was just a form of abuse that we used. But we did use them and they were, um, directed specifically at this one boy, so, uh, whoever was, whoever originally thought up the term of abuse for him must have known what it meant or if they . . .

Dave: Yeah.

Teresa: . . . associated it with him, I don't know, but we just, we just followed on whatever was being said and used it as a way of insulting him.

DE: What was, what was he like?

Teresa: He was like really quiet and he was, um, he always used to get his homework done, used to have his school uniform on and then, none of us had a school uniform. He did. And this sort of thing. So he was just different I think, just different. I mean, it was just one of these forms of abuse that he, he just started . . .

Here we see a dynamic going on which is both about masculinity and about class. This boy was neat; he had a school uniform and a satchel; he kept his books neat; and 'he always used to get his homework done'. In Teresa's account these come to signify a middle-classness which the girls in her group saw as fey and not masculine, and which resulted in the boy being labelled 'queer'. In this sense, her narrative brings to mind Paul Willis's 'ear'oles' and 'lads' (Willis 1977) with differences in approach to work representing something about class aspiration as well as something about a perceived deficit in 'proper masculinity'. In fact, Teresa herself uses the term 'lad' to signify something very similar to the 'lads' of Willis's *Learning to Labour* – the opposite of all that was represented by the boy whom she bullied: not only playing football, but, presumably, untidy in person and work and failing to do homework.

Máirtín Mac an Ghaill (1994) has also drawn attention to the position of the group of boys he calls the 'Academic Achievers'. These boys, too, talked about the problems they encountered as a result of being academically successful:

Parminder: Sometimes you wonder if all the learning and study is worth it, you just get down in yourself. You lose mates and you can't really get on with the snobs. I mean you wouldn't want to, would you?

MM: So what keeps you going?

Parminder: I don't know. I like the work a lot of the time and I want to get on and that's what my family wants. I wouldn't like to be like the dossers here. My brother's like them. He's just wasting his life.

(1994: 62)

Again there is both a class and a gender dynamic to this account, as well as a racialized one. Parminder is not just 'doing boy'. Rather he is 'doing Asian, working-class boy', distancing himself from the, presumably middle-class, 'snobs' with whom he 'can't really get on', but being divided from his 'mates' – those who 'do boy' in more traditionally macho ways than through academic success – by virtue of his ability with those things the school values (academic work) but his peers do not. He also acknowledges the role which the aspirations of his family play in his affiliation to academic achievement ('I want to get on and that's what my family wants').

Mac an Ghaill points out that this particular group of boys differed from the 'Macho Lads' (1994: 56–9) because of their aspirations to professional careers and from the 'Real Englishmen' (pp. 64–7) who, with the cultural capital of the middle class, could manage to achieve with little apparent effort; as Mark, one of Mac an Ghaill's respondents, put it 'with their background, it's easy for them to be clever' (p. 63). According to the 'Academic Achievers', it is not just the other pupils who taunted them for being feminized and/or gay because of their evident work, but also the teachers:

Tony: I think we're more confident now. You have to be in this school. It wasn't just the low-set kids but the men teachers would always be getting at you in little ways.
MM: Like what?
Tony: Oh, stupid things, like put away your handbags or stuff about marrying us off because we stuck around together. . . . Like in a school like this, a lot of the male teachers are very defensive, very macho and they've got a lot of power to put you down in front of everyone.

(Mac an Ghaill 1994: 61)

Mac an Ghaill points out that, while these boys managed to negotiate the heterosexist jibes of both teachers and other pupils in imaginative ways, they nevertheless worked within conventional essentializing discourses of gender, in which 'men [are] more intellectual and women more emotional' (Parminder, quoted in Mac an Ghaill 1994: 61). What is interesting to me in this example, is the way that insults are made through feminizing the boys ('put away your handbags') and implying that they are gay ('marrying us off') and that, according to the boys, this comes from the teachers who, in theory, should have an investment in encouraging the boys to engage in academic work and achieve academically. Indeed, it would be almost unthinkable for a teacher to say 'Well, actually, I don't like boys who work hard at their school work. It's not an acceptable way for boys to behave', but this is, in fact, the 'between the lines' meaning of the kinds of insults reported by the 'Academic Achievers'.

It is also important to note, in this context, the complexity of the power relations brought into play here. On the one hand, the 'Academic Achievers', aspirant middle-class professionals, seem to be destined, at least if they achieve their ambitions, to occupy relatively powerful positions in their future careers. In this sense, they echo Willis's 'ear'oles'. They distance themselves from their less aspirant, working-class peers, who adopt more 'laddish' positions and are more likely to end up either unemployed or in working-class jobs, and work hard to build up the cultural capital that they will need to achieve their ambitions. On the other hand, within the culture of the school, their position is, at best, ambiguous: they are certainly subordinated within the cultures of masculinity prescribed by their peers (apart from one young man whom Mac an Ghaill describes as having moved from being part of a macho gang to becoming an 'Academic Achiever'); they are also subordinated as pupils within the power/age relations of teacher-taught and, it seems, many of the teachers, particularly the male teachers, validate the less scholarly, more macho versions of hegemonic masculinity which tend to dominate within schools.

There is, furthermore, a racialized as well as a sexualized account of academic achievement noted by both Mac an Ghaill (1994) and Sewell (1997). Sewell lists many indicators of 'acting white' used by African-Caribbean boys in Township School, described by Sewell (1997, see also this volume, page 111) as an inner-city comprehensive school which was experiencing some considerable difficulties at the time he did his research. These range through speech, dress, dating white girls and, with regard to schooling:

> you suck up to the teachers
> grovelling to teachers
> get good grades
> always do your work
> bunk off lessons

(Sewell 1997: 185)

It is interesting that the first four of these are not only in contradiction to the last, but that they also describe characteristics which my respondents and Mac an Ghaill's group of 'Academic Achievers' found to be used as indicators of femininity, or homosexuality. Indeed, in Chapter 7 of this book (p. 120) Sewell quotes one of his interviewees as saying that: '[T]he white boys are just pussies, they haven't got the balls like a black man, most of them go on as if they are batty men [homosexual].'

He concludes his study by pointing out that:

> There were many examples of the way that African-Caribbean boys in Township School contested their feelings of powerlessness through phallocentric responses. This was shown in the way that the Rebel

students positioned the Conformist boys as sexually deficient or unmasculine when they chose not to contest the school processes.

(1997: 220)

My point, here, is that phallocentrism, misogyny and homophobia are not the recourse of African-Caribbean boys only, but pervade the cultures of masculinity which are dominant in schools. That these cultures of masculinity are racialized and classed (and that 'race' and class are sexualized), should not come as a surprise, for those differences that make a difference are lived out in ways which are complexly connected. However, it does seem as if the linking of masculinity and homophobia may be associated with the harassment of non-macho and/or studious boys, at least in secondary schools.

Who gets bullied? The primary phase

I have considerably less evidence of the bullying and harassment through the exercise of homophobic abuse and name-calling of boys who 'work hard' at the primary school level, but it certainly does exist. For example, one primary school teacher, talking about the ethos of her school, commented:

Ruth:[3] There is quite a lot of bullying . . .
DE: Is that very male, or, you know, is it boy-to-boy, boy-to-girl?
Ruth: No, it's, it tends to be, yeah, within peer groups, boy-to-boy or girl-to-girl. It doesn't tend to be male dominated, the bullying. The male bullying tends to be more aggressive and violent, and confrontational. The girl-to-girl bullying tends to be more sort of, you know, insidious, nasty remarks you know, um, trying to make people gang up on somebody else verbally, that sort of thing. . . .
DE: Uh, who gets bullied? I mean what, is there, is there a kind of child that you could say that this child is likely to get bullied?
Ruth: The child who doesn't hit back, um, the child who doesn't interact particularly well, who doesn't have such a lot of social skills, tend to be on their own. The child who's, not necessarily physically small, but sometimes the child who stands out, who doesn't fit in with the crowd, the boy who settles down to work, it tends to be, certainly.
DE: And in terms of name-calling, are there, what kinds of names do they use?
Ruth: Oh yeah, we have, um, 'gay boy', that old favourite. 'Gay boy' comes up quite often actually, between the boys as a term of abuse.

(Interview, 2 July 1993)

Here we see the 'boy who settles down to work' listed alongside a range of other children who '[don't] fit in with the crowd'. It is interesting to note the change from the ungendered 'child' to the 'boy', clearly identified by his gender in the context of not fitting in by virtue of 'settling down to his work'. It does not follow that the term 'gay boy' as a term of abuse is applied only to those boys who settle to work. Rather, Ruth seems to be saying that it is a generalized form of abuse, applied indiscriminately to the 'square pegs'. Certainly, in my observation of primary school classrooms and playgrounds, I have witnessed many different forms of racist, sexist and homophobic name-calling and abusiveness and it seems that the names associated with being gay ('sissy', 'poof', 'gay boy' and 'queer' are common at this age) or lesbian ('lezzie', 'lemon', 'dyke', 'lesbian') are used in a more generalized way than some of the racist names which are prevalent. Racist names are more likely to be used towards children with particularly phenotypic characteristics in terms of skin colour, hair and so on, than as a general form of abuse towards someone you do not like (though that does happen as well).

Homophobic and anti-lesbian abuse does seem to have a more general application at primary level, but I have seen it mainly hurled at girls who resist masculinist definitions of their roles (for example, by playing football) and at boys seen as sissies, either because they want to play 'girlish' games, or because they dislike the rough and tumble which characterizes much boys' play, preferring gentler pursuits. Indeed, it seems that feminized boys come in for a major portion of abuse in both primary and secondary schools, and that this abuse is conflated with both misogyny and homophobia. In the primary-school context, the worst thing a boy can be called is a 'girl', even worse than being called 'gay boy', 'poof' or 'sissy'. It is clear, however, that both taunting a boy by calling him a 'girl' and calling him more specifically homophobic names are closely related and are generally applied to boys who seem to be feminized in some way. And it is certainly feminized to be seen to work in most schools, both primary and secondary.

Changes at sixth form

What is set up during the years of compulsory schooling (5–16 years in the United Kingdom), then, seems to be a particular set of discursive strategies within which boys can 'do boy' without risking homophobic and misogynist abuse; and visibly working at school work is not one of these. However, the move from the final compulsory year of schooling into the lower sixth form[4] brings about a change in which being good at academic work, and working hard becomes available, even desirable, as a marker of hegemonic, middle-class masculinity. Peter Redman and Máirtín Mac an Ghaill (1997) suggest that the sixth form allows the expression of what they call 'muscular intel-lectualness', the ability to 'push people about with one's mind', as a new form of school-based masculinity:

However, the accessibility of muscular intellectualness as an alternative form of masculinity was also dependent upon a sixth form reconfiguration of the masculinities validated in the pupils' cultures and the formal culture of the school. . . . We would argue that this move from Year 11 to Year 12 (in effect, the move from compulsory state education to the labour market/further and higher education) marks a key cultural transition that involves young people in new social relations (in particular those of the labour market) and requires new forms of identity to handle these. . . . Muscular intellectualness was . . . a discourse – a cultural code – that circulated in and through the meanings and practices of further/higher education, and the newly reconfigured pupils' cultures of [the] sixth form.

(Redman and Mac an Ghaill 1997: 169)

Connell (1995: ch. 7), in his discussion of 'hegemonic' and 'complicit' masculinities also points to the importance of the workplace, especially for middle-class men, and links this to the importance of rationality in late capitalist cultures (Habermas 1976) – and rationality has long been seen as a masculine property, in comparison to the irrational emotionality of the feminine. As Connell says,

Hegemonic masculinity establishes its hegemony partly by its claim to embody the power of reason, and thus represent the interests of the whole society; it is a mistake to identify hegemonic masculinity purely with physical aggression.

(1995: 164)

For professional, middle-class men, he points out, post-secondary, usually university-based, education has become essential. It would be wrong to assume that the cultural change in the sixth form indicated by Redman and Mac an Ghaill is a completely conscious choice for the students. There is, none the less, a discursive shift at this stage of schooling, which acts as preparation for higher education, and which enables working to become an acceptable form of masculinity.

In the focus group discussion quoted above, Dave describes the shift in the following terms:

Dave: Up to 16, um, I was like a complete write-off. All of the boys in my school were a complete write-off. All we used to do was just riot and really hassle the student teachers and that sort of stuff and the girls used to be the ones. The girls used to be the ones, y'know, it was the girls who got ten O levels, or whatever, got As and the boys used to get like . . . y'know, half a dozen, or whatever and then at A level everything changed and there was a big difference.

Rachel: Mm.

Dave: I'd say there was a big difference. The boys got As, Bs and Cs and went to university. The girls didn't and, uh, that was a big change, but it was definitely, clearly, like a gender thing, y'know and the girls used to work really hard and [before the sixth form] the boys didn't, basically... It's quite complicated. It's all to do with streaming and stuff as well, but, in the sort of circles I mixed it was girls always used to work hard, almost universally and the boys that never used to work hard almost universally.

Others: Mm. [other sounds of agreement]

Dave: There was the odd, like, boy who was a bit odd, who used to work all the time, but no one used to talk to him anyway... [laughter]

Alistair: [I] remember, some boys did work hard... [but] they had some image to maintain, y'know, and they had t', um, work hard and appear like they weren't.

Dave: Yeah. Well, um, I felt like I had to do both, d'ya see what I mean? I had to, um, do well and get good grades and all that sort of stuff and, at the same time, still like, when I was in the sixth form, I was a bit older, still go out drinking on a Friday night and all that sort of stuff.... After a while... there was this, like, status attached to academic achievement.

(Focus group discussion, 16 January 1992)

Dave's impression of the change which took place between O (now GCSE) and A levels is confirmed by other evidence (Murphy and Elwood 1998; Power *et al.* 1998), and Alistair repeats, here, the assertion that boys had to maintain an image of not working hard, even if this was misleading. Dave, however, points out that, while academic achievement does come to have a certain status at this stage, the image of the 'hard man', who still goes out drinking on a Friday night remains important, at least in his particular group of working class young men, on their way to middle-class professions via higher education. Indeed, taking part in a heterosexist, patriarchal pub culture (Hey 1986), was part of the price that Dave had to pay to avoid being identified as gay before he was ready to take the major step of coming out, and for academic work to be seen as acceptable.

Conclusion: paradoxes and contradictions

In trying to think through the question of cultures of masculinity and boys' affiliations (or lack of them) to schooling, their investments in certain versions of masculinity, and difficulties in being 'other' to dominant versions of school-based macho-ness, certain paradoxes and contradictions become apparent. There is no single version of masculinity; rather, we need to speak in the plural, of 'masculinities', even among very particular groups. Among school students, the 'superman' does not include 'Clark Kent'. The main demand on boys from within their peer culture (but also, sometimes, from teachers), up to the sixth form at least, is to appear to do little or no work, to be heavily competitive (but at sport and heterosex, not at school work), to be rough, tough and dangerous to know. But this is something that changes somewhere along the line, for among adult men, especially those of the professional middle classes, the harder a man appears to work within the public sphere of jobs and careers, the more 'masculine' he becomes. Indeed, some of the competitiveness among men which, during childhood and adolescence may be attached to sporting and (hetero)sexual 'achievement', may be shifted into competition about who works the hardest, longest hours.

This is in striking contrast to the ways that girls and women are supposed to appear and behave. For them it seems as if working hard at school is not only acceptable, but is, in fact, wholly desirable. Whereas boys, if they achieve success (in the narrow academic sense) at school, are supposed to do so without the appearance of working, girls' success has, historically, been written off as being due to their hard work rather than their 'ability'. However, the work of adult women in looking after homes and families, working on themselves and their bodies, doing the emotional work of relationships is, generally, not defined as work (Delphy and Leonard 1993). Women, must do all this 'non-work' work, therefore, without apparent exertion, and, if they also have careers and/or paid jobs outside the home, these must not interfere with their family work. Furthermore, for adult women to appear to work compromises their femininity: to make home/ family work visible is to become a 'drudge', while to become invested in a career and work hard at it is seen as masculinizing.

The problematic of 'boys' underachievement' is, then, called into question. Jo Boaler (1998) argues, deliberately controversially, that:

> The heightened position that girls now occupy with regard to general GCSE achievement is no more than they deserve. This . . . is because the superior position that boys traditionally held was caused by the systematic barriers that were placed in the paths of girls; now that these barriers are, in some places, being removed, the attainment of girls is a more accurate reflection of their interest, motivation, and ability . . . [G]ender patterns are shifting, not because of a climate of boy-disadvantage, but because of a climate that is moving closer to equality of opportunity, in which girls are being *allowed* to achieve. I would like therefore to turn a popular media perspective on its head and propose a history of male *over*achievement, gained at the expense of the oppression of girls, that is now being replaced by a more equitable system of opportunity in which the group that works hardest and longest is allowed to achieve the greatest awards.
>
> (Boaler 1998: 119–20, original emphasis)

What my work would suggest, though a great deal more research is needed in the area, is that many boys achieve acceptable forms of masculinity both at the expense of their own academic success, prior to the sixth form, and at the expense of girls and of boys perceived as 'not real boys'. This research would fall into a number of areas, but would need, in the first instance, to focus on understanding how different versions of masculinity are put in place and how boys experience themselves as boys. A further step would be to examine, in detail, the costs and benefits to the boys themselves and to others (for example, girls, other boys, teachers, parents) of the different possible ways of being a boy. Another stage in the required research would be to investigate how unequal gender relations and compulsory heterosexuality are implicated in the different things that boys do at school, the different ways they negotiate their schooling, and their differing levels of academic attainment. This is a path more likely to produce rewards than simplistic and/or managerialist 'solutions'.

Acknowledgements

This chapter was first given at the ESRC funded seminar series, Gender and Education: Are Boys Now Underachieving? held at the University of London Institute of Education on 15 November 1996. I would like to thank all those who took part in the discussion which was wonderfully supportive and helpful in the further development of the chapter. Remaining faults are, of course, my own.

Notes

1 It is beyond the scope of this chapter to deconstruct that programme and the media coverage of 'boys' underachievement' more generally, but this is an interesting task and one we regularly undertake with our Women's Studies and Education MA students at the Institute of Education.
2 An edited version of this discussion can be found in Alastair *et al.* (1994).
3 In the interests of confidentiality, names of interviewees have been changed unless they specifically requested that their own names be used.
4 This anachronistic label is left/taken over from the earlier nomenclature of the public (private) schools, where pupils moved through lower and upper first, second, etc. years beginning when they started at preparatory schools.

References

Alastair, Dave, Rachel and Teresa (1994) So the theory was fine, in D. Epstein (ed.) *Challenging Lesbian and Gay Inequalities in Education.* Buckingham: Open University Press.
BBC1 (1994) *Panorama: The Future is Female.*

Boaler, J. (1998) Mathematical equity – under achieving boys or sacrificial girls?, in D. Epstein, J. Maw, J. Elwood and V. Hey (eds) *International Journal of Inclusive Education: Special Issue on Boys' 'Underachieveiment*, 2(2): 119–34.

Connell, R. W. (1995) *Masculinities*. Cambridge: Polity.

Daniels, H., Hey, V., Leonard, D. and Smith, M. (1996) *Gender and Special Educational Needs: End of Award Report*, no. R000235059, Economic and Social Research Council.

Delphy, C. and Leonard, D. (1993) *Familiar Exploitation*. Cambridge: Polity.

Epstein, D. and Johnson, R. (1998) *Schooling Sexualities*. Buckingham: Open University Press.

Habermas, J. (1976) *Legitimation Crisis*. London: Heinemann.

Hey, V. (1986) *Patriarchy and Pub Culture*. London: Tavistock.

Mac an Ghaill, M. (1994) *The Making of Men: Masculinities, Sexualities and Schooling*. Buckingham: Open University Press.

Mahony, P. (1989) Sexual violence and mixed schools, in C. Jones and P. Mahony (eds) *Learning Our Lines: Sexuality and Social Control in Education*. London: The Women's Press.

Murphy, P. and Elwood, J. (1998) Gendered experiences, choices and achievement – exploring the links, *International Journal of Inclusive Education*, 2(2): 95–118.

Power, S., Whitty, G., Edwards, T. and Wigfall, V. (1998) Schoolboys and schoolwork: gender identification and academic achievement, *International Journal of Inclusive Education*, 2(2): 135–53.

Redman, P. and Mac an Ghaill, M. (1997) Educating Peter: the making of a history man, in D. L. Steinberg, D. Epstein and R. Johnson (eds) *Border Patrols: Policing the Boundaries of Heterosexuality*. London: Cassell.

Sewell, T. (1997) *Black Masculinity and Schooling: How Black Boys Survive Modern Schooling*. Stoke-on-Trent: Trentham Books.

Walkerdine, V. (1989) *Girls and Mathematics: New Thoughts on an Old Question*. London: Virago.

Willis, P. (1977) *Learning to Labour: How Working Class Kids Get Working Class Jobs*. Aldershot: Saxon House.

PART III

Boys, which boys?

7

Loose canons: exploding the myth of the 'black macho' lad

TONY SEWELL

Not all black boys are the same. This may seem a simple or common-sense assertion but in terms of teacher perception and the popular discourses that underpin 'black masculinity' there is evidence of an acceptance of cultural and ethnic essentialism. This chapter is written with data drawn from an ethnographic study of an inner city boys' school. It seeks to challenge the homogenization of black (i.e. African-Caribbean) boys into one big lump of rebellious, phallocentric underachievers. I want to point to the differences between those who conform to the requirements of schooling and those who do not. Within this, I want to show the fluid, multifarious, shifting and hybrid constructions of black masculinities that operated in this school. I will argue that a more heterogeneous perspective of black boys has been missing from the literature which has failed to look at class, context and the complex inter-sections of masculinity and ethnicity. Emancipation from the canon of 'black masculinity' gives us a more sophisticated understanding of 'underachieve-ment' and the survival strategies of these children. Those teachers who were most successful with African-Caribbean boys were aware that too many boys were tagged with the label of 'black machismo'. Their success was not in the ignoring of masculinity and ethnicity but in realizing the complex identities of the boys in a context where racism worked on a number of levels.

The key part of my empirical evidence is drawn from Township School, an inner-city boys' comprehensive school in the Greater London area. The school faced an ongoing battle to avoid closure. It had a roll of 500 but this had been falling over the last five years. The school was unpopular because of its exam results and reputation of having a poor discipline record. It is located in a rich suburb, uncomfortably nestling between a number of public (i.e. private) schools. The appointment of the school's first African-Caribbean head teacher marked a new start for the school with the expectation that this new leader would change its fortunes.

At the time of research there were 61 students of Asian origin, 63 of African origin, 140 of African-Caribbean origin, 31 mixed-race students, 127 white boys and 23 others. African-Caribbean boys were six times more likely to be excluded from school compared to other groups. In spite of this disproportionate amount of punishment, African-Caribbean boys adopted various strategies to survive the problems of racism and the inadequacies of teaching and management in the school. In order to understand the range of responses I reworked Merton's (1957) typology of the four ways in which subjects negotiated their schooling. These were: the 'conformists' who accept both the means and goals of schooling; the 'innovators' who accept the goals but reject the means of schooling; the 'retreatists' who reject both; and the 'rebels' who reject both but replace them with their own agenda. I was aware that Merton's typology could easily be seen as four stereotypes. The Merton model presupposes that student behaviour can be regimented into these fixed categories. I argue to the contrary, that students are decentred subjects changing their social identity depending on the context and their role(s) within it.

There is a need to look at positions around different discourses and cultural forms and regard Merton's categories not as fixed entities but as rooted in positions that come from an acceptance or resistance to the various discourses and cultural forms of the school and the boys' subculture. A reworked model would be as in Table 7.1:

Table 7.1 Reworking of Merton's typologies

Typology	Meaning
Positioned	Discourse and cultural forms of the school and the way they are perceived as goals and means.
Position themselves	Communities and subculture; producing discourses of acceptance or resistance.
Categories	From a multiplicity of axes for the production of possibly conflicting subject positions and potential practices and interactions.

It is impossible to talk of 'goals' and 'means' without first unpacking the cultural influences or relationships available to different students. The 'categories' then become the result of different discourses and cultural forms and the way individuals are positioned and position themselves in relation to them.

The conformists: the ultimate sacrifice or doing your own thing?

By far the largest single category (41 per cent) was conformist. This meant that most African-Caribbean boys were not rebelling against school and most accepted its means and goals. There has been a concentration in the literature on so-called 'black underachievement' and black conflict with school but little on those boys who say they like school and do relatively well. Therefore we have the danger of perceiving African-Caribbean boys as a single entity who are all disillusioned with schooling. 'Conformist students' were united through the conflict between the 'black fictive culture' (Fordham 1988: 56) of the peer group and the goals, values and expectations of the school. It was this characteristic which helped me develop the conformist type. This is not necessarily the boy who does very well academically but from observation and their own perceptions we get a picture of boys who feel that they cannot embrace both the values of school and those of their own black peer group.

Conformists tended to have a mixture of friends from different ethnic backgrounds, unlike the exclusively black peer group of the rebels. Some of these conformists tended to go to the extreme in their break from the collective, so much so that the discourse borders on the racialized. Kelvin, who is a Year 9 student, gives this 'individualistic' perspective as the reason why he has avoided exclusion:

TS: Do you belong to a gang or posse?
Kelvin: No, because my mum says I shouldn't hang around students who get into trouble. I must take my opportunity while I can.
TS: What students in this school do you avoid?
Kelvin: They are fourth years, you can easily spot the way they walk around in groups, they are mostly black with one or two whites. They're wearing baseball hats and bopping [black stylized walk].
TS: Don't you ever 'bop'?
Kelvin: Sometimes for a laugh, but it's really a kind of walk for bad people. I might walk like this at the weekend with my mates but not in school in front of the teachers. It sets a bad example.

Kelvin has not only linked group or community dynamics with bad behaviour, but is also using a racialized discourse. It is this perceived anti-school subculture of African-Caribbean fourth years that Kelvin links with 'bad people'. He cannot reconcile an 'innocent' cultural expression, which he shares even if it is only on weekends, with the values and norms of being a 'good' student. There is a cost to doing well in Township and that sacrifice is made by Kelvin and his mother.

Fordham (1988) describes the collective identity that Kelvin resists as 'fictive-kinship'. In her study of black American children she looks at how a sense of racialized 'brotherhood' and 'sisterhood' affects their attitude to schooling. This desire to flee from the black collective and cut an individual path is shown not only in attitudes to work but in music and cultural tastes. Kelvin echoes this in his comments on black music:

TS: What music do you like?
Kelvin: I like UB 40 and Meatloaf.
TS: What do you think of rap and ragga music?
Kelvin: It's not my favourite because some of the rappers are offensive
        to women and cuss. It makes you want to dance to the beat, but
        the words about women are bad. It's not fair.
TS: What do the rest of the kids in your year think about your
        musical tastes?
Kelvin: They think I'm weird, but I say to them 'I don't have to listen to
        the same music or dress up like you.' I am my own person. My
        mum told me to be my own person and not copy other people.
        I just follow that.

In Fordham's study, the students who conformed to the schooling process
also felt they could not share the same music as the students who were
anti-school. Although Kelvin does express some of these attitudes, he is too
complex an individual to be categorized simply as 'acting white' in order to
progress. The information from his parents could easily be interpreted as a
'survival' or 'tactical' strategy in a racist context as distinct from an act of
self-denial or what Fordham calls 'racelessness'. The problem with Kelvin's
rationale is that he sees little that is good in the black collective identity. It is
perceived as oppositional to schooling and therefore bad. One of the most
important attributes of fictive-kinship is the blanket of security it gives in a
hostile context. Weis (1985: 125) notes this ambivalence when she argues
that being a conformist is more than just an act of individual will:

The ethic of co-operation is deeply rooted among the urban poor, and
individuals do not break these ties easily. While individualism may be
a desired goal, it may be impossible to live out in a context of scarce
resources. It must be stressed that the desire for dominant culture embod-
ies its own contradictions: while dominant culture may be desired on
one level, it is white, not black. Given that student cultural form at Urban
College [located in the urban ghetto of a city in the north-east of the
United States] acts largely to reproduce the urban underclass, success in
school represents a severe break with the underclass community. Since
the collective offers the only security students have, the individual must
carefully weigh his or her chances for success against the loss of security
that the community provides.

There was in Township a capacity among many of the conformist students
to work at a compromise between the tensions that Weis describes. The
tragedy in Township is that too many of these students did not have the
capacity or the 'luck' to fine-tune the balance between keeping their distance and at the same time staying 'in' with their friends.

This tension was not just an example of student weaknesses; often there
were times when conformist students would attempt to claim the 'individual'

ground but this was taken away by negative teacher expectation. Stephen, an African-Caribbean Year 10 student, was determined not to be linked with the 'posse' (African-Caribbean gang) but his teachers were not prepared to separate him from the group when it came to punishments. Stephen shows some similarity to Gillborn's (1990) student, Paul Dixon:

> Like the members of the clique discussed earlier, Paul Dixon recognised and rejected the negative image which some staff held of him. Rather than reacting through a glorification of that image within a culture of resistance, however, Paul channelled his energies into succeeding against the odds by avoiding trouble when he could and minimising the conflicts which he experienced with his teachers.
>
> (Gillborn 1990: 63)

Like Paul Dixon, Stephen was too often perceived as being in the same category as the anti-school students, despite his efforts to claim individual ground. This individuality was also challenged by his peer group and, most strongly, by the Year 10 posse:

TS: What do the 'posse' think of you?
Stephen: I think they think I'm part of them, even though I'm doing my own things now. When I go to my class and they bunk off, they will say to me I'm a goody goody. But I turn to them and say that when I get my flash car and you're begging for money then you wished you had behaved like me.
TS: What do they say when you tell them this?
Stephen: They call me a pussy.

Being called a 'pussy' Stephen suffers the ultimate attack for being a conformist, which is a charge against his masculinity. Being pro-school cannot be reconciled with the machismo of the subculture. Mac an Ghaill (1994) comments on how some anti-school African-Caribbean boys have linked academic achievement with being gay or effeminate (see also, Epstein this volume).

The category of 'conformist student' becomes, in Township, a fluid context with these students positioning themselves and being positioned by others. Their own stance in school may come from a series of influences: parental, class and even religion. However, no conformist student was really allowed to 'be himself'. In fact this 'individualistic' stance was seen to be most objectionable not only by the fictive-kinship of the peer group but ironically by many teachers. Although these boys claimed to share the dominant ethos of the school, which saw black peer grouping as a negative, many were still perceived as part of a wider African-Caribbean challenge. They could never really escape the castle of their skins and gender. However, the important point is that many of them wanted to. The kind of escape path that many of them desired was not a denial of their race and gender but from the restrictive 'positioning' that came from the teachers and the peer group. Loury (1993: 6–7), a black American academic, talks about this challenge to the 'black psyche':

> I now understand how this desire to be regarded as genuinely black, to be seen as a 'regular brother,' has dramatically altered my life. It narrowed the range of my earliest intellectual pursuits, distorted my relationships with other people, censored my political thought and expression, informed the way I dressed and spoke, and shaped my cultural interests. Some of this was inevitable and not all bad, but in my experience the need to be affirmed by one's racial peers can take on a pathological dimension. Growing into intellectual maturity has been, for me, largely a process of becoming free of the need to have my choices validated by 'the brothers.' After many years I have come to understand that until I became willing to risk the derision of the crowd I had no chance to discover the most important truths about myself or about life. I have learned that one does not have to live surreptitiously as a Negro among whites in order to be engaged in a denial of one's genuine self for the sake of gaining social acceptance. This is a price that blacks often demand of each other as well.

Innovators: learning to balance on the tightrope or a step too far for 'mankind'

The second largest grouping (35 per cent) of African-Caribbean boys surveyed came under the category of innovation. This category accepted the goals of schooling but rejected the means. The origins of their pro-school values are mostly parental. However, they reject the means of schooling. At the heart of 'innovation' is a conflict; you are positive about the wider values of education but you cannot cope with the schooling process. I arrived at this category by looking first at the research done on black girls. Fuller (1980: 59) has shown how the black girls in her study managed subtly to resolve this dichotomy. She describes their attitude as 'pro-education' and not 'pro-school'. They managed to distance themselves from conformists (keeping themselves close to their peer groups) and yet achieve academic success.

The category of innovation as applied to the boys in Township is really about their 'desire' or 'struggle' rather than a successful accomplishment of this positioning. In other words we need to examine why black girls have been more successful at 'innovation' compared to African-Caribbean boys?

Frank Sinclair was a Year 10 student and a key member of the clique in his year called the 'posse'. He was expelled from two schools before coming to Township. He has already had five short-term exclusions since he has been at his new school:

TS: What did your mum say when she found out about your latest exclusion?

Frank: She just sent me to my Dad's house. And my Dad would talk long, long, long.

TS: What did he say?

Frank: He says it would be harder for me to get a job than a white man. He's always talking about this; it's like when he starts he can never finish. Most of the time I go up on Saturdays, get my pocket money – I only want to speak to him. He would just keep on about education. Then as I'm about to go he would get a book out and I would have to sit down and do some weird maths. And if I can't do a sum he would start getting mad.

TS: Do you think it is worth coming to school?

Frank: Yes, I have some friends who are about 21 and they're just loafing around. I just want to go to college do a B-Tec National [a vocational qualification for students of 16+] and go and work in a bank.

Frank is representative of many boys at Township School who were positive about education but rejected the schooling process. These boys were unable/disabled to fine-tune these two opposing instincts in order to avoid open conflict with teachers.

One popular reason given for why 'innovation' may never be successfully accomplished is that black boys face greater pressure and teacher racism compared to girls. This might be the case, but the work of Mirza (1992) shows black girls, too, having to work against the racist discourses of their teachers and experiencing more exclusions compared to their white counterparts.

Another popular reason given is the power and pressure of a peer group that demands an anti-school hypermasculinity. Mac an Ghaill (1994: 87–8) points to this pressure:

> The Black Macho Lads were particularly vindictive to African-Caribbean academic students who overtly distanced themselves from their anti-school strategies. In response, the Black Macho Lads labelled them 'batty men' [a homophobic comment]. As Mercer and Julien (1988, p. 112) point out, a further contradiction in subordinated Black Masculinities occurs, 'when Black men subjectively internalise and incorporate aspects of the dominant definitions of masculinity in order to contest the conditions of dependency and powerlessness which racism and racial oppression enforce.' Ironically the Black Macho Lads, in distancing themselves from the racist school structures, adopted survival strategies of hypermasculine heterosexuality that threatened other African-Caribbean students, adding further barriers to their gaining academic success.

These two popular reasons for the difficulty of 'innovation' can both be reduced to notions of underachievement and hypermasculinity. However, there is a danger of overplaying the achievement of black girls and making an exaggerated comparison. Also, Mac an Ghaill's analysis needs to be balanced by the fact that there were boys who did successfully negotiate the pressures of peer group and the demands of school. For them there was no psychic pressure between the so called 'two worlds'. To use a cliché they 'worked hard and played hard'.

In Township a combination of teacher racism and peer-group pressure led to 'innovation' being a tightrope that many, but not all, of these boys failed to cross. What we need to take from the innovators is not simply an analysis of them as victims, but their reasons for feeling that the 'means' of schooling cannot work for them. In many cases, these reasons centred on individual teachers' class management, and a curriculum irrelevant to them and their interests.

'Retreatism:' an invisible resistance or glad to be unnoticed?

There were a minority of African-Caribbean students in my sample who can be classified as 'retreatist' (6 per cent). These are students who reject both the goals and means of schooling but for whom these are not replaced by the subculture. In fact schooling is replaced with no significant alternative: their task is simply to reject work. The characteristics behind this typology stem from a psychological perspective where a student is marginalized within the margin. In Township we have already established that the black male presence itself could be perceived by some teachers as threatening. For 'retreatism' to be successful it needs an additional characteristic to 'accommodate' this negative teacher expectation. Therefore the African-Caribbean boys who best avoided exclusion were those who were perceived as non-threatening. In physical terms they were either very slight or very overweight and usually had special educational needs.

Joseph is a third-year student. He spends most of his day walking around the corridors. He claims never to have been 'picked up' by his class teachers who regard him as a 'slow learner'.

TS: Why do you spend so much time outside lessons?
Joseph: It's just boring and the teachers that I have are weak and they can't control the class.
TS: Do you ever hang around with the 'posse'?
Joseph: You must be joking. I hate them. They go around trying to bully students and get their dinner money. They just want to start trouble.
TS: Have you ever been excluded?
Joseph: No.
TS: Why?

Joseph: Because I'm not that rude when I'm around teachers.
TS: How long can you get away with not turning up to lessons?
Joseph: Weeks. Teachers sometimes see me on the corridor but they
            don't say anything. They don't think I'm a bad boy because I'm
            not aggressive.

Joseph is not only opposed to teachers; he also hates the subculture of the 'posse'. It is because he is not visibly rejecting the schooling process that he avoids open conflict with teachers. Retreatists are never seen in groups of more than two and they resist schooling through subversion. For example, they might walk the corridors pretending that they are on an errand for a teacher. In Township it was significant that this form of resistance was open to only a minority of black boys. However, it is more evidence of the qual-itative difference of the 'black masculine' experience in the school. Joseph was overweight for his age and the teachers perceived him as 'soft and cuddly' (to quote his form teachers). The physically aggressive signals that teachers picked up from the posse were not present in a student like Joseph. He was therefore more likely to be ignored because he was perceived as non-threatening.

In the case of the retreatists, their experience was not one of a phallocentric charged rebellion. They resisted school through subversion. They add another complex layer to any notion of a uniform 'black masculine' experience in Township school. Even their relationship to the dominant values of the black peer group is different from that of many other boys; they refuse to give the posse any legendary status. They claim an invisible ground marginalized by the schooling process and despised by the dominant peer group.

Rebels: phallocentric revenge or exploding black canons?

At the heart of some black feminist critique (e.g. hooks 1992) is a debate about the motivation and consequences of black male rebellion to racist oppression. It is suggested that because of the sexualized way in which black males are excluded from mainstream society, the only way they can find an alternative power is in an exaggerated phallocentricty which exploits women. What is interesting about this debate is that there are some black scholars (e.g. Staples 1982) who read this as an 'understandable' response and others, like bell hooks (1992: 112), who feel that this is an internalized oppression:

> If Black men no longer embraced phallocentric masculinity, they would
> be empowered to explore their fear and hatred of other men, learn-
> ing new ways to relate. How many Black men will have to die before
> Black folks are willing to look at the link between the contemporary
> plight of Black men and their continued allegiance to patriarchy and
> phallocentrism?

It is my argument that neither Staples nor hooks have allowed for the complex nature of black male rebellion, particularly when it manifests itself in the context of school. Rebellion in Township was really a rather damp squib affair. There were a number of boys who did translate their experience into a phallocentric discourse but there were other forms of rebellion which were more sophisticated and were not a form of internalized oppression. Those boys who did fit into bell hooks' category I call 'hedonist'. They replaced the goals and means of schooling with their own agenda. They were frequently excluded and found comfort in an anti-school black machismo. One afternoon, I showed a video of a programme by the comedian, Lenny Henry, to a group of Year 9 and 10 African-Caribbean students, in which Henry plays the feckless Delbert who makes his living doing scams. This was their response:

> TS: Why does Delbert have to keep using 'scams'?
> *Michael*: It's the only way he, as a black youth, can survive.
> *Donald*: Check it, no one is going to give him a job, he has to do a bit of illegal business or else he's going to go hungry.
> *Michael*: Most black kids do scams.
> TS: Why?
> *Dennis*: It's how we are – we have to go crooked because the system is like that.
> TS: What do you mean?
> *Dennis*: The police and employers, let's face it, they don't like black people.
> *Allan*: I don't think it's just black kids that pull scams. Loads of white boys always do it. They just do it differently.
> TS: What do you mean?
> *Allan*: Yes, the black kids do it up front and they don't care.
> TS: Do you think that the white boys are more clever with their sneaky scams?
> *Allan*: No way, the white boys are just pussies, they haven't got the balls like a black man, most of them go on as if they are batty men [homosexual].
> TS: Do you all agree with that?
> [There is universal agreement.]

These responses do confirm an attitude that has internalized oppression and that sees black masculinity in a narrow patriarchal and phallocentric framework. What is particularly interesting is the contemptuous attitude that these boys have for white boys. This again must be contextualized, with many black students having close relationships with white students. However, as part of the construction of hedonistic rebellion, white students are perceived as effeminate and featuring low in terms of the values of the dominant peer group (see also, Epstein this volume).

African-Caribbean boys constituted just under one-third of the school (at 31 per cent of the school roll), while white boys constituted the second largest ethnic group with over a quarter of the school (at 28 per cent); however, many of the white boys thought that the school was 90 per cent black. As one white boy said to me 'to get on in this school you have to act black'. This point is made by Hewitt (1996: 40):

> For some white English pupils, the celebration of cultural variety actually seems to include all cultures that are not their own. It is not surprising that white children – especially, it seems, young people from working class homes – experience themselves as having an invisible culture, even of being cultureless.

My problem with this analysis is that a neutral culture can also stand for the normal or the unproblematic. All too often 'ethnic minority' or 'African-Caribbean' is linked with deprivation or underachievement.

Although there was no overt racial tension between black and white students, the white boys operated in a discreet manner. Their racism was kept between themselves or with their white friends outside of school. The rebels were aware that they were admired by some white boys who felt that 'acting black' was being anti-school and this was fuelled by a masculinity that they envied. Therefore there were the white 'wannabees' who hung around the fringe of the posse, yet they would also confess to having white friends who were involved in racist attacks. As Hebdige (1979) noted, the impact of African-Caribbean youth culture on white youth was ambiguous but not progressive – as, for example, skinheads in the 1960s incorporated Jamaican music to bolster their white nationalism. However, it is admiration of a phallocentric black masculinity that most disturbs the psyche of white youths, as remarked by Back (1994: 179) in his essay, 'The "White Negro" revisited':

> For white young men, the imaging of black masculinity in heterosexual codes of 'hardness' and 'hypersexuality' is one of the core elements which attracts them to black masculine style. However, the image of black sexuality as potent and 'bad' is alarmingly similar to racist notions of dangerous/violent 'black muggers'. When racist ideas are most exposed, in situations where there is intimate contact between black and white men, stereotypical ideas can be reproduced, 'dressed up' as positive characteristics to be emulated. White identification with black people can become enmeshed within the discourse of the 'noble savage', which renders blackness exotic and reaffirms black men as a 'race apart'.
>
> (Back 1994: 178–9)

Black phallocentrism has a mirror effect on the black male subject. He positions himself in phallocentric terms and this is confirmed by the obsessive jealousy of other groups. African-Caribbean boys are not passive subjects in the face of racialized and gendered stereotyping. They are active agents in discourses which appear to be seductively positive but are in essence racist. This leads to a strong confirmation of an identity that has its source in the dislocation of black and white masculinity. It points to a more complex formation of black masculinity that relies often on 'reputation' rather than substance and has its roots not in a crisis among black boys but an 'insecurity' in white masculinity.

The Lenny Henry response also points to the need, in schools, to deconstruct stereotypes of black males; I do not mean by swapping 'bad' images with 'nice' black middle-class new men. This is equally unrealistic. There is a need to look carefully at the processes that have constructed these images, in particular, a need for an analysis of the media and how it has exploited black male sexuality. The ways in which these boys have been gendered within the school context has left some of them both alienated from 'caring' and 'responsible' notions of masculinity, and victims of the commodification of black culture. This is an argument that Gilroy (1993: 228) develops in his book *Small Acts*:

> The popularity of materialism and misogyny is partly a result of the fact that those images of blackness are the mechanisms of the 'crossover' relationship. They are in a sense the most comfortable representations of blackness. They are the images that the dominant culture finds easiest to accept, process and take pleasure in. So often the medium of their transmission is a discourse on black masculinity that constructs black men as both sources of pleasure and sources of danger to white listeners and spectators.

The problem with Township is that no one had the insight or courage to take on the issue of how black masculinity is constructed and its influence on the wider society. The nearest that the students came to any sort of discussion about these issues was when the new black head teacher (Mr Jones) took a group of boys for their personal and social education class; however, he failed to grasp the opportunity. He felt too threatened by the boys' phallocentric subculture:

TS: What do you think about the African-Caribbean boys' attitude to women?

Mr Jones: During a social education class, we were talking about children's reading books and we were trying to identify stereotypes. I told them I had 10-year-old twins, one boy, one girl, and my wife and I decided we would not create this gender divide in the twins. Then one of the boys in the class said to me, 'You've only got two kids sir?' I said 'Yes, that's right.' He then asked, 'What about the others back in Jamaica?' I said, 'I've only got two children.' He said, 'Well sir, you're not really a true Yard Man!'

The term 'Yard Man' is a reference to Jamaicans who are from 'back home' or affectionately the 'back yard'. He is linked with a street 'hard-man' life-style and he is notorious for fathering many children with different mothers and taking no responsibilities for his actions. Mr Jones had an ideal opportunity to deconstruct the 'Yard Man' and examine the cultural process that goes into his construction. Instead, he saw this as just more evidence of lost youth, who have become irresponsible and who worship destructive role models.

Rebellion in Township was not just phallocentric; there were those who articulated their rebellion on a political level. Calvin is a Year 10 pupil. His dad died, leaving his mum to raise five boys. He has good contacts and a strong network of friends outside school who are a lot older. This helps to bolster his reputation in the posse as a man who does business with 'big people'. He has most conflict with a white teacher named Ms Kenyon. In one class, Calvin was sharing a joke with a group of boys at the back of the class. Ms Kenyon's response was to seek confrontation in a battle of the wills:

Ms Kenyon: Calvin, will you shut up. I don't know why you come to my lessons because you're not interested in doing any work.
Calvin: I would do if you didn't give us rubbish work. Look around, half the class haven't got a clue what you're on about.
Ms Kenyon: And you have, have you?
Calvin: The lesson is boring and so are you.

Calvin does not see a link between schooling and getting a good job. He has already set up his own small business as a 'mobile barber', cutting hair at people's homes. He said he could make up to £300 a week. He carries a mobile phone in school so that clients can make appointments:

TS: How important is it for you to own your own business?
Calvin: It is important for black people to make money because white people don't take us seriously because we're poor.
TS: Is education important to you?
Calvin: Not really, I know what I need to know from the street. I'll give it 3 years and I bet no one will bother with school. There ain't no jobs for no one and they don't want to give jobs to black people.

The national figures on levels of unemployment for black youths compared to white confirmed Calvin's claims that job prospects were bleak for school-leavers. Calvin has rejected the world of schooling and replaced it with his alternative source of income and his most valued contact with the adult world in his community. He spoke about 'real' education which gave black people economic independence and pride in their race.

Calvin has contempt for what Dhondy (1978: 46) calls the functions of school:

The reaction of Black youth to discipline, grading and skilling processes is substantially different and potentially more dangerous to schools. And it is precisely because the education of Black youth starts and continues within the communities of which they are still a part.

Although Calvin exercises individualism in terms of his contempt for many of his peers and his desire to be his own boss, he looks positively towards his local black community for inspiration, guidance and success. He has not distanced himself from power and knowledge; it is school knowledge that he despises. He firmly believes that knowledge can be used for collective action and the eventual betterment of the condition of black people, showing that students in this category do not necessarily close off the possibility of pursuing an emancipatory relationship between knowledge and dissent. He has realized that there are other sources of knowledge which meet his material and psychological needs and they can be found within his community.

The emphasis on framing all the rebels as phallocentric is incorrect. Indeed, much theory and analysis of phallocentrism seems always to point to black boys and ignores the sexist and misogynistic attitudes which have been the inspiration for white working-class rebellion. Furthermore, many teachers seem to find these problems only with black boys. The category of rebel has a wide spectrum, much of which is political and pedagogic. It is simply an analysis and rejection of an education system that works against many black boys. This more sophisticated response has often been silenced by the 'obsessive' preoccupation with the dynamics of the black phallus.

Conclusions

In this chapter I have tried to unpack some of the oversimplifications that exist in the current debate about boys' underachievement. African-Caribbean boys are seen in research (e.g. Mac an Ghaill 1994) and popular discourse as the tip of the iceberg in a general doomsday scenario of male disillusionment with school. This analysis links gender identity to an anti-school attitude. Boys, the argument runs, try to show their maleness by being as unfemale as possible and, in doing so, contrast themselves with girls, who are generally more committed to school work. This has been made worse by peer-group pressure which boys are highly sensitive to, and this allows generalizations to be made about boys as a group. African-Caribbean boys have been seen in this context as a unified lump, who underachieve academically and are driven by a phallocentric revenge impulse to repair their oppressed maleness. There is a need to question seriously this overall pessimism of boys' alleged failure and in particular examine the complex, ambivalent and contradictory male identities that are constructed in school.

I have stressed that there are a number of costs and benefits to the boys in occupying each ideal position and this impacts on other relations (i.e. with male and female teachers, parents, other black boys and white boys). If we look at the parents of conformist students we see them divided on the issue of whether Kelvin should 'bop' (black stylized walk) in front of the teachers. I put the example to many black parent groups and it divides them. Some say he should curb his cultural style in order to 'get on' and not draw attention to himself, while others are adamant that for teachers to see his cultural expression as a threat is really racist and the teachers should change their attitudes. This example shows that even when African-Caribbean boys occupied the ideal of conformist, it was not unproblematic.

What we can say which goes against the tide of pessimism is that there was no evidence that boys were less positive towards school work than girls. Most of the African-Caribbean boys positioned themselves in the pro-school categories of conformist and innovation, while only 24 per cent saw themselves as rejecting the goals and means of schools. Even those boys who could be categorized as rebels were not a simplified and unified group. Rebellion was complex and was not solely based on a phallocentric revenge as in many cases the boys had adopted a political position to explain their rejection of school.

In trying to solve the problems of teaching black boys, teachers need to avoid two falsehoods. The first is to deny that African-Caribbean boys face a disproportionate amount of punishment in school which is based on a wider myth of a greater African-Caribbean male challenge. Second, that African-Caribbean boys are a homogenous lump of rebellious phallocentric under-achievers. There are a number of particular areas of school policy and practice which would merit attention, which I will mention briefly here. (See Sewell 1997 for a fuller discussion.)

In practical terms, schools and teachers need to confront the ways in which they confirm African-Caribbean boys as 'rebellious, phallocentric underachievers'. A start would be a school policy on social justice that was democratically developed and not tokenistic. Another practical approach for schools is for teachers and pupils to learn the art of conflict resolution. This will entail teachers being mindful of their own contribution to the negative behaviours of some African-Caribbean boys. In particular, it would be useful if teachers were to:

- avoid negative comments on cultural styles (e.g. hair styles and dress)
- respect students' personal space
- use friendly gestures, not aggressive ones
- use the students' preferred name
- get on their level physically (e.g. by kneeling or bending down, ask questions rather than make accusations)
- deal with problem behaviour in private
- listen carefully when students speak.

The respect factor is not only important when teachers are relating to students. What is also crucial is that students learn that there is an appropriate behaviour for a particular context – the idea that all situations do not deserve the same response.

Finally, the creative adaptation of the National Curriculum is needed to take on the interests and perspectives of African-Caribbean boys. Personal and social education should have courses that examine how identities are constructed, particularly on the level of race and gender. Many white teachers have complained that they are not equipped on the level of resources or experience to engage black children with their own culture. My response to teachers who say this to me is usually a question: 'What topic work are you doing with your children?' They may answer, 'The Greeks.' My response is 'Are you an Ancient Greek?' Clearly in order to do this work they have to research and prepare. It is now probably easier to find resources to do a topic called the 'Caribbean people' than it is to find material on the Greeks. What the teachers also often forgot is that the best resource is the children themselves.

The use of black male mentors and other outreach initiatives remain important but must never undermine the particular context of each school. Indeed, the notion that black boys need a black male presence in order for them to learn because they cannot learn from women (Holland 1996) remains problematic. It assumes that all boys are turned off school, which is not true, and that the cause of this disillusionment is solely rooted in their inability to relate their 'maleness' to female teachers. There is a need to acknowledge the particular needs of boys – especially in relation to reading – but this should never make us resort to policies and practices that reinforce patriarchy and sexism.

References

Back, L. (1994) The 'White Negro' Revisited: race and masculinities in south London, in A. Cornwall and N. Lindisfarne (eds) *Dislocating Masculinity, Comparative Ethnographies*. London, Routledge.

Dhondy, F. (1974) The black explosion in schools. *Race Today*, 6(2): 44–50.

Fordham, S. (1988) Racelessness as a factor in black students' school success: pragmatic strategy or Pyrrhic victory? *Harvard Educational Review*, 58(1): 54–84.

Foucault, M. (1982) *Discipline and Punish*. London: Peregrine Books.

Fuller, M. (1980) Black girls in a London comprehensive school, in R. Deem (ed.) *Schooling for Women's Work*. London: Routledge and Kegan Paul.

Gillborn, D. (1990) *Race, Ethnicity and Education*. London: Unwin Hyman.

Gilroy, P. (1993) *Small Acts: Thoughts on the Politics of Black Cultures*. London: Serpent's Tail.

Hebdige, D. (1979) *Subculture: The Meaning of Style*. London: Routledge.

Hewitt, R. (1996) *Routes of Racism: The Social Basis of Racist Action*. Stoke-on-Trent: Trentham Books.

Holland, S. (1996) Interview on Choice FM Radio, London.

hooks, b. (1992) *Black Looks: Race and Representation*. London: Turnaround.

Loury, G. (1993) Free at last? A personal perspective on race and identity in America, in G. Early (ed.) *Lure and Loathing: Essays on Race, Identity and the Ambivalence of Assimilation*. New York: Penguin.

Mac an Ghaill, M. (1994) *The Making of Men: Masculinities, Sexualities and Schooling*. Buckingham: Open University Press.

Mercer, K. and Julien, I. (1988) Race, sexual politics and black masculinity: a dossier, in R. Chapman and J. Rutherford (eds) *Male Order: Unmasking Masculinity*. London: Lawrence and Wishart.

Merton, R. (1957) *Social Theory and Social Structure*. Chicago: Free Press.

Mirza, H. S. (1992) *Young, Female and Black*. London: Routledge.

Sewell, T. (1997) *Black Masculinity and Schooling: How Black Boys Survive Modern Schooling*. Stoke-on-Trent: Trentham Books.

Staples, R. (1982) *Black Masculinity: The Black Man's Role in American Society*. San Francisco: Black Scholar Press.

Weis, L. (1985) *Between Two Worlds: Black Students in an Urban Community College*. London: Routledge and Kegan Paul.

8

Boys' underachievement, special needs practices and questions of equity

VALERIE HEY, DIANA LEONARD, HARRY DANIELS
AND MARJORIE SMITH

Boys incontestably dominate special needs provision in the United Kingdom (Cooper *et al.* 1991; ILEA 1988; Malcolm and Haddock 1991). Yet this has not been theorized within previous debates about equality of opportunity, nor has it emerged as a theme in recent popular or government constructions of 'boys' underachievement'. This chapter explores these contradictions in the light of the new gender politics of educational opportunity.

The current discourse of equal opportunity is all about boys needing more help because they are underachieving. This is, however, framed by the paradox that boys have in fact always received more resources, albeit that they are said now to need even more because they are not improving as fast as girls. Whereas girls are no longer entitled to attention on the grounds that they (briefly) received some (limited) additional resources, now read as 'more favourable treatment', as a result of feminist activism in the recent past.

The first part of this chapter discusses possible reasons for these contradictions. The second section briefly characterizes the design of an ESRC-funded study we recently undertook into gender and special needs provision in one local education authority (LEA) in London[1] and then summarizes some of the findings on differences in the social construction of special needs; and the final section calls for a more sophisticated view of matters of equity in special needs systems than has been realized in current debates on equality of opportunity.

'Boys' underachievement' as the new discourse within equal opportunities

> [H]ow can we say that ours is a society organized by men for the benefit of men? . . . If it is true that men throughout Europe live seven

years less than women, commit suicide in the ratio of three to one . . . are imprisoned in the ratio of 50 to one . . . receive less than half as much medical attention, get less favourable attention at school; and with or without educational qualifications, are less likely to get a job, how does anybody imagine that ours is a patriarchal society?

(N. Lydon, in *Guardian*, 14 May 1996)

If we consider previous claims around educational underachievement, we can clearly see how different groups have been positioned within and against its political purchase: 'underachievement' has been owned and *dis*owned by different groups in pursuit of their competing demands on educational resources.

Black and feminist groups initially made a liberal case for improving education in respect of race and gender by speaking within a discourse of black or girls' underachievement (Williams 1987). However, both groups later moved to more radical anti-deficit positions by identifying failure as institutionally and socially constructed. This shift was promoted by a recognition of the social control and pathologizing effects of applying notions of either 'low self-esteem' to black pupils or 'fear of success' to girls (Kenway, Willis and Nevard 1990).

In contrast, the new 'boys' underachievement' position implies a more complex set of ideological and political moves. Importantly, initially at least, blame for boys' relative lack of success was attributed not to something intrinsic to, or culturally produced *in*, boys, but, on the contrary, to the 'feminine' culture of primary schools, or feckless single mothers, or the media. Any 'masculine' attribution has arisen only in discussions of the male underclass. For while all masculinities are apparently at risk in these postmodern and 'disorganized' times (Lash and Urry 1989), it is inner-city, disaffected, black and white youth who are the focus of social control.

Moreover, when it appears that it is boys who are losing out, it has been easy for those who are newly interested in equality of opportunity[2] to 'liberate' equal opportunities, because earlier work had failed to construct a political language – and an activism – around equity beyond competing claims about oppression. We seemed in the 1980s in Britain to be unable to 'think through more than one difference at once' – as Kobena Mercer so powerfully phrased it (1990: 33) – and as a consequence produced a 'politics of difference' which did not recognize that, while most girls were having a hard time in school, Bangladeshi, Turkish, African-Caribbean and white working-class boys were also not doing well. As Mirza comments, 'For the ILEA [Inner London Education Authority], gender was distinctly a white issue and race clearly a male matter' (Mirza 1992: 20). An important and related consequence of this conceptual and political failure was the systematic exclusion of special educational needs (SEN) from the field of equal opportunities, and vice versa (see, Delamont 1989; ILEA 1985).

The separation of questions of special educational needs from questions of equity is also related to the discourse of SEN having been historically shaped by the disciplines of medicine and psychology. The adherence of these two fields to measuring physical and mental competence in order in both cases to determine 'normality', invariably conveys assumptions about deviance and failure, and these labels have become attached to both individuals and groups which have failed to measure up/conform. This legacy of a dominant in-person theory of causation has inhibited the development of a fuller understanding about the social and contextual determinations of SEN. So, while more sociological accounts have emerged (see Tomlinson 1982), the prevalent focus of SEN practice still tends to rest with 'in-child' explanations (Ainscow and Tweddle 1988: 13) and in junior schools to consist substantively of a focus upon 'reading ability' and 'acting-out behaviour' (Daniels *et al.* 1995).

Where questions about equity have been raised, these have been concerned with teachers' and society's general ability to 'integrate' and 'include', rather than with the social characteristics of the special needs groups themselves. In particular, the lack of concern until recently with the predominance of boys *qua* boys in SEN provision (see Delamont 1989; Riddell 1996) suggests gender has been given little attention beyond the cosmetic. Moreover, the early feminist goal of getting girls into the high-status parts of the curriculum may have effaced recognition of boys' domination of the most stigmatized provision – the disparity confirming rather than challenging some unreconstructed notions of inherent male inferiority, or the inferiority of particular males.[3]

Research on gender and SEN in mainstream schools

In our recent project, we sought to discover the nature of resource allocation practices in SEN provision in the primary schools of one inner-city local education authority. Our focus was on non-normative categories of SEN (Tomlinson 1982) and thus on children who had come to the attention of teachers as having or being problems, but who were not seen as sufficiently problematic as to need a statement of special educational needs.[4] The study had three interdependent phases designed to accumulate different types of information to enable us to 'triangulate' much of the material.

Phase 1

In phase one, we conducted an audit of special needs provision in the authority. We surveyed the type, amount and location of special needs help available in all Year 6 (10-year-old) classes. We also sought to establish the social characteristics of pupils in SEN provision in relation to their socio-economic circumstances, ethnicity, gender and home language (Daniels *et al.* 1996, 1998).

Phase 2

From this data set we identified a purposive sample – a subset of four contrasting schools selected on criteria derived from our research interests in the problematic of social inclusion, gender and equity: namely, high or low gender ratios within SEN provision; high or low visibility of equal opportunities (EO) policies and practices; and high and low additional educational needs (AEN)[5] funding.

All four schools were situated within the inner city. School 1 had a population that was mainly African Caribbean, schools 2 and 3 were both predominantly white and working class, while school 4 also had a preponderance of working-class children but was more diverse in terms of its social and ethnic mix.

Phase 3

It proved difficult to elicit teachers' views concerning girls' special needs, since boys and their problems dominated both the formal interviews and informal staffroom conversations. So in order to generate teachers' (and pupils') views about both girls and boys, we collected a further subset of data in two of our case-study schools in a final phase using a video-based interactive technique which we called 'classroom mapping'. This involved presenting teachers (and later, groups of children) with magnetic boards and sets of magnetic buttons with pupil names or photos on them, and asking questions about classroom organization and who needed and who gave help, and how patterns of help-seeking and giving had changed during the course of the school year, while the interviewee moved the buttons around. This captured well both children's and teachers' accounts of how the 'helping' systems operated within their classroom.

Our overall findings suggested a systematic 'skewing' of SEN resources in favour of boys in a ratio of nearly 2 to 1, including an even higher proportion of the most expensive support.[6] This is in line with patterns in special schools (Cooper, Upton and Smith 1991; ILEA 1988)[7] and one interpretation of it could be that this is a relay of reality: that boys do indeed *have* more special education needs than girls. However, within this overall figure, we found boys-to-girls ratios of resource distribution varying from as much as 7 to 1 to 0.4 to 1, in schools with broadly similar intakes. There were also some remarkable differences by race: black pupils appeared to be systematically 'diverted' from the category of 'specific reading difficulties' and allocated to general 'mild to moderate learning difficulties', and black boys to 'emotional and behavioural difficulties', while white boys dominated reading support resources.

This variation between schools suggested there were social, including specifically school, effects in operation. So in the second phase of the research we looked at how selected case study schools established who had

SEN, looking in particular at local definitions of the causes of SEN and the ways in which these were expressed in resourcing decisions and classroom practices. This chapter concentrates on this second phase, and focuses specifically upon heads' and teachers' understandings of causation. We suggest that schools exhibit different patterns in the way SEN is constructed and hence resources allocated, which are linked to the discourses invoked to explain SEN.

Case studies in the local construction of SEN: 'readings' and responses

In theorizing schools' diverse framings of special needs, we have found work influenced by post-structuralist accounts of the role of language in setting relations of power and position in place to be particularly useful, especially work looking at the relations of gender and classroom practice (e.g. Davies 1989; Jones 1993; Kenway *et al.* 1996). Such an approach allows us to identify the positions that different discourses construct, at the same time as suggesting how different positions secure their specific gendered effects.

We are seeking to analyse the following factors which, taken together, constitute the school's local framing of SEN:

- the orientations of the school's managerial culture – the degree to which the head teacher and her staff can be said to work within democratic or autocratic modes, and the degree to which staff feel empowered to effect change
- the staff's theories of causation – the extent to which SEN attributions are described as psychological, sociological, moral or pedagogic in origin
- the staff's focus for intervention – the site or type of response
- the resultant nature of the provision – the form, extent and duration of the provision.

In the following discussion we shall present an initial analysis of just one of these elements: the staff's theory of causation, that is, effectively, the stories the staff tell about the children with special needs. We give brief examples of the statements made by practitioners in respect of pupils, policy and practices in the domain of SEN, but must stress that all we can provide here are indicative findings, rather than a fully worked analysis of a school-based system of SEN resource management.

We can briefly summarize the four schools as advancing the following 'ideal types' of belief in their construction of special needs:

- In school 1, SEN was thought to be an indicator of social injustice manifested in pupils' emotional and behavioural problems.
- In school 2, SEN was understood to arise as the result of the social damage inflicted in hopeless and hapless families. This damage was 'acted out' by children in inappropriate behaviour.

- In school 3, SEN was currently being redefined. It was seen as an outcome of a misalignment between teaching and classroom management strategies and pupils' needs – the result of inexperience on the part of new teachers, as witnessed in differential identification rates of SEN by different teachers.
- In school 4, SEN was thought to result from a mismatch between educational provision and the child's present performance. SEN support was provided to those children identified as doing poorly against teacher expectation.

We do not want to overstate the extent to which these beliefs could be said to be uniformly distributed within any single school. They were discursive tendencies, not absolute, fixed and uncontested sets of beliefs supported by all members on all occasions. Moreover, there were also other accounts to be found within each school; and obvious overlaps between school 1's social-justice model and school 2's therapeutic approach, and between the emphasis on pedagogic aims in the third and fourth formulations. In other words, neither teachers nor pupils merely 'took up' their places within whichever discursive regime (and its associated practices) was dominant. On the contrary, both teachers and to a lesser extent pupils could (and did) rework, resist or invert dominant positions. But what they could not do was ignore them.

The following set of brief vignettes, taken from interviews with heads and class teachers, offers illustrative examples of how these beliefs about the derivation of SEN were expressed and worked out in practice.

School 1: SEN as a product of social injustice

Right, well basically I will start by saying that we are a very tough inner-city school, partly because we are a county school. We have got church schools on either side of us, and we don't have a uniform. So I actually think this is a [name of area] catchment and that this school ends up getting probably the toughest kids. Also, because we are not popular as such, in that we are not a church school, we do not have a uniform, and we are not a centre of excellence as such, we tend to have spaces. And because we have spaces, we have a high turnover. There is a lot of temporary accommodation. We also get kids who have been excluded from other schools. [...] So because we are a typical, fairly tough inner-city school, I believe that the number of special needs children in each class is going to be very similar.

(Interview with head teacher)

One of the research team likened this head teacher's commentary to the 'roll-call' sequence which opens the American police series *Hill Street Blues*, notably the coda: 'Just be careful out there people!' However, the school had a high profile within the authority for its equal opportunities work and was the only school in our study to foreground equality policies. The head sought to recruit staff from minority ethnic communities and advertised posts in appropriate black newspapers. She had managed to secure several African-Caribbean members of staff. The school also prominently displayed work with equality or oppression as a theme. For example, it celebrated International Women's Day, and had a mural about political refugees which included children's accounts of the political persecution of the refugees' families.

But, while the approach to pupils' SEN clearly drew upon earlier formulations of equal opportunities work, particularly in concerns about sex, class and race, in practice teachers' talk was characterized by a concern that their time and energy in the classroom was being dominated by the demands of African-Caribbean boys.

It became apparent on closer scrutiny that while racism was said to *stipulate* the conditions for the emergence of SEN, in practice there was not the same concern for African-Caribbean girls. They were positioned outside of concerns about underperformance. Instead they were frequently cited as positive forces for good because they helped with the management of 'unsettled African-Caribbean boys'.

> So you find you have to make a conscious effort to try to make sure the girls aren't swallowed up by the boys, 'cause they're very dominating. But right from the start it was a case of . . . there are only eight girls . . . fortunately we've got . . . I could say half of them [are] very strong girls so, they're [able to look after themselves] . . . they've actually been used to help settle some of the more unsettled boys and they've been wonderful. I mean it's hard work getting him [Keith] to sit down and do anything and Naomi's brilliant. We're talking about strong girls like Natalie and Charmian who sit on people like Keith . . .
> (Interview with class teacher)

The existence of successful, competent and 'tough' black girls suggests a more complex story about the impacts of racism than can be carried by a rudimentary additive social-injustice account. Can African-Caribbean girls be seen as tough but also fully able to learn? Some teachers clearly welcomed girls' toughness and saw them as allies in controlling the deviant boys,[8] but this also seemed to affect their view of the girls' academic ability. Self-evidently, once we rework gender into the account, the rationale for SEN that links racism with toughness and with disadvantage becomes problematized. Such outcomes also suggest that the ungendered discourse of 'SEN is a product of social injustice' may in fact further position some African-Caribbean boys within problematic (but prestigious) forms of masculine identification that are anti-education (Sewell 1997). It is difficult to envisage how, in this context, such boys could easily seek help with learning difficulties, since this is a position associated with a pro-school (feminine) position of 'weakness'.

School 2: SEN as a product of damaged families

He wasn't having any. He's the one who witnessed his father hitting somebody over the head with a hammer. He's the one who yesterday was outside holding the hammer and the pigeon got hurt – not in the playground [but] after school, where they're doing the gas work. So, you're very aware of this and ... thinking, dear me, poor kid. You know if I get angry about this, I mean, there's nothing to take personal[ly] anyway, because you know he's come to school with his own set of agendas ... He's got his own agenda. He's got everything going on in his head. He's just gone into care. His mother's a victim – nice woman – whose brother abused [name of child] in my class, who's the one that can flip at the slightest thing. And he's bright ... You can only talk really about not [letting him use] ... a pair of scissors, just because of the example that he's had.

(Interview with deputy head teacher)

The above extract from an interview represents a typical misbehaviour anecdote from school 2. The deputy head had been called to deal with a child who had absconded from a classroom having confronted another teacher with a pair of scissors. The dominant story the staff told here was of working with 'difficult' children in deprived circumstances. A major theme was the link between inadequate parenting, emotionally damaged children, and inappropriate behaviour. Teachers' (metaphorical) language offered powerful insight into their values and practices. The deputy head's use of the phrase 'own agendas' encodes an exemplary awareness about the child's particular social deficits. The senior staff often spoke about 'familial dysfunction', male violence, acrimonious divorces, and 'inappropriate parenting' when explaining children's behaviour and predispositions. The school presented itself, in contrast, as a safe space – a compassionate extended family to set against the emotionally impoverished 'other' of their pupils' biological families. Yet it would seem that these effects were unevenly distributed, since *boys* heavily dominated SEN provision.

Moreover, in this school there was also an assumption that sorting out behaviour came before attention to pedagogy and learning, and the staff preferred defusing rather than fully resolving discipline matters. Thus early in our fieldwork we observed the following incident. An experienced teacher[9] was dealing with a group of children sent out of their class for misbehaving. She produced what she called 'magic dust' from her pocket and sprinkled some over the children's heads to dispel their 'silly behaviour'. The children, duly penitent, colluded in the fiction and apologized.

All the teachers were encouraged to take up an understanding, 'healing' approach; but some new staff could not manage its emotional demands,[10] and even those who could work in this way expressed reservations about being seen as 'soft' by parents. Nevertheless, senior staff instructed others in the recuperative approach and supplied (therapeutic?) support to those teachers who found it hard. For instance, one in-service (INSET) session began with a covert 'role play', where the head 'acted out' parental (and thus deviant) anger at a member of her staff. The staff were then told that this was part of the session and asked to disclose their 'feelings' about witnessing a colleague being criticized so publicly. This scenario was said to be an analogy for the impact of disruptive pupils on teacher self-esteem. The main message of the session was an encouragement to teachers to see pupil behaviour as a reaction, as 'acting out', rather than as bad behaviour directed at the actual individual to whom it was addressed.

Pupil interviews showed that the majority of pupils fully understood this therapeutic model, and in one notable instance a white working-class girl was repeatedly validated in a helping role that consisted primarily of expressions of maternal concern. She was credited both with 'making pupils feel better' as well as with providing individual forms of learning assistance. Conversely, many boys spoke of themselves as needing to 'focus' or 'concentrate', miming their teacher's characteristic language.

However, there is some evidence, in the numbers of African-Caribbean girls labelled as having behavioural difficulties, that they were alienated by this therapeutic model. This was supported by the discovery that several African-Caribbean girls had been excluded or had parents who had 'voluntarily' chosen to remove them from the school roll. They may have found it equally unacceptable to be positioned as either in need of 'understanding' or as providers of 'understanding' for others.

School 3: SEN as a product of school and classroom mismanagement

The children [were] running in and out of the staffroom and screaming things, going to the head's office without knocking and barging through, no respect for hardly any of the adults that were in here. And my friend came on a visit and she walked through the playground and she asked somebody really nicely 'Would you tell me where Miss Mansfield is?' and the boy replied 'How the f . . . should I know'!

(Interview with deputy head teacher)

School 3, like school 1, had fewer pupils than its official roll and so had to take any children removed from other schools. It also had a reputation as a very challenging school. The local authority had recruited a new senior management team in an effort to 'turn the school around'. The new head described the situation when she arrived as 'volatile and demoralized' and said that the previous regime was one of containment/entertainment. The newly appointed Deputy Head described finding filing cabinets full of confiscated knives. The new Head was trying to shift the school's SEN culture away from a reactive mode that responded to 'boys behaving badly', towards the creation of more systematic special needs procedures. She had longer-term aims of raising pupil aspirations and standards, and she was fully aware

of the gender imbalances within SEN provision. She had initiated a streaming system in maths and also taught the top class, both in order to raise the
status of the subject and to signal to her staff the importance of the need for
educational improvements.

SEN provision in this school was focused on what the head termed 'tur-
bulent' classes and on reading and literacy failure. She felt that inheriting a
chaotic school probably meant some children were currently completely
missing out on their entitlement to SEN provision, but she insisted that the
school could improve and she was intent on trying to make a difference
through staffing and management changes. She offered no 'excuses' about
structural disadvantage or familial deprivation. Instead, she attributed far
more significance to teachers' local power to establish appropriate pedagogies.
In practice, she and her Deputy had to handle the competing claims of
effective crisis management (including support to inexperienced teachers)
and consideration of their long term development goals.

> [T]he classes . . . all of them have got children who have needs. There's
> not really a class that doesn't. But what I do find is, depending on the
> quality of the teacher that's in there, um, it really has profound impact
> on the way that the children cope in the school and whether they stand
> out because the child has a special need. And I've got a year 6 class who
> have an excellent teacher – she's my deputy, and when she's in there
> no, none of the children will stand out.
>
> (Interview with head teacher)

The Head spoke about staff motivating pupils through appropriate curriculum pitching and pacing as the key means to ensure the optimization of
learning and pupil engagement. With the help of her deputy, she was determined to stop SEN being dominated by default by those boys who 'stood
out' as disruptive.

School 4: SEN as a product of a mismatch between educational provision and a child's performance

> Historically, genetically, boys are more inclined to play rough and there
> are a lot more behavioural problems with young males. It's physically
> rough play rather than aggression. When I first arrived there was a lot
> of very aggressive behaviour amongst the males and the females – and
> that is the first thing I worked on and that is the behaviour policy.
> And I worked with all the children in the school, at assembly time
> and in each class, asking the children what kind of school they would
> like. Right – first I got all sorts of things out which were negative
> about kicking and hurting; and then, brainstorming with them, getting
> the things they were negative about, I turned them around into being
> positive.

> We don't stereotype and we don't classify a boy who has behavioural
> problems as having SEN.
>
> (Interview with head teacher)[11]

Although this school also had its share of the same problems as the other
schools – the surrounding catchment area included a lot of short-term housing accommodation so it took in many recently arrived political refugees,
and turnover in the school was often as much as 30 per cent of pupils each
year – it differed from all the rest in being the only school (among our case
studies and indeed in the LEA) with a gender ratio in SEN provision that
favoured girls. The head attributed this to its SEN practice being organized
against dominant ways of identifying pupils with problems, that is, to its distinguishing 'educational' from 'behavioural' issues: it was the school policy and
practice to split the management of behaviour from the resourcing of SEN.

The school had well developed policies and procedures in place for the
management of behaviour. The behaviour policy arose out of the Head's
discussions with all the 'stakeholders': children, parents, teaching and support staff. She took a 'hands-on' approach to issues of child-to-child dis-
agreements, specifically seeing the resolution of these incidents (name-calling,
exclusion from social games, playground bad-mouthing) as *central* to her
working through of both behavioural and social justice policies. This was
also evidenced in the way class teachers moved to resolve interchild antag-
onisms. The existence of a pro-active, inclusive regime meant that children
did not need to 'stand out' to obtain (learning or other) support.

Children echoed school policy, noting that if they misbehaved, 'going to
see the head was very serious'. Yet this disciplinary role was also seen positively: as a concern for their safety. For example, two boys in the children's
group interview encouraged another of their number to 'go and see Miss' in
response to his distress over comments others had made about him.

Children whom teachers suspected were experiencing learning difficulties
were assessed, and, if appropriate, a detailed programme of support was put
in place. Literacy and maths help was given to identified groups of children
within a class. The support was described in pedagogic terms and related to
the need to encourage specific skills and competencies. There was also a strong
emphasis on making distinct provision for children for whom English was a
second language and for those with other special needs. Individual progress
was regularly monitored by the Special Needs Coordinator (SENCO), who had
time allocated to visit classes and record the progress of the child on individual education plans (IEPs). The school was thus well placed to comply with
the recording and monitoring demands of the new *Code of Practice* introduced
in 1994 (DfE 1994), and indeed the discursive framing of SEN as practised
here approximated to the ideal type envisaged in the *Code of Practice* (DfE).

This school had the most systematic planning documents of any within
the case studies. Planning was seen as the key to enabling the school to
learn from its own practice:

It has been hard work implementing planning cycles and consistently getting them to work. We have to keep going until we have a clear system. Now there is evidence that it is happening but we kept a high focus all the time for 5 years. Now we use them. Because of the number of bilingual learners some of them are learning really quickly . . . there is this sort of thing of letting the bilingual learner go through stages 1 and 2 [of the *Code of Practice*] and saying it's patently obvious that some of these kids are struggling with the work and saying well this isn't the developmental process – it's language that is the issue here.

(Interview with head teacher)

The head stressed the centrality of learning and having systems in place that allowed both her and her staff to learn about which children were not able to benefit fully from the school's teaching. Attention to teaching quality was monitored at many levels: from recruitment – the head seeing would-be teaching candidates in their current school – through to teachers' own record-keeping (they were asked to prepare weekly schemes of work). In addition, the senior management team had the capacity to work with the available statistical information. For example, the Head had analysed the latest SATs (Standard Assessment Tasks) results by gender and the length of time the child was in the school. She was confident that the girls were performing well in maths and science.

Like the Head from School 3, the Head of School 4 construed the management of children's behaviour as teachers' responsibility and as best managed through ensuring sufficient degrees of differentiation of curriculum and pedagogy. She emphasized the need for careful planning in the grouping of children and argued for a consistency of approach across all the levels of educational planning.

Children in school 4 shared the expectation that learning mattered. Their talk about helping behaviour reflected the pedagogical emphasis. It was full of references to children 'having second-language needs' and of children with 'specific learning difficulties'. Equally they recognized those children who were very good at particular curriculum subjects. Field notes record, for instance, Phawin being described as a 'brilliant mathematician' and Resha as an 'excellent artist'. The children offered little talk about their classmates' psychosocial predispositions.

Discourse and practice

It is important to understand that such local, differently inflected, school-based discourses also lead to different decisions being made about how to distribute resources. The belief in school 1 that SEN derived from social injustice, and particularly that it was a product of racism, resulted in a decision to spread SEN resources evenly across the teaching groups because racism was a generic feature of all the children's lives. This decision was also held in place by a conviction that the African-Caribbean community saw it as stigmatizing and/or the result of racist practices for children to be given an SEN designation. The school 2 construal, with its focus on 'acting-out' behaviour, led to the employment of a half-time behaviour support teacher to work in rotation with other staff on developing behaviour management strategies. The third 'transitional' school and classroom management definition was being carried forward by shifting resources from individual classes towards a more systematic, planned, whole-school approach, while the final, pedagogically defined approach of school 4 implied the targeting of resources on individual children and then monitoring individual progress, and a switching of resources in response to changing learning needs.

It is nevertheless significant that, despite the differences between them, the first three SEN regimes all provided help predominately for boys, while only the last orientation identified slightly more girls than boys as needing SEN provision within the school population.

Recognizing multiple inequalities rather than focusing on the underachievement of 'boys'

In the light of our (and other people's) evidence that boys are already receiving the majority of SEN resources within schools, we should resist simplistic arguments that (all) boys now need *more* money spent on them at the expense of (all) girls because boys are doing less well than girls. Instead of joining the rush to affirm 'boys' underachievement', we need to construct a more sophisticated awareness of the sets of relations that exist between wider social inequalities; local systems of beliefs about learners and learning; schooling cultures; and differential achievement. We need, in short, a form of language that allows us to think through 'more than one difference at once'.

If we were to look at the domain of SEN with the gaze of equal opportunities, we would ask questions about the effects of homogenizing differences within each group (gender, race and class) which are produced by simplistic 'identity-based' or 'compensatory' targeting on girls (or boys), minority ethnic children, or those from poor backgrounds. We could also reflect on the gendered implications of taking up prevalent definitions about 'acting-out' behaviour, which is largely a problem with and/or for boys, since many forms of girls 'acting out' distress (withdrawal, anorexia, flirtatiousness or overcompliance following sexual abuse) are not considered.

As the discussion of the four case study schools clearly shows, different schools manage pedagogy differently in the face of similar types of masculine behaviour. School 4, however, explicitly prevented boys from commandeering almost all SEN support by separating behavioural from academic needs; having explicit whole school policies through which behaviour is

managed; and having objective criteria for assessing SEN together with dedic-
ated monitoring. This school, therefore, could establish a more discriminating
pattern of provision. Moreover, within this school, which was organized to
support learning improvement (as opposed to social control or social rescue),
we found an atmosphere which allowed staff to learn explicitly from pupils
and from each other about how the organization was working.

Most schools in our study, however, did not have the capacity to check
the continuous tendency for boys to demand and get more teacher time,
attention or other resources (accepting of course that not all teachers' attention is positive attention). Consequently such schools were not able to check
a tendency towards inappropriate allocation of scarce resources.

One of our initial findings from the third phase of this project, where we
looked at teachers' and pupils' self-reported accounts of learning support,
was that boys are generally less inclined to seek help from, or to give help
to, their male peers.[12] Overall, boys appear willing to ask girls for help, and
girls routinely support both each other *and* boys, but boys do not seem to
want to look to each other for assistance. Boys thus seem to compete with
each other for the teacher's time and attention; and given all the other
compelling demands on teachers' time this is a scarce resource. When they
do not get teacher's (as opposed to peer) attention, boys may be tempted to
go 'off task' and/or to respond with inattentive and disruptive behaviour.

We suggest that this is a powerful complex. A masculine orientation which
sees learning as sissie, combines with a school orientation to learning support which focuses on behaviour and (above all other curriculum areas) on
literacy support, to produce resource allocation heavily tipped towards provision for boys. Within this overall bias, teachers also hold beliefs about learning that result in the raced attribution of labels. Poor reading performance
in black boys and girls is read as an indicator of general (mild to moderate)
learning difficulties, while white boys have 'specific reading difficulties'
(Daniels *et al.* 1998) and white girls have no problems because they are quiet
and get on with their reading.

Teachers may believe that their assessments are the best (or only necessary)
means of decision making about special needs. But our research suggests
that this is problematic. Such judgements are subjective and promote a relay
into SEN of common-sense assumptions about different pupils' abilities and
behaviour based on gender, class and race.

However, whether a school is driven by social-justice, therapeutic or strictly
pedagogical concerns in its allocation of resources, and whether the subsequent positions it makes available to its pupils, larger ideological forces are
not simply transmitted into the school. Schools can themselves affect dominant expectations if they organize their practices in ways that work *against*
powerful 'common sense'. As school 4 shows, an insistence on systematic
assessment, resource targeting and child-sensitive interventions can work
to create powerful 'school effects' which do not result in practices in which
'boys will be boys' and girls will be overlooked. We suggest that schools

need to turn the gaze upon their own identification practices; and (provisionally) that the use of objective diagnostic measures and follow-up monitoring of support result in more gender-equitable identification of SEN within school populations. Leaving it to the workings of local ideologies, however well intentioned, is not fair. In the light of shrinking educational budgets, some very tough choices have to be made. We will be far better placed to make them for girls and certain boys if we consider the implications of our current practices. This chapter is an attempt to stimulate such critical thinking.

Acknowledgements

An earlier version of this chapter was presented at the Economic and Social Research Council funded seminar on 17 May 1996. This was part of a series on Gender and Education: Are Boys Underachieving? held under the auspices of the Centre for Research and Education on Gender (CREG) at the University of London Institute of Education.

Notes

1 'Gender and Special Educational Needs Provision in Mainstream Schools', ESRC grant number R000235059, directed by Diana Leonard and Harry Daniels, with Valerie Hey and Marjorie Smith as research officers. The project was based at the University of London Institute of Education.
2 See Jane Kenway's (1995) critique of what she terms 'the Lads' Movement' – those who position men and boys as victims.
3 It was of course the suspicion that African-Caribbean boys were disproportionately placed within special schools on just such biologist (racist) grounds that led Coard (1971) and others (see Tomlinson 1982) to challenge the *status quo*.
4 A statement lays down a mandatory right to receive certain designated additional support. The *Code of Practice* (DfE 1994) governing the current special needs policy sets out five stages within which the teacher, school and local authority (as appropriate) should respond to a child identified as not making progress. The minimum intervention requires the teacher to monitor the child and offer help, and each stage implies increasing levels of help.
5 Additional educational needs are determined by a series of proxy indicators and form the basis of an allocation of extra resources to a school. In the LEA in our study, eligibility for free school meals was used as one of the main proxy indicators for poverty.
6 A fuller discussion of the quantitative data is available in Daniels *et al.* (1998).
7 In our sample, four categories of need predominated: mild and moderate learning difficulty, specific learning difficulty, and emotional and behavioural difficulties. All these categories lack precise definition and are inevitably context-bound. Emotional and behavioural difficulties (EBD) show the greatest, and mild learning difficulty the smallest gender differences (which is consonant with earlier reports from other studies, e.g. Cooper, Upton and Smith 1991). But what was striking

was the interaction of gender and race: the differences between black boys and girls are very different from those between white boys and girls.

8 Compare the positioning of African-Caribbean girls in school 3, where they refused both the 'understanding mother/therapist' and the 'victim' positions.

9 The teacher had been drafted into the school from a special school for emotional and behavioural difficulties to support the staff in developing behaviour-management strategies.

10 Two new members of staff left after one year in the school.

11 The above data extracts reflect extracts from the Head teacher's views given in an interview. They were reassembled from extensive field notes made at the time and written up almost immediately – short verbatim comments were taken down during the interview. She would not give permission for taping.

12 We are currently investigating this further in a new ESRC-funded project on gender and learning.

References

Ainscow, M. and Tweddle, D. A. (1988) *Encouraging Classroom Success*. London: Fulton.

Coard, B. (1971) *How the West Indian Child is Made Educationally Subnormal in the British School System*. London: New Beacon Books.

Cooper, P., Upton, G. and Smith, C. (1991) Ethnic minority and gender distribution among staff and pupils in facilities for pupils with emotional and behavioural difficulties in England and Wales. *British Journal of the Sociology of Education*, 12(1): 77–94.

Daniels, H., Hey, V., Leonard, D. and Smith, M. (1995) 'Standing out': a preliminary report of an ESRC supported gender and special needs project. Paper presented at the British Educational Research Association Annual Conference, University of Bath, 14–17 September.

Daniels, H., Hey, V., Leonard, D. and Smith, M. (1996) Equal to the challenge *Special*, Autumn: 15–17.

Daniels, H., Hey, V., Leonard, D. and Smith, M. (1998) Differences, difficulty and equity: gender, race and SEN. *Management in Education*, 12(1): 5–8, special issue ed. M. Arnot.

Davies, B. (1989) *Frogs and Snails and Feminist Tales: Preschool Children and Gender*. Boston: Allen and Unwin.

Delamont, S. (1989) Both sexes lose out: low achievers and gender, in A. Ramasuk (ed.)*Whole School Approaches to Special Needs*. London: Falmer.

Department for Education [DfE] (1994) *Code of Practice on the Identification and Assessment of Special Educational Needs*. London: DfE.

ILEA (1985) *Educational Opportunities for All? Report of the Committee Reviewing Provision to Meet Special Educational Needs* (The Fish Report). London: ILEA.

ILEA (1988) *Characteristics of Pupils in Special Schools and Units*. Research and Statistics Branch, RS 1270/90, mimeo.

Jones, A. (1993) Becoming a 'girl': poststructuralist suggestions for educational research. *Gender and Education* 3(2): 157–66.

Kenway, J. (1995) Masculinity and education. Paper presented at a joint Centre for Research and Education on Gender and Social Science Research Unit Seminar, SSRU, University of London Institute of Education, 12 July.

Kenway, J., Blackmore, J., Willis, S. and Rennie, L. (1996) The emotional dimensions of feminist pedagogy in schools, in P. F. Murphy and C. V. Gipps (eds) *Equity in the Classroom: Towards Effective Pedagogy for Girls and Boys*. London: Falmer.

Kenway, J., Willis, S. and Nevard, J. (1990) The subtle politics of self-esteem programmes for girls, in J. Kenway and S. Willis (eds) *Hearts and Minds: Self-Esteem and the Schooling of Girls*. London: Falmer.

Lash, S. and Urry, J. (1989) *The End of Organized Capitalism*. Cambridge: Polity.

Malcolm, L. and Haddock, L. (1991) Make trouble – get results: provision for girls in Southwark's support services, mimeo.

Mercer, K. (1990) Welcome to the jungle: identity and diversity in postmodern politics, in J. Rutherford (ed.) *Identity, Community, Culture and Difference*. London: Lawrence and Wishart.

Mirza, H. (1992) *Young, Gifted and Black*. London: Routledge.

Riddell, S. (1996) Gender and special educational needs, in G. Lloyd (ed.) *'Knitting Progress Unsatisfactory': Gender and Special Issues in Education*. Edinburgh: Moray House Institute of Education.

Sewell, T. (1997) *Black Masculinities and Schooling: How Black Boys Survive Modern Schooling*. Stoke-on-Trent: Trentham.

Tomlinson, S. (1982) *A Sociology of Special Education*. London: Routledge and Kegan Paul.

Williams, J. (1987) The construction of women and black students as educational problems: re-evaluating policy on gender and 'race' in M. Arnot and G. Weiner (eds) *Gender and the Politics of Schooling*. London: Unwin and Hyman in association with the Open University.

PART IV

Curriculum, assessment and the debate

9

Language and gender: who, if anyone, is disadvantaged by what?

JOAN SWANN

Introduction

In this chapter I am concerned with language as an essentially social phenomenon: one that is closely bound up with the development, negotiation and
maintenance of speakers'/listeners' and readers'/writers' personal and social
identities. I shall focus on one important aspect of this: the relationship
between language and gender.[1] Since the publication, over 20 years ago, of
several important feminist studies on language and gender, there has been
increasing interest in the area. The interest has been at both a theoretical
and a practical level. Many studies of language and gender have been carried
out in educational settings, and several of those with an interest in the area
have been concerned about the educational implications of their work.

I shall review some changing perceptions of both 'language' and 'gender',
and consider how these relate to educational concerns about gender in/
equity. In using terms such as 'inequity' (as well as 'inequality' and 'disadvantage') I am adopting a broader focus than educational 'underachievement'
narrowly defined in terms of examination or test results. Although the formal
assessment of girls' and boys' language is clearly an important issue (I have
discussed this in earlier papers – e.g. Swann 1993; Swann *et al.* 1992) language is also bound up much more generally with the process of schooling,
with how girls and boys experience schooling, and (more crudely) what they
get out of it.

I shall look first at approaches that have associated educational language
use fairly directly with inequalities between female and male students (the
main focus being on disadvantages faced by female, relative to male students);
and then at approaches that would see the relationship between language

and gender as operating in a rather more complex manner. I shall also look at recent research on electronic communication that raises important questions about potential inequalities between female and male language users in education and in other contexts.

A final point to mention at this stage is that, while language and gender has been a matter of professsional interest to many English teachers, the research I shall refer to is concerned not specifically with the English curriculum, but with the routine use of language in schools and classrooms, and across subject boundaries.

Gender difference and inequality in language: a brief overview

A large volume of the empirical research on language and gender carried out since the 1970s and 1980s, in educational and in other settings, has been concerned to document differences between female and male language users. Within education, many studies of classroom talk have shown male students occupying disproportionate amounts of teacher time and attention. Gender differences in interactional style have also received some attention, a major focus being on male students' tendency to 'dominate' in class discussion. In a review that draws on this established body of work, the New Zealand linguist Janet Holmes argues:

> women and men talk differently. Research in Britain, America and New Zealand reveals similar gender-based patterns of discourse. Women appear cooperative, facilitative participants, demonstrating in a variety of ways their concern for their conversational partners, while men tend to dominate the talking time, interrupt more often than women, and focus on the content of the interaction and the task in hand, at the expense of attention to their addressees . . .
>
> The strategies which typically characterise female interaction can be described as 'talk-support' strategies, while at least some of those which characterise male talk function as 'talk-inhibition' strategies. In the classroom these have obvious implications for learning opportunities. In the second language classroom they can either promote or restrict language learning opportunities.
>
> (Holmes 1994: 156)

Holmes is concerned here with 'improving the lot' of female students in ELT (English language teaching) classrooms. Her observations are, however, consistent with evidence of male dominance of talk, and (consequent) disadvantages for female speakers in many subject areas (see Swann 1992 for examples and further discussion). Holmes argues that women and girls 'are getting less than their fair share of opportunities to practise using English'

(1994: 157) – an echo of earlier claims made by Dale Spender on the basis of observations in British classrooms:

an enormous amount of research has been undertaken which establishes the primary importance of learners being able to talk about their own experience as a starting point for learning. Yet we have an education system where not only is it extremely difficult for half the population to find an opportunity to talk – particularly to the teacher – but where the experience about which they could talk is seen as inappropriate, as not sufficiently 'interesting' to be talked about.

(Spender 1982: 60)

Concerns about girls' educational disadvantage have been prominent across the curriculum, even in areas noted for high academic achievement among girls. Janet White suggests that girls' very aptitude for English-related activities (she focuses on writing) is harmful to them. She argues both that girls are channelled into English at the expense of their success in other subjects, and that girls' success in school English is not reflected in their subsequent achievements. White notes that women write novels, but make up a small proportion of writers studied on literature courses; they write as journalists, particularly in magazines, but it is men who are more often promoted to top jobs; women work in advertising, but often behind the scenes. She comments:

The English Department which operates with a punctilious view of 'good' writing (a matter of prescriptive correctness) and enshrines only a few types of writing as the 'best' (fictional narrative, varieties of 'creative' description) is ultimately doing as great a disservice to its predominantly female students as are the overtly 'unfriendly' male-dominated subject areas.

(White 1986: 570)

Similarly, in a more recent review of gender differences in reading, Myra Barrs considers the generally accepted finding that boys perform less well than girls, but she also warns of girls' 'underachievement', at least in certain aspects of reading:

girls' generally higher levels of achievement in reading may reflect the nature of the reading demands made of them, and may in fact mask substantial under-achievement in some areas of reading which, for a complex of reasons, are less carefully monitored in schools, such as the reading of information texts.

(Barrs 1993: 3)

Concerns about language use informed the 'equal opportunities' and 'anti-sexist' policies and practices that were developed in several British schools and local authorities, particularly during the 1980s. In relation to language as in other areas of classroom life, such initiatives frequently emphasized the needs of girls and sometimes explicitly targeted girls' language.

Hordyk (1986), for instance, discusses how girls can be encouraged to be more verbally assertive – by implication, adopting patterns of language more usually associated with boys. Such strategies, and the evidence they were based on, have been the subject of debate among feminist teachers and researchers. In a discussion of girls' and boys' writing, Gemma Moss questions 'anti-sexist' preoccupations with the problems faced by girls, whereas boys escaped such close scrutiny:

> By worrying about all the negative pressures on girls and their ability to cope, whilst insisting on the importance of our help, aren't we turning them into the passive, helpless victims we came to save? Meanwhile, the security of boys' identity is not subject to the same sort of scrutiny, the same doubts.
>
> (Moss 1989: 54–5)

Some feminist educationists have used writing as a means of questioning boys' behaviour, albeit occasionally expressing qualms about devoting time to an already privileged group (e.g. Reay 1993).

A great deal of the evidence of boys' interactional dominance in the classroom has come from whole-class and/or teacher-directed talk. Rather than changing girls' behaviour in these contexts, some teachers have advocated changing the nature of classroom talk to make it more hospitable to girls. Strategies have included providing more (verbal) space for girls/quiet pupils in whole-class talk (e.g. Bousted 1989); and encouraging collaborative talk in pairs or groups – in which, for instance, pupils would be required to take turns to speak and listen to their partner(s) (Claire 1986). Holmes (1994) advocates tackling the language behaviour of male students more directly, focusing on their 'inadequacies' and teaching them to be 'good conversationalists'. This reflects her concern that male students' behaviour (rather than females') constitutes a problem, albeit one that adversely affects female students.

Alongside such debate among those with an interest in language and gender, the educational context itself has shifted dramatically. The introduction of the National Curriculum in England and Wales has been associated with the marginalization of gender issues, or 'equal opportunities' initiatives in language, as in other aspects of school and classroom life. Within the English curriculum, for instance, the initial proposals drawn up by the English working group chaired by Brian Cox (Cox Report, DES/WO 1989) contained a chapter on 'Equal opportunities' which discussed, among other things, some educational implications of gender differences in language use. Subsequent non-statutory guidance for English reduced this to a few passing references (e.g. NCC 1989). And there was no mention at all of gender, or 'equal opportunities', in the streamlined 1995 version of the curriculum (DfE/WO 1995).

Public debate about male 'underachievement' has also increased concern about boys' language behaviour in the classroom. A report from Ofsted (Office for Standards in Education) on *Boys and English*, written when boys' 'underachievement' had beome a highly salient issue, recognized that boys often dominated oral work in the classroom (1993: 3, 15–16), but argued that this did not work to their advantage – it inhibited their own learning as well as that of others. Ofsted's recommendations on boys' participation in classroom discussion, while designed to benefit all pupils, nevertheless focused primarily on the needs of boys themselves:

> *When boys took part in class discussion or worked together in pairs or groups the pattern of their talk was often different from girls'.* They were more likely to interrupt one another, to argue openly and to voice opinions strongly. They were also less likely to listen carefully to and build upon one another's contributions. Teachers did not take account of such characteristics in a planned approach to oral work intended to encourage boys to be more considerate and girls more confident. In many cases the large size of classes made detailed planning and orchestration of this sort of work difficult. Nevertheless, such features of boys' and girls' talk need to be allowed for in planning and evaluating group work and class discussion. *It is particularly important for boys to develop a clearer understanding of the importance of sympathetic listening as a central feature of successful group and class discussion.*
>
> (Ofsted 1993: 16, emphasis as in original)

As well as identifying boys' language behaviour as a problem for boys, Ofsted suggests boys need to develop certain kinds of talk (e.g. sympathetic listening) that are consistent with the collaborative and supportive speaking styles associated with girls and valued by many feminist researchers. Ofsted's motivation here is unlikely to be a feminist one. Educationists concerned to promote 'oracy' in the classroom have, from the 1960s onwards, emphasized the educational and social value of collaborative talk in which pupils listen to others and build upon their ideas (e.g. Johnson 1990; Wilkinson *et al.* 1965; Wilkinson *et al.* 1990).[2] Whatever the motivation, however, Ofsted is setting a high value on talk associated with female speakers and seeing its absence, among boys, as a problem that needs to be addressed.

Such concerns about boys' language behaviour reflect different interests and emanate from a different political and educational context from the feminist work I mentioned earlier, which documented educational language practices that seemed, broadly, unfavourable to girls. They have in common, however, a focus on girls and boys as relatively distinct social groups whose language behaviour is characterized by certain differences. I want now to look at alternative approaches to language and gender which would question this focus on gender difference, and which would see the relations between gender and language as operating in a more complex manner. The educational implications of these approaches need to be more fully worked out. At the very least, however, they are unlikely to articulate well with current trends in educational policy and practice.

More complex models of 'language' and 'gender'

Empirical research on gender difference and inequality in language has always acknowledged variation among female, and among male language users. Nevertheless, such research depends on the identification of general patterns – in the case of interactional style, for instance, that, in the contexts investigated, female speakers tend to talk in one way and male speakers in another. This in turn depends on an assumption that categories such as 'girls' and 'boys' (or 'women' and 'men') are relatively fixed and distinct, and that they may be related, fairly unproblematically, to language use. The more complex models of gender and language I turn to below, which might broadly be termed postmodernist,[3] and which are characterized by an emphasis on context, diversity and provisionality, would challenge any such general claims about difference and inequality.

In terms of language, there has been a general shift away from a reliance on formal linguistic categories, with researchers frequently adopting a more contextualized model of language. This shift may be illustrated by taking as an example interruptions, a frequent indicator of gender differences in spoken language. (Interruptions were identified by both Janet Holmes and the Ofsted report as being more common in male speakers.)

In order to make any claims about the gender-differentiated use of interruptions, one needs some agreement on what an interruption actually is. Early research on language and gender accepted the common-sense assumption that an interruption occurs when a new speaker talks over a continuing speaker's turn, overlapping their speech by more than a limited extent (precise measures of interruptions have differed between studies). A problem with this formal definition is that the meaning, or function, of overlapping speech will vary considerably in different contexts. In a study of conversations in all-female groups, Jennifer Coates (1996) found that the talk was characterized by large amounts of overlapping speech which, in this context, could not be said to constitute interruptions. Coates argued that a more valid interpretation was to see the speakers as jointly constructing speaking turns. Overlapping speech was used in a collaborative or supportive way, rather than as a (hostile) incursion into another's speaking turn. Such an interpretation may still suggest that, on any occasion, features such as overlapping speech have a single function. However, linguistic features often fulfil more than one function simultaneously. In certain contexts, for instance, overlapping speech could support certain speakers while also excluding others from the discussion.

This focus on language in context highlights subtle aspects of language use. The meaning of language is seen as relatively fluid; meaning is not simply 'in the language' but may be negotiated between speakers; individual utterances are often multifunctional, and may be ambiguous. This model of language is encapsulated in the following statement of 'integrational linguistics' from the linguist Deborah Cameron:

language is *radically* contextual. It is not just a matter of context affecting the system, the system has no existence outside a context. Thus language cannot be abstracted from time and space, or from the extralinguistic dimensions of the situation in which it is embedded. Just as modern biologists regard even simple organisms' behaviour as produced by incredibly complex interactions of genetic and environmental phenomena, so even the simplest linguistic exchange involves a constellation of factors – linguistic, contextual, social and so on – which is always more than the sum of its parts. And this also implies, of course, that meaning is radically indeterminate and variable.

(Cameron 1992: 192)

Alongside this problematization of language, gender as a social category has increasingly been rendered problematical. Recent studies emphasize the socially constructed nature of gender, and tend to see this as context-dependent, relatively fluid and variable (for examples, see the papers in Bergvall *et al.* 1996; Hall and Bucholtz 1995; Johnson and Meinhof 1997). In a discussion of language and masculinity, Sally Johnson argues:

Work within pro-feminist approaches to masculinity has explored men in terms of 'multiple subjectivities', and this has led writers to abandon the idea of 'masculinity' in the singular, in preference for the pluralized 'masculinities'. The concept of 'male power' is then dislodged by the notion of 'hegemonic' or 'hierarchical' masculinities, perhaps best characterized as those forms of masculinity able to marginalize and dominate not only women, but also other men, on the grounds of, say, class, race and/or sexuality . . .

According to this view of masculinities, where gender identities and power relations are seen as highly contextualized practices, it becomes rather more difficult to make clear and generalizable statements about how men are or what they do.

(Johnson 1997: 19–20; the model of masculinity here is derived from the work of Robert Connell, e.g. Connell 1987 and 1995)

This rather fragmented model of gender has several parallels in work more explicitly related to educational settings – for example, Alison Jones's discussion of the notion of 'girls' in educational research:

the language of discourse and subjectivity offers ways of talking about complexities and contradictions in understanding girls' schooling. However, there are problems. A focus on women's/girls' multiple and fragmented experience calls into question any straightforward – and compelling – notion of power, and it also challenges the use of the term 'girls' in educational research.

(Jones 1993: 157)

Both Johnson and Jones are trying to work with a model of gender that is internally differentiated (so that 'masculinity' and 'girlhood' are seen as plural and diverse). Both researchers, however, discuss fairly well-documented factors that distinguish different forms of femininity/masculinity. Jones asks when, in New Zealand, it is appropriate to talk about 'girls' and when about 'Maori girls'. Johnson mentions distinctions between men, made on the basis of 'class, race and/or sexuality'. We are left with categories that still seem a little too solid and obvious. A socially constructed, fluid and context-dependent model of gender would suggest that several aspects of a speaker's identity, not all readily specifiable, would be bound up with their language behaviour, and that any combination of these might be salient on a certain occasion.

In terms of linguistic research, as in other areas, such a model leads researchers not to start with gender, or any other aspect of identity, as a 'given', but to focus instead on how a person's sense of identity, and their relations with others, are worked out in interaction – the moment-by-moment negotiation of gender, and/or race, power, or whatever. The use of phrases such as 'doing gender' indicate that gender is seen as a process, rather than as a fixed category that somehow 'explains' language behaviour. Despite the attractiveness of this approach, however, it poses a number of challenges for empirical enquiry. In practice, language researchers do not, and probably cannot, dispense with gender as an a priori explanatory category. The perception that someone is 'doing gender' (or masculinity, or an aspect of masculinity) seems necessarily to depend upon an observer's prior assumptions about the potential salience of gender/masculinity. (This point is discussed more fully in Swann 1997.)

There are further challenges in relation to educational policy and practice. Whereas earlier approaches to language and gender seemed able to articulate fairly readily with the practices and policy making of the day, these more recent approaches sit uneasily alongside current educational debate and policy-making. There seems, in fact, to be a divergence of interests. Research that takes on board complex, and highly contextualized models of language and gender will be wary of 'quick and easy' generalizations about gendered language behaviour. On the other hand, in the current educational climate, with its emphasis on the speedy identification of problems (such as 'underachievement') and the provision of immediate and straightforward solutions, some research interests will appear, at least, rather esoteric.[4]

It is not immediately clear how researchers should respond in this situation. Ian Stronach and Maggie MacLure, in a discussion of postmodernism in educational research, argue strongly against giving in to what they term 'populist rhetorics':

At a time when the English educational research community is contemplating setting up a charter to enhance its status by policing its membership, standards and practices (Deem 1996), and issuing admonitions to researchers who fail to 'write in a readily understood language' (Bassey 1993: 21)[5] it seems to us that a better strategy for educational research might be to see how far it can get by failing to deliver simple truths. Such calls for 'clarity' (see also Ranson 1996) fail to address the possibility that some forms of plain speaking amount to a surrender to populist rhetorics about education.

(Stronach and MacLure 1997: 6)

In strategic terms, however, this relatively 'purist' stance runs the risk of being ineffectual. Whether (and if so, how) researchers, including language researchers, should seek some accommodation with educational policy interests that they may find uncomfortable is clearly a matter for continuing debate.

New forms of communication

So far, I have focused on gender issues in what might be termed 'traditional' forms of language behaviour: face-to-face spoken interaction and, to a lesser extent, reading and writing. There is, however, a growing interest, within 'language and gender' research, in various forms of electronic, or computer-mediated communication (CMC). These relatively new forms of communication offer alternative possibilities for interaction between people that, some would argue, subvert traditional notions of personal and social identity. Their use in education may also challenge conventional hierarchies and transform teaching and learning practices.

CMC has given rise to a wide range of diverse texts and practices. Some of these, such as e-mail, electronic discussion lists and computer conferences, while they use the written mode, have been found to include some of the properties of spoken language (e.g. Yates 1996). There are differences, however, between CMC and face-to-face communication. Many of the cues that accompany face-to-face communication are lost electronically: contributors to an electronic discussion list cannot see the people they are talking to and cannot hear the way they speak. There has been some speculation about whether this relatively new form of communication might therefore transform traditional interpersonal relations, including gender relations; or on the other hand whether it might simply reinforce existing gendered practices.

Some commentators (e.g. McAdams 1996) have suggested that, because there are no obvious indicators of a person's gender on-line, gender can be a matter of choice. Sherry Turkle (1995) also discusses highly complex behaviour among student computer users in the United States, who may have several windows open on their machines at the same time, interacting in the form of different personae in different windows. Such personae may be gendered in a variety of ways, or their gender may be uncertain. Turkle comments that many users feel they are taking on different identities as they interact in each window on their computer screen.

Dale Spender, an influential contributor to earlier debates about gender and language, draws a favourable comparison between certain uses of CMC and the kinds of talk traditionally associated with female speakers, such as 'gossip' and chat (emphasized in the title of her book, *Nattering on the Net*). Spender is also enthusiastic about the potential of the computer to revolutionize information exchange, 'knowledge making' and interpersonal relations within education. She sees the use of computers as, potentially, a liberating development, with students able to access huge amounts of information and use this to their own ends, without the gatekeeping function of educational institutions. Spender compares the scope of the changes brought about by the 'electronic era' with the earlier transition from manuscripts to printing; our beliefs about what constitutes knowledge, about teaching and about learning, she argues, will require radical restructuring. She gives the example of a school in Australia, where the provision of personal laptop computers to students led to greater enthusiasm and sharing of ideas, but also changed students' approaches to learning, teaching practices, teacher–student relations, subject boundaries and the overall organization of the school.

On the evidence so far, CMC would seem, at least for some, to function as an archetypally postmodern medium that allows people considerable flexibility in how they present themselves to others, and in the terms on which they interact with others. It poses severe challenges to the notion of discrete personal identity, allowing a kind of 'identity-hopping' that would be difficult to match in face-to-face communication. Within education, it is set to revolutionize learning, as well as interpersonal relations. In this new context, traditional gender relations might seem increasingly irrelevant.

A note of caution, however, is sounded by Spender herself. She argues that women who use the Internet have to contend with 'the men who are already there: the men who have written the rules of the road' (1995: 192). Spender argues that men's electronic interactional dominance may be similar to their dominance in face-to-face interactions. They may, in fact, behave in a more abusive way in contexts in which they are guaranteed anonymity (she gives several examples of electronic sexual harassment).

There has been a limited number of empirical studies of gender and interaction in electronic communication (none yet, as far as I know, involving students in educational settings). Such evidence as is available suggests that, at least when people communicate overtly as female or male, relations are surprisingly traditional. Studies of communication styles in electronic discussion lists give rise to a sense of *déjà vu*, with accounts of male dominance and assertive or aggressive interactional behaviour that bear a remarkable similarity to studies of face-to-face communication carried out in the 1970s and 1980s.

Susan Herring (1993) claims that, despite suggestions that CMC might encourage democratic participation from contributors, in practice men dominate electronic interaction – they 'talk' more, take an 'authoritative stance' in public discourse, and frequently harass or intimidate women. In a later study, Herring, Johnson and DiBenedetto (1995) focus on occasions when women took control of the discourse in two electronic discussion lists. They argue that male participants used various strategies (e.g. ignoring a contribution or diverting attention away from it) to silence the women and to regain control of the interaction. (This behaviour may have been related to the subject matter – in each case, aspects of sexism.)

Other researchers have produced similar findings. Margie Wylie, for instance, reports that in electronic discussions:

> More often than not . . . women's ideas are simply met by silence from men and women alike. A female-initiated subject gets roughly less than a third of the replies that a male-initiated thread does . . . And even women-initiated threads that survive are taken over by men . . . so the eventual fate of the conversation isn't guided by women. What's more, men tend to post longer messages more frequently.
>
> (Wylie 1995, cited Spender 1995: 197)

Within education there is also a need to address female students' relative exclusion from this medium. There is well-documented evidence, going back over several years, of girls' low take-up of computing, and of boys' dominance of computing resources where these are meant to be available to all in the classroom (e.g. Beynon 1993; Culley 1988; Hoyles and Sutherland 1989). As familiarity with computing becomes more essential, considerable concern has been expressed about girls' potential disadvantage in this area. Dale Spender speculates on whether new communication practices may actually reverse girls' educational achievements and swing the balance back in favour of boys:

> After five hundred years, women were just beginning to look as though they were drawing even with the men. They have reached the stage in countries like Australia where, for the first time, more women than men have been gaining higher education qualifications. But this success has been achieved in an education system still based on print, where the skills needed to succeed have been reading, writing and memory – all things that women are good at.
>
> And just when it looks as though equity is about to be realised – the rules of the game are changed. The society (and soon, the education system) switches to the electronic medium. And 'everyone' knows that girls are not as good as boys – with machines!
>
> (Spender 1995: 185)

While CMC offers startlingly new opportunities, then, it also raises some rather 'old' concerns about gender differences and inequalities. At issue, as electronic forms of communication become more prevalent in education, is whether they are likely to offer a range of alternative positions to both girls and boys; or whether, as Spender suggests, they will reinforce traditional gender inequalities, reversing the trend towards girls' educational success and boys' (relative) 'underachievement'.

Conclusion

I have tried to broaden out from a narrow focus on 'underachievement' to look at girls' and boys' language use in more general terms, and to ask to what extent perceived gender differences in language might be said to disadvantage girls or boys. Traditional interpretations of girls' and boys' language use have been fairly clear on this point. To take spoken language as an example, features of language have been identified that are associated either with girls or with boys. In many cases, gender-differentiated use of language has been seen as disadvantageous to girls (for instance, boys' 'dominant' behaviour along with girls' 'supportive' behaviour mean that girls have less opportunity to contribute to discussion). The recent focus on boys' 'underachievement', however, may lead to the reinterpretation of boys' behaviour, seeing this as posing problems for boys themselves.

Such judgements rest, at least by implication, on a relatively undifferentiated notion of gender and a relatively fixed view of the meaning, or function of language. They downplay differences between girls and between boys, as well as the complexity of how people relate to one another in specific contexts. Research on electronic forms of communication runs this risk as much as research on more traditional language use. The empirical observations of CMC that I discuss above seemed to hark back, in some respects, to earlier preoccupations among researchers studying face-to-face communication. (Such research is, of course, looking at new forms of communication, and in this case it may be useful to establish fairly general patterns of behaviour before exploring more subtle aspects of interaction.)

More contextualized approaches to language and gender provide a useful emphasis on the provisional and often uncertain nature of any interpretation of language meaning, as well as challenging any straightfoward dichotomy between 'girls' and 'boys' (or 'women' and 'men'). Within education, for instance, one might be led to look more closely at boys' verbally 'dominant' behaviour (whether face-to-face or electronic): to explore how different boys behave in specific classroom contexts, and to what ends. Such approaches do, however, pose problems of their own for empirical research – for instance, they may lead to some analytical uncertainty about whether gender (or any other aspect of identity) is salient in an interaction. At worst, we may seem to be left with a set of context-specific individualisms. Without wishing to return to monolithic perceptions of masculinity/femininity, or of language, it seems important to undertake at least some reconstruction work: within educational and other forms of research, to try to identify both differences and commonalities, and to establish connections and continuities between individuals and contexts.

Notes

1 This chapter focuses on the educational implications of language and gender re-search. More general overviews of the field can be found in Coates (1993), Crawford (1995), and Graddol and Swann (1989).
2 I have discussed elsewhere (Swann and Graddol 1995) the extent to which this may be considered a process of 'feminization'.
3 I am using the term 'postmodernist' quite loosely here, to refer to a general shift in conceptions of language and gender. Some researchers draw directly and explicitly on postmodernist or post-structuralist theories; others do not, but the models of language and gender they adopt are similar.
4 I am referring here to the situation in Britain. Recent publications from Australia (e.g. Alloway 1995; Gilbert 1994) suggest that policy contexts elsewhere may, to some extent, be more favourable to current research interests.
5 These references are to contributions to *Research Intelligence*, the newsletter of the British Educational Research Association (BERA).

References

Alloway, N. (1995) *Foundation Stones: The Construction of Gender in Early Childhood.* Carlton Vic: Curriculum Corporation.

Barrs, M. (1993) Introduction: reading the difference, in M. Barrs and S. Pidgeon (eds) *Reading the Difference.* London: Centre for Language in Primary Education.

Bassey, M. (1993) Some FRIPPERIES AND FLAWS of research papers suggested by Michael Bassey. *Research Intelligence*, 48(Winter): 21.

Bergvall, V. L., Bing, J. M. and Freed, A. F. (eds) (1996) *Rethinking Language and Gender Research.* Harlow: Longman.

Beynon, J. (1993) Computers, dominant boys and invisible girls: or, 'Hannah, it's not a toaster, it's a computer!', in J. Beynon and H. Mackay (eds) *Computers into Class-rooms: More Questions than Answers.* London: Falmer.

Bousted, M. (1989) Who talks? *English in Education*, 23: 41–51.

Cameron, D. (1992) *Feminism and Linguistic Theory*, 2nd edn. London: Macmillan.

Claire, H. (1986) Collaborative work as an anti-sexist process, in C. Adams (ed.) *Primary Matters: Some Approaches to Equal Opportunities in the Primary School.* London: ILEA.

Coates, J. (1993) *Women, Men and Language*, 2nd edn. Harlow: Longman.

Coates, J. (1996) *Women Talk.* Oxford: Blackwell Publishers.

Connell, R. W. (1987) *Gender and Power: Society, the Person and Sexual Politics.* Cambridge: Polity Press.

Connell, R. W. (1995) *Masculinities.* Cambridge: Polity Press.

Crawford, M. (1995) *Talking Difference: On Gender and Language.* London: Sage Publications.

Culley, L. (1988) Girls, boys and computers. *Educational Studies*, 13: 3–8.

Deem, R. (1996) BERA Council Consultation: chartered status for educational researchers? *Research Intelligence* (Newsletter of the British Educational Research Association), 56(April): 22.

Department for Education and the Welsh Office [DfE/WO] (1995) *English in the National Curriculum.* London: HMSO.

Department of Education and Science and the Welsh Office [DES/WO] (1989) *English for Ages 5–16: Proposals of the Secretary of State for Education and Science and the Secretary of State for Wales* [Cox Report]. London: Department of Education and Science and the Welsh Office.

Gilbert, P. (1994) *Divided by a Common Language? Gender and the English Curriculum.* Carlton Vic: Curriculum Corporation.

Graddol, D. and Swann, J. (1989) *Gender Voices.* Oxford: Blackwell.

Hall, K. and Bucholtz, M. (eds) (1995) *Gender Articulated: Language and the Socially-Constructed Self.* New York and London: Routledge.

Herring, S. (1993) Gender and democracy in computer-mediated communication. *Electronic Journal of Communication*, 3; repr. in R. Kling (ed.) *Computerization and Controversy*, 2nd edn. New York: Academic Press, 1996.

Herring, S., Johnson, D. A. and DiBenedetto, T. (1995) 'This discussion is going too far': male resistance to female participation on the internet, in K. Hall and M. Bucholtz (eds) *Gender Articulated: Language and the Socially-Constructed Self.* New York and London: Routledge.

Holmes, J. (1994) Improving the lot of female language learners, in J. Sunderland (ed.) *Exploring Gender: Questions and Implications for English Language Education.* London: Prentice Hall.

Hordyk, A. (1986) Assertion and confidence training with girls, in C. Adams (ed.) *Secondary Issues: Some Approaches to Equal Opportunities in Secondary Schools.* London: ILEA.

Hoyles, C. and Sutherland, R. (1989) *Logo Mathematics in the Classroom.* London: Routledge.

Johnson, J. (1990) What is the project saying about assessment? *Oracy Issues*, no. 5: 1–4.

Johnson, S. (1997) Theorizing language and masculinity: a feminist perspective, in S. Johnson and U. Meinhof (eds) *Language and Masculinity.* Oxford: Blackwell.

Johnson, S. and Meinhof, U. (eds) (1997) *Language and Masculinity.* Oxford: Blackwell Publishers.

Jones, A. (1993) Becoming a 'girl': post-structuralist suggestions for educational research. *Gender and Education*, 5: 157–66.

McAdams, M. (1996) Gender without bodies. *Computer-Mediated Communication Magazine*, 1 March.

Moss, G. (1989) *Un/Popular Fictions.* London: Virago.

National Curriculum Council [NCC] (1989) *English Key Stage 1: Non-Statutory Guidance.* York: NCC.

Office for Standards in Education [Ofsted] (1993) *Boys and English.* London: Ofsted.

Ranson, S. (1996) The future of educational research: learning at the centre. *British Educational Research Journal*, 22(5): 523–35.

Reay, D. (1993) 'He doesn't like you, Miss!': working with boys in an infant classroom, in H. Claire, J. Maybin and J. Swann (eds) *Equality Matters: Case Studies from the Primary School.* Clevedon: Multilingual Matters.

Spender, D. (1982) *Invisible Women: The Schooling Scandal.* London: Writers and Readers Publishing Cooperative.

Spender, D. (1995) *Nattering on the Net: Women, Power and Cyberspace.* North Melbourne: Spinifex Press.

Stronach, I. and MacLure, M. (1997) *Educational Research Undone: The Postmodern Embrace.* Buckingham: Open University Press.

Swann, J. (1992) *Girls, Boys and Language*. Oxford: Blackwell.

Swann, J. (1993) Assessing language, in H. Claire, J. Maybin and J. Swann (eds) *Equality Matters: Case Studies from the Primary School*. Clevedon: Multilingual Matters.

Swann, J. (1997) Yes, but is it gender? Paper presented at conference on Language and Gender, University of Lancaster, July.

Swann, J. and Graddol, D. (1995) The feminization of classroom discourse?, in S. Mills (ed.) *Language and Gender: Interdisciplinary Perspectives*. London: Longman.

Swann, J. with Brown, G. and MacLure, M. (1992) *Assessing Speaking and Listening*. CLIE Working Papers in Linguistics. London: Committee for Linguistics in Education.

Turkle, S. (1995) *Life on the Screen: Identity in the Age of the Internet*. New York: Simon and Schuster.

White, J. (1986) The writing on the wall: beginning or end of a girl's career? *Women's Studies International Forum*, 9: 561–74.

Wilkinson, A. with Davies, A. and Atkinson, D. (1965) Spoken English, *University of Birmingham Educational Review*, Occasional Papers 2.

Wilkinson, A., Davies, A. and Berrill, D. (1990) *Spoken English Illuminated*. Buckingham: Open University Press.

Wylie, M. (1995) No place for women. *Digital Media*, 4(January).

Yates, S. (1996) Computer-mediated English: sociolinguistic aspects of computer-mediated communication, in J. Maybin and N. Mercer (eds) *Using English: from Conversation to Canon*. London: Routledge in association with the Open University.

10

Gendered learning outside and inside school: influences on achievement

PATRICIA MURPHY AND JANNETTE ELWOOD

Introduction

The divergence in girls' and boys' interests and pastimes outside of school has been established by many national and international studies. What has rarely been examined is how these gender differences emerge and their consequences for students' learning both within and without school. The issues considered in this chapter is not what girls and boys can or cannot do but what it is that girls and boys *choose* to do; what lies behind their choices; and how gendered choices influence achievement. To address this, we examine the sources and nature of gender differences and how they are related to learning outside of school and learning in school. The chapter concludes by looking at the way achievement is defined in subjects, how these definitions shift between the phases of education and the consequences of this for how 'girls' and 'boys' as groups are perceived both by teachers and students.

Background

Research into sex differences in intellectual abilities continues to show a female superiority on certain verbal abilities. The female advantage is largest for pre-school and adult samples. In relation to quantitative abilities, evidence indicates a male superiority which emerges in adolescence and appears to increase particularly on tests of mathematical problem solving. These findings remain controversial as the measures and the samples used vary between studies and over time (Gipps and Murphy 1994; Halpern 1992). A consistent finding however, is that the similarities in males' and females' performance far outweigh any differences observed. Many of the major reviews of studies into cognitive sex differences have revealed empirical trends in the size and extent of differences (Hyde and Linn 1988; Hyde, Fennama and Lamon 1990). Findings such as these have been seen to provide support for psychosocial explanations for gender differences in performance.

The social and psychological factors cited to explain gender differences are derived from the different socialization processes that research indicates girls and boys experience from birth. Wilder and Powell's (1989) review of the research in this regard is particularly useful. Briefly, their review highlights the different ways parents respond to boys and girls and encourage them to interact with the world and with people.

Parents' expectations differ for boys and girls. These different expectations are reflected in the activities and toys they provide for them and in their reactions to them. Consequently, boys and girls engage in different hobbies and pastimes from an early age, and their interests continue to diverge with age. An outcome of these different socialization patterns is that children develop different ways of responding to the world and making sense of it, ways which influence how they learn and what they learn. These different treatments also influence children's views of what constitutes appropriate behaviours for them and what others' expectations of them are.

Clearly parents are not a homogeneous group nor are children passive in this process. Other adults and children are also influential, as is the media and market pressures. How does this general picture relate to what young children do and what might be the consequences for children entering school?

Gender differences and the pre-school child

Browne and Ross (1991) concluded from observations of a large number of pre-school children that from a very young age children develop clear ideas about what girls do and what boys do. The activities girls choose to take part in more than boys were labelled by Browne and Ross as *creative*. Boys on the other hand opted for *constructional* activities.

In a more recent study (Murphy 1997) pre-school staff in day-care centres were interviewed about their perceptions of gender differences. Some key findings emerged that overlap with Browne and Ross's observations and extend them. For example, staff talked of the importance of role play for children aged 2 to 4 years but commented on the differences between girls' and boys' preferred roles:

> You see the maternal instinct in girls from a very early age and this does tend to motivate their play.

> Boys bring their own agendas – they get into some very active, very physically involved games – they do a lot of role play.

Boys like to be people in authority, policemen, fire fighters or super heroes.

(Murphy 1997: 120)

In playing out different roles children automatically become involved in the activities related to the role. These activities in turn afford children with different learning opportunities. For example, how a mother might interact with the environment will be very different from the way a firefighter or super hero interacts. The roles children play also involve them in dressing up. What constitutes an appropriate costume will vary depending on the role. As one member of staff observed, girls like to be the 'grand ladies'. Clearly the needs of a grand lady differ from those of Batman so children from a very early age are paying attention to different details and developing a different view of salience.

Role play also engages children in talk. Again the kind of talk will vary with the role. If one imagines a mother–child discussion and compares it with an exchange between a policeman and a 'baddie' it is clear that during role play children will practise different types of talk. A recent study of pre-schoolers' communication style found significant gender differences (Thompson 1994). In particular girls' and boys' talk in terms of help seeking were found to vary dramatically. When children were observed making jigsaw puzzles, it was found that girls more than boys said such things as 'I can't do this', 'Will you do this one?', 'Where does this piece go?' However there were no differences in girls' and boys' ability to solve the puzzles. When adults were shown videos of the children, they were of the opinion that the girls were less confident than the boys and believed boys' performance to be superior to girls'. Girls' equivalent performance was later put down to 'luck'. Thompson (1994: 129) suggests that when 'communicative style does not reflect ability, observer bias seems very likely to occur'. Furthermore, 'adults' beliefs about the ability of girls particularly at the early developmental ages, may not come in the form of overt disapproval but more often will occur as a subtle shaping of the children's self-concepts' (Thompson 1994: 129).

Emerging from the interviews in Murphy's study was a picture of the boy whose interests had to be either captured or suppressed. In contrast, girls' predispositions were considered more congruent with typical nursery activities. There was a consensus among staff about young boys' interest in mechanical things: 'As soon as you have a sort of machinery, gears or something, the boys are interested straightaway' (Murphy 1997: 121).

These interests were then exploited to get boys interested in reading and were developed to maintain their interest in other activities. Two potential effects arise from this. First, it can orientate boys towards particular experiences and to observing only certain aspects of their environment and phenomena within it. Second, because books about vehicles and structures are usually written in a particular style, from an early age boys may be involved with different types of text from girls. It was evident from the study that girls' lack of interest in mechanical things was not considered problematic for them. Although one teacher observed about boys' interests 'I think it inclines them more to the sort of mathematical side of things, science' (Murphy 1997: 122).

Girls' interests were characterized by staff in similar ways to Browne and Ross:

> Girls are much more interested in drawing and as a result quite often are more forward than boys when it comes to using pencils and scissors.

> Girls seem to enjoy the colours and the process of drawing. Boys just aren't interested.
>
> (Murphy 1997: 122)

Here girls' interests are also focusing them on different aspects of their environment and engendering the development of particular skills. When asked if boys and girls went to school equally well prepared, most staff were not sure but some clearly felt that boys were at a disadvantage.

Reception classes in England are increasingly dominated by the requirement for children to learn the basics of reading, writing and numeracy (Thornton 1990). If boys go to school having taken longer than girls to settle to listening to stories and with an interest in information type books already developed then it is likely that they will find the reading schemes for young children, based largely on stories about people, harder to access. Similarly, boys' less-developed skills with using pencils may put them at an initial disadvantage when beginning to write. Baseline assessment of children in school reveals a close correspondence between girls' preferred activities and achievement (Arnot *et al.* 1996). The largest performance gaps in favour of girls were in the areas of social skills, letter identification, writing and drawing. The implication of these gender differences discussed is that boys entering school are potentially more vulnerable than girls to becoming disaffected. As Walkerdine commented from her study of nursery schools, 'classroom practices, then, might be for boys a site of struggle where they must work to redefine the situation as one in which the women and girls are powerless subjects of other discourses' (1989: 71).

Davies and Brember's (1995) longitudinal study of children's attitudes in six primary schools in England found that while all infant children were positive about school, girls were more positive than boys. The only topics where boys were more interested than girls in infant school included 'weighing and measuring', 'games' and 'listening to the teacher read'. Browne and Ross (1991) observed that children in infant classes continued to pursue their gendered interests even when participating in the same activity. Girls and boys observed playing with Lego (a construction kit) were found for example to make different things. Girls made houses and boys made vehicles or guns using the wheels and rotatable connections in the kits. Browne and Ross commented that boys were using constructional materials in schools in sophisticated ways incorporating movable parts and focusing on movement and balance. Girls on the other hand were observed to make simple structures as a 'foil for social play'. Thus both boys and girls continue to develop their pre-school interests and learning in school. These observations were consistent across 'cultural and social groups' (Browne and Ross 1991: 46).

Gender effects in performance: evidence from national surveys

In Murphy and Elwood (1998) a review of national and international survey findings established systematic gender effects across countries in relation to the types of measures used. Shifts in the size of this effect over time also supported the view that sociocultural factors were at play. This was reinforced by the absence or reversal of the patterns in certain countries where different curricula and cultural contexts obtain. A great deal of research has been, and continues to be, undertaken to explain measured gender differences in performance. However, very little research has examined these gender differences at the level of item characteristics. At this level of analysis it is possible to discern systematic effects unrelated to the achievement purported to be being assessed or to the abilities of the students.

Both UK (Assessment and Performance Unit) and US (National Assessment of Educational Progress) surveys showed that girls' and boys' experiences of scientific equipment and apparatus out of school differed. Where gender differences in the use of apparatus arose in the surveys they were in favour of boys and for precisely those instruments which boys reported more experience of outside school (DES 1988a, 1988b). These performance differences increased in range and magnitude as students progressed through school (Johnson and Murphy 1986).

The Davies and Brember (1995) study referred to above, found that boys' early interest in school in 'weighing and measuring' continued through primary school. The Assessment and Performance Unit (APU) maths surveys also found that 15-year-old-boys' performance was superior to girls' on tests of measures which included 'units and mensuration' (Foxman *et al.* 1985). However this performance difference disappeared in later surveys when students were *asked* to use particular instruments rather than being expected to choose the appropriate instrument (Foxman *et al.* 1991). The different experiences students acquire not only affect the skills and knowledge they develop but also their understanding of the situations and problems in which to apply them. For example, boys in the APU science surveys were better able than girls at ages 13 and 15 to use ammeters and voltmeters yet they did not report experience of these instruments outside of school. Boys, however, continue to play more than girls with electrical toys and gadgets outside of school. Such play allows boys to familiarize themselves with the effects of electricity and to develop a tacit understanding of how it can be controlled.

Confidence and alienation

Browne and Ross (1991) refer to gender domains and discuss the effect on children when placed in situations which were perceived by them as out of their 'territory'. In situations which children perceived to be part of their territories they behaved with confidence, whereas being out of territory rendered them diffident. Children's early years experiences are crucial in forming their perceptions of what constitutes 'girls'' and 'boys'' domains.

The APU science surveys used 600–800 questions at each age. Spanning the question banks revealed that patterns in gender differences occurred in ways not associated with the tasks set. Questions were labelled by several dimensions, one of which was referred to as the content, that is, what the task was about. For example the task for the student might be to interpret a table of data but the content could be to do with spare parts for cars or the ingredients and nutritional values of a snack bar.

The APU results showed that girls and boys reacted to the same content differently irrespective of the task. Questions which involved content related to health, reproduction, nutrition, and domestic situations were generally found to show girls performing at a higher level than boys across the ages. It was also the case that more girls than boys would attempt such questions. Hence the gender gap in performance arose because of the increased confidence of girls combined with the lower response rate of boys. In questions where the content was more overtly 'masculine' the converse occurred. Typical 'masculine' contents included cars, building sites, submarines, machinery and so on. Talking to students revealed that they had definite views about content areas where they expected to be competent and content areas where they anticipated failure. Many boys and girls typically avoided those contents which they judged were outside their realm of competence – their territory.

Exactly the same response was found with questions involving electrical content where girls more than boys anticipated failure. In the APU practical investigation tasks, although girls were found to be equally as competent as boys, more girls than boys lacked confidence in handling the equipment. This effect has been linked to observations of boys' and girls' behaviours in laboratories where boys typically dominate the use of apparatus and equipment (Whyte 1986).

In a recent study of differential performance at 18 plus, A level physics teachers overwhelmingly identified electrical circuits, electromagnetism and mechanics as areas more difficult for females than males, indicating that these differences in experience continued to influence both teachers' and students' perceptions (Elwood and Comber 1996).

The content-related performance effects can be traced to the different learning opportunities that children's gendered play affords them. As children engage with activities outside of school, they develop skills, knowledge and confidence in them. Faced with similar activities in school, children tackle them with confidence. However, faced with features of activities they judge to be outside their gendered domain of competence leads children to withdraw from them. Hence children unwittingly build on the strengths and interests they bring to school and continue to develop them both within and out of school. The downside of this is that children's alienation from certain content areas is similarly unremarked by children and teachers alike. It is very difficult to observe the effects of children's withdrawal from learning activities. They may appear to be pursuing an activity but actually have a very low level of cognitive engagement with it. Task engagement is an essential prerequisite for learning. Unfortunately lack of confidence is all too often interpreted as a lack of ability. Consequently the effects of alienation go unchecked and lead to underachievement as children 'opt out' of certain learning opportunities.

Gendered views of salience

Earlier in the chapter it was noted how children's play led them to attend to different features in phenomena. Girls across the ages in the APU science surveys were found to outperform boys consistently on the practical tests of making and interpreting observations. It was not the case that girls' perform-ance was higher than boys' across all tasks. Indeed closer review revealed that girls more than boys took note of colours, sounds, smells and texture, while boys, on the other hand, took note of structural details. Thus when asked to observe phenomena or objects and events without any cues as to what was salient, girls as a group and boys as a group paid attention to different details given the *same* circumstances. A review of gender differences at 15 years of age in the APU design and technology survey showed that on tasks of a quite different nature but which similarly allowed students to determine what was salient, girls again focused on *aesthetic variables* and empathized with users' needs. Boys more than girls focused on *manufacturing issues* and were more competent than girls in their application of knowledge of *structures* (Kimbell *et al.* 1991). These findings show a close correspond-ence with those in science. Girls' and boys' observations indicate their differing views of relevance rather than competence. For example, if boys were directed to observe sounds and so on, they were perfectly capable of doing so, but the relevance of these observations had to be pointed out more often for boys than for girls.

Research into the nature of observation has demonstrated that observers pay attention only to those objects or features that are familiar to them. When people observe, there is always more information than they take note of. Observation is fundamentally a selection process. Our knowledge of the world, our expectations and our purpose for observing all influence the selections we make and the sense we make of them. Students' gendered socialization influences what becomes 'familiar' to them. Just as it is difficult to detect content effects it is very difficult for teachers to be aware of students' differing perceptions of what is 'familiar' and how this in turn might influence their learning. Students and teachers alike need strategies to identify the way they filter and select data in different circumstances. A simple strategy which has been used to this end (Murphy 1991a) is to set students open tasks to elicit their initial perceptions of what might be salient.

For example, one task asked students to imagine they were designing a boat to go around the world; another asked them to design a vehicle of their choice. They were told in both cases to give details of things they thought were important. The students' designs covered a wide range, but primary and lower secondary girls' and boys' responses reflected different views of salience. The boys designed powerboats, battleships, army-type vehicles, secret agent transport and sports cars. The girls mainly chose cruise ships and family cars for travelling, agricultural machines or children's play vehicles. The detail the boys included varied but generally there was elaborate weaponry and next to no living facilities but detailed mechanisms. The girls' designs focused on social, domestic details but rarely included mechanisms. Using such responses as stimuli for discussion can open up to children and teachers how they view the world and others' alternative perceptions of it.

In another such task primary children were involved in a language lesson looking at different forms of writing for different purposes (Murphy 1991b). The teacher had selected estate agents' use of language when selling houses as a focus of study. Prior to showing children typical estate agents' literature the children were given the opportunity to be estate agents first. Again there were striking differences in the detail children considered relevant in their houses which was also evident in their written descriptions of the selling points of their houses. The girls focused on aesthetic and domestic issues in contrast to boys' focus on structures and 'masculine' spheres of activity, for example, garage space for cars.

The APU surveys found that girls more than boys tend to value the circumstances in which tasks are set and take account of them when constructing meaning in the task. They do not abstract issues from their context. Conversely, as a group, boys tend to consider issues in isolation and judge the content and context to be irrelevant (Murphy 1991a). The consequences are that girls and boys perceive different problems and solutions to them – given the same set of circumstances. Again it is difficult for teachers to recognize when such a gender effect occurs and the consequences of it for students' learning.

The task in Figure 10.1 was given to a class of 9–10 year olds as part of the normal work in science. The scenario of dissolving sugar in tea was the context for the task in the box. A mixed group of three children was observed tackling the task. It became clear that the girl in the group (Rachel) took the context and integrated it into her task. She was trying to find out the time taken for sugar to dissolve in tea under 'normal', that is, domestic circumstances. One boy in the group (Billy) paid no attention to the 'tea

Figure 10.1   Science task given to 9 to 10-year-olds

Dissolving

Molly always teased her dad that he would stir a hole into the bottom of his teacup. He said that he wanted to make sure the sugar had dissolved properly. Molly suggested that if he put the sugar into the tea as soon as it was poured (instead of five minutes later), it would dissolve quicker and not need so much stirring.

Find out how the time taken for sugar to dissolve depends on the temperature of the liquid.

Check that your investigation is sensible – for instance, use reasonable temperatures and use a reasonable amount of sugar for each test.

When you have finished, write a short account of what you did. Did you stir the tea? Explain why you did this (or didn't do it).

---

drinking' context. He did not reject it, it just had no salience as far as he was concerned. For him the task in the box was a 'science' task and so he wanted to test a range of temperatures starting with a low temperature. The girl disagreed as it made no sense to her in terms of Molly and her father's dilemma. As she said on numerous occasions 'Nobody drinks cold tea.' Neither the boy nor the teacher could understand the girl's perception of the task. The teacher intervened and directed the group to do the 'science' task, that is, Billy's task. The teacher in interview described his concern about Rachel's behaviour, labelling her as being 'difficult and quirky'. For Rachel who had to pursue a task the purpose of which she could not understand, the experience was profoundly alienating as she reported in interview (Murphy *et al.* 1996). Cooper's (1996: 7) research similarly reveals the effects of context on performance and he suggests that the effects may be 'systematically distributed across the socio-economic structure'.

In science and in mathematics 'realistic settings', as Cooper (1996) refers to them, are increasingly used to indicate the relevance of subject knowledge and skills in everyday life. However, it is assumed that the relevance is universal, and so interpreted by all students in the same way. To be successful in learning or assessment activities, a prerequisite demand is that students interpret contexts in the same way as that intended by the teacher or the assessor. This assumption fails to take account of sociocultural differences between students. Gender differences in performance in other domains provide further evidence in support of this. For example, while a girl's typical contextualized response might be devalued and misinterpreted in a science and maths situation, the converse occurs in design and technology. The APU surveys in design and technology found, for example that girls were ahead of boys on identifying tasks, and investigating and appraising ideas. Girls, in addition, dramatically outperformed boys on evaluating products. Many assessment tasks in design and technology give value to responses that reflect a broad perspective and which recognize human needs. Boys on the other hand, were ahead of girls at generalizing, an achievement that requires students to abstract from specifics.

Expectations and achievement

In most of the chapter so far, attention has been drawn to the consequences of children's learning out of school for their subsequent achievements in school. In the final sections, consideration is given to the consequences of gender differences for children's evolving attitudes to school and to achievement in domains. Teachers' role in this will also be touched on.

In recent years in England and Wales since the introduction of (a) a national curriculum which reduced students' opportunity to opt for certain subjects at 14 years of age; and (b) the General Certificate of Secondary Education (GCSE) which broadened both the definition of achievement and the means of assessing it for students at 16 years of age; there has been a trend for girls to outperform boys in that girls achieve more GCSE grades A*–C than their male counterparts (Elwood 1995, 1998). Table 10.1 shows the mean difference between male and female performance for each of the major curriculum subjects for 1995.

What these figures show is that in biology only are boys substantially ahead of girls and that the gap is very narrow between the two genders in the traditionally male subjects. Girls are now 8 per cent ahead of boys in terms of the proportion of A*–C grades obtained overall. This gap has been increasing steadily since the introduction of the GCSE in 1988. As a general summary of the overall picture of outcome patterns, these figures challenge the old assumptions about male and female performance in examinations at age 16 and highlight the underachievement of boys relative to girls at this age. Media coverage of these results have made much of this perceived underachievement of boys and have contributed to the growing backlash against girls' success (e.g. Bright 1998; Lepkowska 1998). However, we should be cautious when interpreting these results as they are aggregated from numerous syllabuses, all of which have different result patterns and the figures are even less transparent in relation to certain assessment structures that are used within the public examination system.

Trends such as these are not restricted to the UK context. Concern about the underachievement of boys has been voiced in many countries of the world, recently in the United States and Australia, for example. Davies and Brember (1995) found that by the end of primary schooling girls' and boys'

Table 10.1 Percentage of male/female entry and grades A*–C (all GCSE groups) in main GCSE subjects 1995

Subject	% Entry male	% Entry female	% A*–C male	% A*–C female	Difference % A*–C male–female
Art/Design	50.4	49.6	48.0	66.5	−18.5
Biology	52.5	47.5	78.2	70.6	7.6
Chemistry	62.8	37.2	83.8	84.6	−0.8
Combined science	49.8	50.2	47.2	48.0	−0.8
English	50.2	49.8	48.8	65.7	−16.9
English literature	47.4	52.6	56.8	70.6	−13.8
French	46.8	53.2	42.9	56.2	−13.3
Geography	56.5	43.5	49.5	55.2	−5.7
History	48.6	51.4	51.9	58.5	−6.6
Maths	49.3	50.7	45.5	44.3	1.2
Technology	52.8	47.2	37.6	51.7	−14.1
Physics	65.8	34.2	85.1	85.5	−0.4
All subjects	49.3	50.7	48.9	57.1	−8.2

Source: Southern Examining Group (1995).

attitudes to school had declined. Girls were less positive about mathematics than when they entered school whereas boys' attitudes remained relatively stable. Boys, on the other hand, were less positive than girls about reading and writing. Importantly, the decline in boys' attitudes to school was related to their views of discipline. By the end of primary schooling boys were less keen to observe rules and were less concerned about being reprimanded. Girls, on the other hand, were anxious to do as they were told and to please their teachers.

Barber (1994) also suggests that boys' disaffection with school, in comparison to girls', is related particularly to their motivation to learn. Girls were consistently more positive, better motivated, better at getting on with their teachers and better behaved than boys in their mid-teens. Evidence from interviews with students (Barber 1994) indicates that it is not 'cool' for boys of that age to be seen by their peers as 'achievers'. Boys' greater disaffection with school and lack of motivation has several sources.

Earlier discussion has highlighted the way boys' behaviours, on entering school, are suppressed and judged inappropriate compared with girls'. Girls' conformity, on the other hand, is valued. Unfortunately girls' conformity has been found to influence negatively teachers' perceptions of their ability. The converse has been found for boys. Ebullient, aggressive, risk-taking behaviour is often interpreted as an indicator of high ability.

Girls' conformity has other consequences for their learning. Evidence from classroom interaction studies indicates that girls and boys typically receive different feedback from teachers: teachers' feedback to girls focuses on their work rather than their behaviour whereas the reverse is the case for boys. Randall (1987) looked at pupil–teacher interactions in workshops and laboratories. She found that girls received more attention from teachers than boys. However, the girls' contacts were mainly seeking help and encouragement. Randall found that teachers accepted girls' low confidence and thus reinforced their feelings of helplessness. Dweck *et al.* (1978) found that this leads girls to have low expectations of their abilities and for boys to overestimate theirs. Many studies have found this to be the case (Barber 1994; DES 1989a; 1989b) with lower motivated young males consistently rating their abilities more highly than females. The 'false' sense of competence that some boys have is confronted eventually in schools when teachers have to make decisions about which level of the GCSE to enter students for. Teachers' judgements may therefore have a significant negative impact on some boys' views of schooling towards the end of the secondary phase.

Differential performance at 16 plus

Stobart *et al.* (1992) investigated the reasons for the gap between males and females in the core subjects of mathematics and English at age 16. This study found that in GCSE mathematics, the gender differences in performance which have generally favoured boys, were shown to have steadily decreased to the extent that boys were gaining only 3 per cent more A*–C grades than girls. A major factor to be considered in GCSE mathematics, however, is a scheme of differentiated entry where teachers have to select candidates for different levels of the examination. The differentiated entry system for mathematics has three tiers of entry each with a restricted set of grades: lower tier (grades D–G), middle tier (grades B–F) and higher tier (grades A*–C). Any candidate not achieving the lowest restricted grade on any tier is unclassified.

Stobart *et al.* (1992) hypothesized that different entry policies for boys and girls might contribute to the differences in performance. They suggested two aspects of differentiated entry that might create and influence differential performance. First, more girls than boys are entered for GCSE mathematics. In 1994 an estimated 95 per cent of the 16-year-old cohort entered for mathematics: 98 per cent of girls and 93 per cent of boys at this age. These figures are not unimportant if they represent differences in entry policy that will bear on the interpretation of the data. For example, although boys were gaining 3 per cent more A–C grades than girls, girls might none the less be doing better relative to boys because fewer low-attaining boys than girls were being entered.

Alternatively disaffection with GCSE mathematics was (and still is) increased by restricted grade ranges and tended to be greater among boys than girls. Hence low-motivated boys rather than girls were less likely to be included. Given the established link between motivation and achievement, this could again account for the small male advantage. In reviewing teachers' comments from surveys and case study interviews, Stobart *et al.* (1992) suggest that it was clear that teachers considered boys who were placed in the foundation tier to be less motivated (and as a consequence disruptive) than girls in the same tier. This greater disaffection shown by lower-attaining boys influenced teachers' decisions about whether to enter them at all.

Second, more girls than boys are entered for the middle tier in GCSE mathematics with its maximum grade B. For example, in 1994, nearly 59 per cent of the female entry were entered for the middle tier as opposed to 54 per cent of the male entry, this 5 per cent difference accounting for nearly 21,000 candidates. The larger female entry in the middle tier may represent the underestimation of girls' mathematical abilities by teachers. Stobart *et al.* (1992) found that teachers perceived girls to be less confident and more anxious of failure in mathematics than boys and believed that they are more adversely affected by final examinations. Consequently teachers tended to place girls in the middle tier rather than the higher tier to protect them from such anxiety. The middle tier provides a safety option to accommodate teachers' perceptions of girls' attainment. It offers the key grade C while avoiding the risk of being unclassified if performance drops below that grade on the higher tier.

Research also shows that schools often demand the attainment of a grade C from the higher tier before taking A level mathematics (in fact grades B and A, even A* are often the criteria) (Elwood and Comber 1996). This therefore marginalizes the candidature taking the middle tier from taking their mathematics any further, especially the disproportionate number of girls who are entered for this tier.

Stobart *et al.* (1992) also examined girls' and boys' achievement in GCSE English. At the time of the study girls were achieving 14 per cent more grades A to C than boys. In reviewing students' coursework folders it was illustrated that only a limited number of types of writing were offered for examination, resulting in folders containing stories, descriptions, pieces of writing about personal life and pieces discussing responses to reading fiction. Higher marks were awarded for descriptive, narrative writing. In collating their folders, students confirmed the value of such genres by placing 'narrative' pieces first and 'discursive' pieces at the end. It was common to find girls' folders containing a majority of imaginatively based work and boys' containing more discursive pieces, or pieces which had some clear basis in fact.

Teachers seemed to reward and encourage narrative and descriptive writing over and above factual and analytical work. Overall, writing which drew on the field of personal affection and emotions was more highly valued than that based in a public or political domain. While girls were able to present contrasting areas of experience, there was little incentive for them to do so; when boys' personal writing was less intimate than that of girls there was a perceived undervaluing of their work by teachers. Hence there was bias in both the selection of pieces of coursework for the examination folder and how these pieces were judged.

Styles of expression and achievement

There is evidence that students' performance in English is strongly influenced by learning outside of school. The APU surveys of English (Gorman *et al.* 1988) described girls' preferred style of written response as 'extended, reflective composition'. Boys' style of response was more often episodic, factual and focusing on commentative detail. The APU language surveys found that the students' preferred style of expression reflected their choice of reading material outside of school. At age 11, more boys than girls enjoyed reading works related to hobbies or which involved finding things out. They were also more likely to choose comic books and annuals at home in preference to stories. At age 15, over half the boys compared to one third of the girls said they preferred reading books which gave accurate facts. Twice as many girls than boys liked to read 'to help understand their own and other people's personal problems' (Gorman *et al.* 1988).

The Language team suggested that there was a link between the imbalance in girls' and boys' exposure to different types of reading material and their preferences and skills in writing (Gorman 1987). There is in addition, a link between the pre-school children's interests and teachers' reactions to them already described and their developing interests in particular reading materials. Certain styles of expression are expected in particular subject areas and influence teachers' judgements of students' ability often in ways that misrepresent students' real achievements. While girls appear to be advantaged by this in English, research indicates that the reverse obtains in science. Furthermore, as students progress beyond compulsory education to advanced level study post-16, a shift in performance patterns arise that can again be seen to link achievement to particular styles of response.

Differential performance at 18 plus

Elwood and Comber (1996) investigated the shift in performance patterns that occurs between 16 and 18. At 18, males leave post-compulsory schooling better qualified, as shown by the higher proportion of top grades obtained, than their female counterparts.

The main examination taken by 18 year olds in England and Wales is the General Certificate in Education Advanced Level (GCE A Level). One of the main changes in the GCE A level examination over the last 20 years has been the increase in the proportion of females entering for this examination. In 1995, females made up 54 per cent of the total entry having been only 38 per cent of the total entry in 1970. However, gendered patterns of entry

Table 10.2   Differences in % A–C grades in A level examinations 1990–95, all GCE groups

Subject	Difference in % A–C grades male–female all GCE groups						Mean difference
	1990	1991	1992	1993	1994	1995	1990–95
Biology	2.3	1.8	2.4	0.5	−0.6	−2.0	0.7
Chemistry	2.0	1.3	2.0	1.5	1.0	0.7	1.4
Physics	0.4	1.0	−1.1	−0.9	−1.6	−1.5	−0.6
Maths	1.8	1.2	0.9	−0.4	−1.4	−2.3	−0.0
French	4.0	3.5	5.2	4.6	3.8	4.1	4.2
English literature	2.9	3.5	2.3	1.9	0.9	1.2	2.1
Geography	−0.1	−3.6	−3.5	−2.9	−4.2	−4.9	−3.2
History	5.4	5.0	3.6	3.2	3.0	1.8	3.7
Total all subjects	2.8	2.3	1.5	0.8	0.1	−0.3	1.2

Source: Associated Examining Board (1990–5).

occur in most subjects at this stage when choice is reintroduced. For example, in English and mathematics, when choice is introduced at 18, only 15,000 boys go on to do A level English whereas nearly 200,000 had taken this subject at GCSE. Conversely, in mathematics only 20,000 girls go on to do this subject at A level from the 300,000 who had taken mathematics at GCSE.

Results from A level examinations show males ahead overall; and in certain subjects at the higher grades, where they had been behind at 16. Table 10.2 shows the difference in percentage A–C grades obtained by males and females in eight popular subjects at A level.

The gender differences in outcomes at A level must be interpreted with reference to the entry patterns. For example, in English literature, males outperform females at A level by 3 per cent grades A–C, where females had been ahead by 13 per cent in the same subject at GCSE, yet, males make up only 30 per cent of the candidate entry for English literature. The male entry for this subject is obviously a highly selective group who have indicated a positive choice in opting for this subject. The other side of this coin is the selective female entry in the science subjects. The females who opt for the science subjects at A level perform well, but not as well as would be predicted from their GCSE results. For example, girls are ahead of boys in GCSE physics by 4 per cent grades A*–C but only maintain a gap of 0.4 per cent grades A–C at A level. Males tend to make more progress, especially when GCSE performance is taken into account, between GCSE and A level, than do females (Goldstein and Thomas 1996).

In trying to understand this shift in performance, Elwood and Comber (1996) analysed examination papers and also surveyed and interviewed teachers and students. The differences in performance found on examinations were small and less significant than those found at GCSE, reflecting the more complex items used in the A level examinations. Data from interviews and case studies provided more substantial clues as to why the patterns of performance change between GCSE and A level.

Teachers offered insights into what may be termed *general characteristics* of males and females, those characteristics which were perceived as general attitudes of male and female students. For example, in English literature, mathematics and physics, boys, by comparison with girls, were seen as relatively self-assured, anxiety-free and relatively unperturbed by exams. Girls on the other hand, were perceived to be more motivated and conscientious. However, male confidence did not appear to necessarily equate with teachers' perceptions of greater ability. Teachers tended to see girls as having the edge when asked about specific elements within the syllabus and about day-to-day participation and performance.

A possibility which arises from this distinction between general characteristics and course-specific ability is that the overall style of A level, rather than particular components, may reward certain approaches and responses more than others. This, in turn, may advantage males more than females. Teachers suggested that males were more likely to take risks, were more willing to sound stupid in front of their peers and more likely to go blindly in with understanding not necessarily a priority. Females, on the other hand, were perceived as taking less chances, keen to understand and generally more circumspect. Such attitudes may mean that boys' faith in their own ability to succeed overrides any lack of knowledge or skill, which may develop later. The fact that girls are seen as generally more cautious may result in them being judged to have less command of a subject and thus restrict the level of their achievement.

Elwood and Comber (1996) suggest that it was not untypical for teachers to explain girls' achievement in relation to diligence rather than ability. Teachers' comments regarding the differing success of boys and girls at A level highlight a shift in the way achievement, that is, success, is defined between 16 and 18:

> I hope she doesn't crack up doing A levels . . . I suppose our expectations are that that particular girl over-performed [seven A* grades at GCSE] because she worked too hard. Because she is not brilliant, she's very very good.
>
> (Female English teacher, quoted in Elwood and Comber 1996: 59)

> it's the boys who will come up with something absolutely unique, that I'd never thought of. They suddenly say 'what about this?' while the girls will listen to every single word, and do it exactly along those lines and they won't take risks. They'll produce a very competent, good piece of work, but it hasn't got that sparkle.
>
> (Female maths teacher, quoted in Elwood 1998: 178)

Moreover, a closer look at the form of response expected in English A level is very revealing as are teachers' comments about male and female students' style of expression at A level.

> The boys go through it like a Panzer division. Their writing is very clinical and clean, you know, point point point. Girls are much more 'if this then that and I might think this and I might think that . . .' The girls tend to like to take a lot of time.
>
> (Female English teacher, quoted in Elwood and Comber 1996: 58)

> He will write you a side-and-a-half where others are writing four or five pages . . . it's like a knife through butter – almost notes but not quite, a very sparse style of writing. I've *never* seen a girl do that. Never.
>
> (Female English teacher, quoted in Elwood and Comber 1996: 58)

While the roots of boys' underachievement in English at 16 plus occur outside of school and are a cause for concern, their preferred choice of reading provides both a content and a style of writing that appears to be valued in science and increasingly in a range of subjects in the later phases of education. This continues into university. For example, history emerges as a subject where males significantly outperform females. A 'women's' style of response was characterized as showing 'a preference for cautious, discursive and synthetic approaches, a willingness to consider a range of views and a strong personal investment in getting it right'. This was contrasted with good undergraduate history writing which was seen to embody, 'an argumentative and self-assertive approach to questions, risk-taking, the bold affirmation of a particular view and a confident dismissal of others' (Gender Working Party, 1994).

Concluding remarks

Students' learned styles of communication and ways of working combined with their preferred choice of reading material exert a powerful influence on the solutions and form of responses they consider to be appropriate. The evidence cited in this chapter has demonstrated a consistency in aspects of males' and females' typical responses and how these are viewed differently in certain subjects at different points in students' educational careers. Speculation on the consequences for students' learning at 18 plus is beyond the scope of this chapter. Nevertheless, it is essential to consider how learning in the early years may influence achievement throughout students' educational experiences.

Boys and girls are equally able to appreciate the value of different ways of working and communicating for different purposes. However, to develop this appreciation they need opportunities (a) to examine their own and others' preferred styles and what lies behind them; and (b) to address a range of purposes the meaning and value of which make sense to them where alternative styles are necessary and appropriate.

The chapter has cited several sources of evidence to show how learning outside of school influences learning in school. Young children's learned gender preferences lead them to pursue particular interests which provide them with different learning opportunities and importantly align them in different ways to schooling and to subject learning. The combination of girls' and boys' differential learning and interests out of school, and teachers' and students' treatment of these in school, lead to differences in performance between girls and boys, often unrelated to students' ability. They also, as the evidence has shown, lead to underachievement, as many children channel themselves away from certain learning experiences. Furthermore, teachers often unwittingly compound this by interpreting aspects of students' behaviour and styles of learning and communication in terms of their ability when these actually reflect differences in opportunities to learn. The strong message that emerges from the research is that teachers, and students from a young age, need to take more account of the interests and learning developed outside of school and of how these influence attitudes to, and learning in, school subjects. In addition, if particular styles of response are agreed to be significant elements of achievement in domains, then this should be made clear to students and become a matter for teaching and not just assessment.

It is also clear that more attention needs to be paid to the potential value of different styles and approaches to ways of working. In areas like science and mathematics a too narrow view of what constitutes appropriate behaviour and responses has evolved, a view that is covert and possibly limits the potential of many students, girls and boys alike. Interventions that have broadened the styles and ways of working allowed and have concentrated on the social derivation and implications of subjects have been found to increase the levels of achievement for both boys and girls but especially so for girls. However, the improvement in female achievement has not occurred for all girls, in particular not those from low socio-economic backgrounds (Hildebrand 1996). More research which looks for systematic effects across the socio-economic structure is needed if we are to better understand how students make sense of learning and assessment situations. This understanding is essential if we are to move towards more equitable teaching and assessment practice.

References

Arnot, M., David, M. and Weiner, G. (1996) *Educational Reforms and Gender Equality in Schools*. Manchester: Equal Opportunities Commission.

Associated Examining Board [AEB] (1990–5) *Inter-Board Statistics*. Guildford: Associated Examining Board.

Barber, M. (1994) *Young People and their Attitudes to School: Interim Report.* Keele: Keele University, Centre for Successful Schools.

Bright, M. (1998) Boys performing badly, *Observer,* 4 January.

Browne, N. and Ross, C. (1991) Girls' stuff, boys' stuff: young children talking and playing, in N. Browne (ed.) *Science and Technology in the Early Years.* Buckingham: Open University Press.

Cooper, B. (1996) Using data from clinical interviews to explore students' understanding of mathematics test items: relating Bernstein and Bourdieu or culture to questions of fairness in testing. Paper presented at the American Educational Research Association Conference, New York, April.

Davies, J. and Brember, I. (1995) Attitudes to school and the curriculum in year 2, year 4 and year 6: changes over four years. Paper presented at the European Conference on Educational Research, Bath, 14–17 September.

Department of Education and Science [DES] (1988a) *Science at Age 11: A Review of APU Survey Findings.* London: HMSO.

Department of Education and Science [DES] (1988b) *Science at Age 15: A Review of APU Survey Findings.* London: HMSO.

Department of Education and Science [DES] (1989a) *Science at Age 13: A Review of APU Survey Findings.* London: HMSO.

Department of Education and Science [DES] (1989b) *Science in Schools Age 13: Review Report.* London: HMSO.

Dweck, C. S., Davidson, W., Nelson, S. and Enna, B. (1978) Sex differences in learned helplessness: the contingencies of evaluative feedback in the classroom. *Development Psychology,* 14: 268–76.

Elwood, J. (1995) Undermining gender stereotypes: examination and coursework performance in the UK at 16. *Assessment in Education,* 2(3): 283–303.

Elwood, J. (1998) 'Gender and performance in the GCE A level: gender equity and the gold standard', unpublished PhD thesis. Institute of Education, University of London.

Elwood, J. and Comber, C. (1996) *Gender Differences in Examinations at 18+: Final Report.* London: University of London Institute of Education.

Foxman, D., Ruddock, G. and McCallum, L. (1991) *Assessment Matters: No 3 APU Mathematics Monitoring 1984–1988 (Phase 2).* London: Schools Examination and Assessment Council.

Foxman, D., Ruddock, G., Joffe, L., Mason, K., Mitchell, P. and Sexton, B. (1985) *A Review of Monitoring in Mathematics 1978–1982 Part 1 and Part 2.* London: HMSO.

Gender Working Party (1994) Men's and women's performance in Tripos examinations, 1980–1993. Unpublished paper, Faculty of History, Cambridge University.

Gipps, C. and Murphy, P. (1994) *A Fair Test? Assessment, Achievement and Equity.* Buckingham: Open University Press.

Goldstein, H. and Thomas, S. (1996) Using examination results as indicators of school and college performance. *Journal of the Royal Statistical Society,* Series A, 159(1): 149–63.

Gorman, T. P. (1987) *Pupils' Attitudes to Reading.* Windsor: NFER-Nelson.

Gorman, T. P., White, J., Brook, G., Maclure, M. and Kispal, A. (1988) *Language Performance in Schools: Review of APU Language Monitoring 1979–1983.* London: HMSO.

Halpern, D. F. (1992) *Sex Differences in Cognitive Abilities.* Hillsdale, NJ: Lawrence Erlbaum Associates Inc.

Hildebrand, G. (1996) Redefining achievement, in P. Murphy and C. Gipps (eds),

Equity in the Classroom: Towards Effective Pedagogy for Girls and Boys. London/Paris: Falmer Press/UNESCO.

Hyde, J. D., Fennema, E. and Lamon, J. S. (1990) Gender differences in mathematics performance: a meta analysis. *Psychological Bulletin*, 107: 139–253.

Hyde, J. S. and Linn, M. C. (1988) Gender differences in verbal ability: a meta analysis. *Psychological Bulletin*, 104: 53–69.

Johnson, S. and Murphy, P. (1986) Girls and physics: reflections on APU survey findings, *APU Occasional Paper 4*.

Kimbell, R., Stables, K., Wheeler, T., Wosniak, A. and Kelly, V. (1991) *The Assessment of Performance in Design and Technology.* London: Schools Examinations and Assessment Council.

Lepkowska, D. (1998) Whatever happened to the likely lads?, *Times Educational Supplement*, 9 January.

Murphy, P. (1991a) Gender differences in pupils' reactions to practical work, in B. Woolnough (ed.) *Practical Science*. Buckingham: Open University Press.

Murphy, P. (1991b) *Assessment in the Primary Curriculum*. Milton Keynes: The Open University.

Murphy, P. (1997) Gender differences: messages for science education, in K. Harnquist and A. Burgen (eds) *Growing up with Science: Developing Early Understanding of Science*, London: Jessica Kingsley/Academia Europaea.

Murphy, P. and Elwood, J. (1998) Gendered experiences, choices and achievement: exploring the links, in D. Epstein, J. Maw, J. Elwood and V. Hey (eds) *International Journal of Inclusive Education: Special Issue on Boys' Underachievement*, 2(2): 95–118.

Murphy, P., Scanlon, E., Hodgson, B. and Whitelegg, E. (1996) Developing investigative learning in science: the role of collaboration, in J. van der Akker, W. Kuiper and U. Hameyer (eds) *Issues in European Curriculum Research*. Oxford: Pergamon.

Randall, G. J. (1987) Gender differences in pupil–teacher interaction in workshops and laboratories, in G. Weiner and M. Arnot (eds) *Gender Under Scrutiny: New Inquiries in Education*. London: Unwin Hyman.

Southern Examining Group [SEG] (1995) *Inter-Group Statistics*. Guildford: SEG.

Stobart, G., White, J., Elwood, J., Hayden, M. and Mason, K. (1992) *Differential Performance in Examinations at 16+: English and Mathematics*. London: Schools Examination and Assessment Council.

Thompson, R. (1994) Gender differences in communicative style: possible consequences for the learning process, in H. C. Foot, C. J. Howe, A. Anderson, A. K. Tolmie and D. A. Warden (eds) *Group and Interactive Learning*. Southampton: Computational Mechanics Publications.

Thornton, M. (1990) Primary specialism. *Early Years*, 11(1): 34–8.

Walkerdine, V. (1989) *Counting Girls Out*. London: Virago.

Whyte, J. (1986) *Girls into Science and Technology: The Story of a Project*. London: Routledge and Kegan Paul.

Wilder, G. Z. and Powell, K. (1989) *Sex Differences in Test Performance: A Survey of the Literature*. New York: College Board Publications.

Index

RESEARCHING RACISM IN EDUCATION
POLITICS, THEORY AND PRACTICE

Paul Connolly and Barry Troyna (eds)

- Is there a place for anti-racist politics in educational research and, if so, what should it consist of?
- Can white people do meaningful research on racism and the experiences of black students?
- What research methods are most appropriate in the study of racism in education?

This book offers a comprehensive overview and assessment of the wide range of debates and controversies concerning the politics, theory and practice of research that have become associated with 'race' and education in recent years. It offers new and original contributions from many of the leading academics within the field together with some of the most promising and influential researchers to have recently emerged. In dealing with these debates, the book offers new lines of enquiry and alternative ways of thinking. It represents both an important text and a timely contribution to the field. The book will be of interests to a wide range of students, teachers and practitioners in education, 'race' and ethnic studies, sociology and research methods.

Contents
Introduction – The myth of neutrality in educational research – Partisanship and credibility: the case of antiracist educational research – Racism and the politics of qualitative research: learning from controversy and critique – Silenced voices: life history as an approach to the study of South Asian women teachers – 'Caught in the crossfire': reflections of a black female ethnographer – 'Same voices, same lives?': revisiting black feminist standpoint epistemology – 'The whites of my eyes, nose, ears . . . ': a reflexive account of 'whiteness' in race-related research – Struggles with the research self: reconciling feminist approaches to antiracist research – 'Dancing to the wrong tune': ethnography, generalization and research on racism in schools – A league apart: statistics in the study of 'race' and education – References – Index.

The contributors
Maud Blair, Paul Connolly, Sean Demack, David Drew, David Gillborn, Martyn Hammersley, Mehreen Mirza, Sarah Neal, Anuradha Rakhit, Barry Troyna, Cecile Wright.

208pp   0 335 19662 4 (Paperback)   0 335 19663 2 (Hardback)

EXPERIENCING SCHOOL MATHEMATICS
TEACHING STYLES, SEX AND SETTING

Jo Boaler

Jo Boaler has written a stunning book: clearly written and carefully researched, it is a model of technical rigour. A wide range of qualitative and quantitative data is marshalled to produce exhaustive case studies of two contrasting mathematics departments – one traditional and one progressive. Boaler's findings represent a major challenge to the 'back to basics' credo. This book should be read as a matter of urgency by politicians, mathematics teachers, and educational researchers.

> Stephen Ball, Professor of Sociology of Education, King's College London

Anyone with an interest in making sure that every child is numerate should read this book.

> Sally Tomlinson, Professor of Educational Policy
> at Goldsmiths College, University of London

Experiencing School Mathematics is the first book of its kind to provide direct evidence for the effectiveness of 'traditional' and 'progressive' teaching methods. It reports upon careful and extensive case studies of two schools which taught mathematics in totally different ways. Three hundred students were followed over three years and the interviews that are reproduced in the book give compelling insights into what it meant to be a student in the classrooms of the two schools. The different school approaches are compared and analysed using student interviews, lesson observations, questionnaires given to students and staff and a range of different assessments, including GCSE examinations. Questions are raised about:

- the effectiveness of different teaching methods in preparing students for the demands of the 'real world' and the twenty-first century;
- the impact of setted and mixed ability teaching upon student attitude and achievement;
- gender and teaching styles;

and new evidence is provided for each.

The book draws some radical new conclusions about the ways that traditional teaching methods lead to limited forms of knowledge that are ineffective in non-school settings. The book will be essential reading for maths teachers, parents and policy makers in education.

Contents

176pp   0 335 19962 3 (Paperback)   0 335 19963 1 (Hardback)

DATE DUE
